OF THE WORLD'S TALLEST BUILDINGS

ONE HUNDRED AND ONE

OF THE WORLD'S
TALLEST BUILDINGS

Edited by **Georges Binder**

Council
on
Tall Buildings
and
Urban Habitat

images
Publishing

Published in Australia in 2006 by
The Images Publishing Group Pty Ltd
ABN 89 059 734 431
6 Bastow Place, Mulgrave, Victoria 3170, Australia
Tel: +61 3 9561 5544 Fax: +61 3 9561 4860
books@images.com.au
www.imagespublishing.com

Copyright © The Images Publishing Group Pty Ltd 2006
The Images Publishing Group Reference Number: 675

National Library of Australia Cataloguing-in-Publication entry:

101 of the world's tallest buildings.

Includes index.
ISBN 1 86470 173 0.

1. Tall buildings. 2. Skyscrapers. I. Binder, Georges.
II. Council on Tall Buildings and Urban Habitat.

720.483

Coordinating editor: Robyn Beaver

Designed by The Graphic Image Studio Pty Ltd, Mulgrave, Australia
www.tgis.com.au

Digital production by Splitting Image Colour Studio Pty Ltd, Australia
Printed by Everbest Printing Co. Ltd. in Hong Kong/China

Contents

Foreword

Before we talk about architecture and design, I would like to begin with a very simple assertion: architecture is about relationships. I know that seems obvious but I think it's important to reiterate this idea before we move on to discuss some very specific kinds of architectural relationships. Our capacity to design is as diverse and as abundant as human creativity itself. Consequently, architecture reflects our multifarious, and seemingly infinite quest to manipulate the environment—built and not yet built. These relationships include the way in which humans perceive a need for shelter; they involve our understanding of community as it relates to that shelter, and also how we link that community to culture, science, and art. Architecture synthesizes all of these components, and, as we consider the socio-economic and socio-political forces that shape our architecture, we must also consider how our architecture shapes our society—its economics, politics, and behavior.

The context is integral to the way we think about the built environment. I have always maintained that architecture is an expression of our mood as a culture. It reflects our interests and it mirrors the preoccupations of our time. Our built environment must not just reflect our culture and the age we live in but it must also delight those who use it and are impacted by it. Our built environment is constantly in transition; it is kinetic and it is at once a reminder of the past and a predictor of the future. It is an expression of our conscious values and the state of our economies. It exposes our egos and reveals the degree to which we are willing to collaborate. Architecture expresses our optimism in the future.

Constructing meaning through contextualism is about how meaning is constructed through a relationship with everything that has gone before and everything that is to come, the simultaneous existence and simultaneous order ... and then, adding to it, changing the sequence somehow, having technology and our contemporary awareness inform our designs ... then a piece becomes contextual to both the historical fabric and the contemporary sense of place. It reveals a unique identity that is singular to its own time.

I view the city as a kind of tapestry in which many people over many years have an imprint and where the structure of the tapestry is inviolate and is similar to the infrastructure of the city. It is this underlying structure that gives the city its lasting memory and it is the manner in which we relate to this infrastructure that forms the character and shape of our building over time. The new must make a connection with the old in ways that respect the essence of a place, a kind of ethos regeneration. A foreign ideology inserted into an environment of strength and harmony can have a cancerous effect on the biology of a city. It may be very apparent in the tapestry, but if it is not the right object or if it is not placed in the correct position in relation to the composition of the piece, it can ruin the continuity of a place.

The super-tall building not only drastically changes the literal landscape, but it changes the symbolic landscape as well, and the meaning of that landscape is changed through the mutual interaction of images. And so we are not typically interested in jarring the civility of a city with buildings that are aesthetically and functionally challenging to the surrounding communities—unless there's a proper spot and reasoning for it. The city's built environment is the physical context within which future architecture will be seen and with which it will interact. I believe that it is important to understand not only the physical context that a building will be designed to relate with, but also the nature of the climate, topography, cultural influences, and the history of a place. There are clues in every city that make that city unique from others. These clues are based in the city's past and are both physical and symbolic, emanating from the culture of the people who inhabit the city.

How has technology contributed to and changed the meaning of the skyscraper? The history of a skyscraper is inextricably linked to its technology. The skyscraper marks time by the use of technologies. If we examine the history of a particular building, we can see how it registers its history piece by piece through the sophistication of its systems and its enclosures. It adopts materials, means, and methods, and engineering principals. The evolution of technology commingled with design ideas to solve complex problems represents a particular breakthrough in our history of architecture.

The first modern tall buildings, post-World War II, were developed as an innovative counterpoint to the skyscrapers in the 1920s. Their formal departure was based on innovation and the emerging philosophy of modernism as practiced by the international school. Modernism was based, in part, on the mass production technologies of all building components. In order to accomplish the design and construction of these new modern structures, the building industry had to be re-tooled to accommodate the tremendous building volume that was to take place. The philosophy was in place but new technologies of building and construction were not as developed. The integration of new building services such as long span structural systems, automated elevator systems, energy efficient exterior wall components and systems, air

conditioning systems, and modular lighting and wiring systems were all in their infancy and had to be designed and integrated into a building whose components were mass produced. Many architects designing tall structures in this period were obsessed with a manifesto to design for the masses. They utilized the components of mass production and the best of these architects refined their designs through endless study of proportion, scale, and material selections to produce architecture as art and a reflection of a modern civilized society.

This movement produced a multitude of large high-rise structures in America, Japan, and Europe that redefined the image of the city. The first of these buildings were highly refined, artistic, and beautifully detailed structures and are considered to be modern classics today. In the 1960s and 1970s, the American city was characterized by a proliferation of bland, poorly detailed, and poorly resolved buildings that were rapidly losing their appeal and falling from the favor of the general public and the corporate world.

In the 1980s modernism in America was dead. In its place arose a new paradigm whose inspiration came from the fundamental principles of pre-World War II architecture. No longer was "less is more" the mantra of the day. Decoration was in, and the composition of classical elements defining entry, base, middle, and top, centered compositions, mannerist façades, and contextual influences became dominant. It was the desire of society to give a face and a personality to each of our buildings, and a character to our cities. Into the 1990s this period produced dramatic variety and unleashed a level of individual creativity never before encountered within a decade of building. New systems were developed for using natural and man-made materials and enhancing building envelope performance, and energy efficient building systems advanced appreciably during this period.

We have now entered a new century and rapid expansion of cities in Asia and the Middle East is seeing a startling abundance of new super-tall structures, many of which defy their context and are indulging in a frenzy of self expression, without rationality. The effect in many cases is a cacophony of individual pieces all striving for attention and recognition. It is yet to be seen if this new approach to city making will create wonderful cities of the future or hideous environments of *Blade Runner* status.

Adrian Smith, FAIA, RIBA
Consulting Design Partner
Skidmore, Owings & Merrill LLP

Introduction

The United States: home of the first skyscrapers

The 1885 Home Insurance Company Building in Chicago, designed by William Le Baron Jenney, is generally considered to be the first skyscraper, with its 10 levels, elevator, metal structure, and cast-iron and steel supporting masonry walls. However, the 21-story, 302-foot Masonic Temple, also in Chicago, completed in 1892 and designed by Burnham and Root, is considered to be the first major skyscraper. The Masonic Temple was demolished in 1939. While Chicago introduced a new building typology, New York City started to witness its own tall buildings, especially in the downtown area near the port.

The first super-tall building is probably New York City's 792-foot, 57-story Woolworth Building, designed by Cass Gilbert in 1913. Its Gothic-style architecture, as well as the lobby interiors and plan, inspired the building's nickname, 'Cathedral of Commerce'.

In the early years of the 20th century, the skyscraper was to become a major force in the economy. Apart from the not-so-rational race to the sky, which is as old as the Tower of Babel, the driving force behind every skyscraper then, as now, was rational economics and ever-increasing land values, demanding larger projects to repay the cost of the land. That would be a rational thought. Or is it the reverse and does the land value increase because of the desire to build tall (and larger) buildings?

At the time there was no limitation on the height or the maximum built area allowed on a site. This led to the construction of projects such as the 37-story Equitable Building, designed in 1915 by E.R. Graham. The footprint of the building covered the full site and the building overshadowed the entire neighborhood. The following year, the City of New York enacted new zoning regulations that introduced setbacks and which had a major impact on the next generation of tall buildings. These regulations allowed sunlight to infiltrate to the street and the same time regulated the density of the urban fabric. The result was a series of buildings with large bulky podiums and slender towers above. As long as the tower was reduced to 25 percent of the site area, there were no height restrictions.

Home Insurance Building, Chicago, Illinois, USA,
William Le Baron Jenney, 1885, 10 stories
(an additional 2 stories were added later)
Reproduced from Francisco Mujica, History of the Skyscraper,
Archaeology & Architecture Press, Paris/New York, 1929

Masonic Temple, Chicago, Illinois, USA,
Burnham and Root, 1892, 21 stories
Reproduced from Francisco Mujica, History of the Skyscraper,
Archaeology & Architecture Press, Paris/New York, 1929

Woolworth Building, New York, New York, USA, Cass Gilbert, 1913, 57 stories
Reproduced from Francisco Mujica, History of the Skyscraper, *Archaeology*
& Architecture Press, Paris/New York, 1929

Ritz Tower, New York, New York, USA, Emery Roth, 1926, 41 stories
Photography: courtesy Robert Sobel

In 1926, the Ritz Tower, a 41-story residential building, was completed at Park Avenue and 57th Street in New York by Hungarian-born architect Emery Roth. The 540-foot tower was then the tallest residential building in the world, three times taller than the typical residential buildings built at the time. The Ritz Tower was an apartment hotel; residents could take advantage of all the services usually found in hotels such as maid service or private dining. This concept was recently revived by developer Millennium Partners in a series of tall buildings that include the 64-story Four Seasons Hotel & Tower in Miami, completed in 2003. In this case, the hotel name is used as a marketing tool to boost the sales of the residences. The Ritz Tower was the first of a series of Emery Roth-designed tall buildings in New York City that combined residential and hospitality; others included the Beresford and the El Dorado along Central Park West. Later, the firm known as Emery Roth & Sons was associate architect to major super-tall high-rise projects including the Citicorp Center, designed by Hugh Stubbins and Associates, and the World Trade Center, designed by Minoru Yamasaki and Associates. In fact, Emery Roth & Sons has been responsible for the highest number of high-rise buildings in New York.

Returning to the timeline of super-tall buildings, in the late 1920s and early 1930s, there was fierce competition between New York City developers to construct the world's tallest building. While the William Van Alen-designed Chrysler Building was advertised at 925 feet high before its completion, the 40 Wall Street building (now the Trump Building) was completed at 927 feet. It was soon discovered that the addition of a 'secret spire' planned for the Chrysler Building would see it become the world's tallest building at 1046 feet, surpassing the Eiffel Tower. But not for long, as the Empire State Building, designed by Shreve, Lamb & Harmon, became the next world's

tallest building a few months later in 1931. The Empire State Building was originally planned as an 85-story 'classic' skyscraper, reaching 1050 feet. Although officially referred to as having 102 levels, it is actually an 85-story building with a metallic tower built on its roof up to the stated height of 102 levels with the observation deck as the only useable floor level of the 200-foot mast.

The Empire State and Chrysler buildings will be paired forever in popular imagery as the epitome of the skyscraper. The fact that very few tall buildings were built in North America in the following 30 years probably accentuated their status as iconic symbols of American culture and economic prosperity. The skyscraper became a symbol of prosperity whatever its location, despite the fact that construction of the Empire State Building in fact began in 1930, after the 1929 economic crisis began. This leads to questions about the reasons why people erect tall buildings, and especially super-tall buildings; the rationale is obviously not always entirely rational. After all, as opposed to other projects, the Empire State Building was a purely speculative project and not built for a specific company; even projects such as the Chrysler Building were also largely speculative.

The 1920s also witnessed a series of unbuilt projects scheduled to become the 'tallest', such as the 108-story Larkin Building in New York designed in 1926 by John A. Larkin & Edward L. Larkin. The project, scheduled to reach 1208 feet, was designed to possibly accommodate double-deck elevators.

The Larkin Building, New York, New York, USA, John A. & Edward L. Larkin, 1926 (never executed), 108 stories
Reproduced from Francisco Mujica, History of the Skyscraper, Archaeology & Architecture Press, Paris/New York, 1929

Progress in Europe

Meanwhile, tall buildings were being erected in Europe. The 11-story, castle-like Witte Huis office building designed by Willem Molenbroek and completed in Rotterdam, The Netherlands in 1898 is usually regarded as the first tall building in Europe. But it was in Antwerp, Belgium in 1932 that the first grand skyscraper was completed on the Old Continent. Built between 1928 and 1932 in the Art Deco style for the Algemeene Bankvereniging, the Torengebouw or Boerentoren (now headquarters of the KBC Banking & Insurance company) became and remained Europe's tallest building until the 1950s. Designed by architects Jan Vanhoenacker, Jos Smolderen and Emiel Van Averbeke, the building is reminiscent of the great early American skyscrapers and comprised a 24-story observatory deck open to the public and now closed.

The skyscraper as a political vehicle

By 1950, the skyscraper, previously a product of private enterprise, became a political issue. Between 1937 and 1940 in the former USSR, architects Iofan, Chtchouko, Guelfreikh, and Merkoulov had designed the Palace of the Soviets. Planned for a site not far from the Kremlin in Moscow, the 1365-foot project, slightly taller than the Empire State Building, was expected to be topped by a huge 328-foot statue to the glory of Lenin, but the project was never built. After World War II, in the late 1940s, a series of eight high-rise buildings planned in the 1930s was scheduled for Moscow. Seven have been completed to date. All these early Russian skyscrapers, which were not to be look-alikes of their American counterparts, can be seen as smaller versions of the plan

Moscow State University, Moscow, Russia, Lev Rudnev, Sergei Tchernitchev, Pavel Abrosimov, Alexander Khriakov, 1953, 36 stories
Photography: Airprint Business Communication, Brussels

proposed for the Palace of the Soviets. In 1953, the most impressive of the seven built projects, the 787-foot Moscow State University was completed, followed in 1955 by the 757-foot Palace of Culture and Science in Warsaw, Poland, still the country's tallest building. Both projects were designed by a team lead by Lev Rudnev and were government initiatives, as were the other Moscow tall buildings completed during the same decade.

50 years of world's tallest records: world's tallest buildings in 1956

		City	Country	Year	Stories	Feet	Meters	Use
1	Empire State Building	New York	USA	1931	102 *	1250	381	Office
2	Chrysler Building	New York	USA	1930	77	1046	319	Office
3	Cities Service Building (now American International Building)	New York	USA	1932	67	952	290	Office
4	40 Wall Street (now Trump Building)	New York	USA	1930	70	927	283	Office
5	RCA Building (now GE Building)	New York	USA	1930	70	850	259	Office
6	Woolworth Building	New York	USA	1913	57	792	241	Office
7	Moscow State University	Moscow	USSR	1953	36	787	240	Educational
8	Palace of Culture and Science	Warsaw	Poland	1955	42	758	231	Educational
9	20 Exchange Place	New York	USA	1931	57	741	226	Office
10	Metropolitan Life Insurance Company Tower	New York	USA	1909	50	700	213	Office

In 1956, the 10 world's tallest buildings were mainly located in New York City, where no building had been completed in the previous 25 years. Two buildings are located in Eastern Europe and they have been built according to urban master plans approved by Stalin.

*The Empire State Building does not actually have 102 levels since the mooring mast atop the 85-story main building structure has only the observation desk as a useable level but there is a wide acceptation of the now-mythic 102 figure.

Source: G. Binder/Buildings & Data SA

Vertical transportation in super-tall buildings

Vertical transportation at the World Trade Center in New York City featured for the first time a system of express elevators and sky-lobbies. It was a way to reduce the volume occupied within the building by the elevator shafts. In relation to the vertical transportation system, the building was essentially three identical towers built atop each other. Sky-lobbies were created on levels 44 and 78, so to reach any level between levels 44 and 77, or to travel from the 78th level to the top, one had to first reach level 44 in one case or level 78 in the other case using one of the appropriate shuttle or express elevator cabs (see R1 and R2 in the WTC plans), traveling non-stop to these two levels. Note that each of the shuttle elevator cabs could accommodate 60 passengers per trip. Upon arrival at the 44th or the 78th level, it was exactly as if someone was taking an elevator at the ground level of any standard high-rise building. Four elevator banks were available (see A, B, C and D in the WTC plans) to reach each building zone within each zone of the tower: ground floor to 43rd (zone1), 44th to 77th (zone 2) and 78th to top (zone 3). If a traditional vertical transportation pattern with all elevators starting their journey from ground level had been used, the added elevators shafts would have used so much of the building volume that not much space would be left for office use, and the project would not be economically viable.

This concept of superimposing groups of elevators on the same vertical axis provides more rentable floor area. The shuttle elevators, by serving only two stops—ground floor and level 44 or ground floor and level 78—reduce the time lost during intermediate floor stops. More round trips can therefore be performed in a shorter period of time and can thus be operated with fewer elevators cabs than in a traditional pattern plan.

Double-deck elevators as used in the First Canadian Place in Toronto, (see schematic diagram) in 1975 or the Citicorp Center (now Citigroup Center) in New York in 1977 are another way of saving rentable space by reducing the number of hoistways: two superimposed elevators cabs using the same hoistway can move twice as many people as single cabs.

The first double-deck elevator was installed in the early 1930s in the Cities Service Building (now American International Building) in New York City but the system never worked properly. This fact has been widely published but Otis.com tells a different story: the system was meant to simultaneously serve a subway station planned for the basement of the building, and the lobby level, but the station was never built, and the double-deck elevator never actually operated.

The Time-Life Building in Chicago, designed in 1968 by Harry Weese Associates, was the first building to feature the double-deck system. With only 30 levels, it is also one of the lower buildings featuring the system, which is usually found only in super-tall projects.

Double-deck elevators require building levels to be at identical distances everywhere the elevator stops so cars always will be even with the floor when passengers enter or exit. That requirement was no longer necessary when Nippon Otis first installed a new kind of double-deck elevators in 2003 in the 54-story Mori Tower at Roppongi Hills in Tokyo, designed by Kohn Pedersen Fox Associates. These double-deck elevators do not require evenly spaced floors and solve the tower's spacing problem with unevenly spaced floors by raising or lowering the elevator up to 6.6 feet to align it with the floor.

In some buildings, such as in C.Y. Lee & Partners' Taipei 101 in Taipei, Taiwan, there may be a mix of double-deck elevators and the sky-lobby concept. This project has sky-lobbies located on levels 35–36 and 59–60 and features the world's fastest elevators, which ascend at a speed of 3313 feet per minute, or 37.7 miles per hour. These Toshiba elevators also feature the world's first pressure control system, which adjusts the atmospheric pressure inside a car by using suction and discharge blowers, preventing uncomfortable 'ear popping' for elevator users.

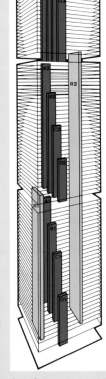

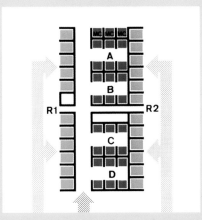

World Trade Center, New York, New York, USA, Minoru Yamasaki and Associates in association with Emery Roth & Sons, 1972/1973, 110 stories
Ground floor plan and axonometric showing the vertical transportation system with sky-lobbies at level 44 and level 78
Plans reproduced from Otis brochure, Coll. G. Binder/Buildings & Data SA

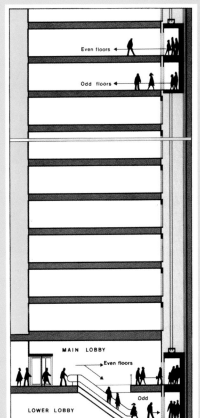

Double-deck elevators at First Canadian Place, Toronto, Ontario, Canada, Edward Durell Stone in association with Bregman + Hamann, 1975, 72 stories
Plans reproduced from First Canadian Place leaflet, Coll. G. Binder/Buildings & Data SA

The plaza emerges

In New York City, the late 1950s saw the creation of a new tall building concept, the 'tower above a plaza'. Two famous examples of this concept are the 38-story Seagram Building, designed in 1958 by Mies van der Rohe with Philip Johnson and associate architect Kahn & Jacobs, and the 60-story One Chase Manhattan Plaza, completed in 1961 by Gordon Bunshaft of Skidmore, Owings & Merrill. Both buildings introduced with panache the plaza concept and One Chase Manhattan Plaza was also the first building to have an address such as 'One ... Plaza', which was to become very popular as a corporate address. A new logo and san-serif lettering was also introduced on the occasion of the new headquarters building. The bank's well-known octagonal logo, designed by Chermayeff & Geismar Associates, became the new company-wide logo. A new tall building became an opportunity to renew the corporate image of a company: tall building marketing was born.

In 1961, these projects led to new zoning regulations in New York City that would eventually have a worldwide impact. While density was lowered in residential areas, a floor area ratio (FAR) of 15 was proposed for dense commercial areas. (FAR is the total floor area divided by the site area.) In addition to the basic FAR 15, bonuses were granted for creating plazas in front of buildings, meaning that building smaller footprints could allow larger projects to be built, with an additional 20 percent allowed, thus transforming FAR 15 into FAR 18, such as in the case of the Citicorp Center (now Citigroup Center). Models such as the Seagram Building and One Chase Manhattan Plaza have been imitated for decades the world over, in many cases badly, both from an architectural and an urban planning point of view as the plaza became the means to build taller ... and larger. It is worth noting that while these two projects were designed as headquarters buildings, they were later copied as models for speculative towers.

Western European initiatives

With built examples already seen in Eastern Europe and new tall buildings built and planned in New York, the first moves in Western Europe toward very tall high-rise projects began. Interestingly, the first major high-rise project in Europe was an initiative by the French government. Eventually developed by a duo of French and American developers, the Tour Maine-Montparnasse in Paris, France (which was the tallest high-rise building in Europe until 1990, with the exception of the Moscow State University and the Palace of Culture and Science, spire included) was part of the urban renewal around the Montparnasse Railway Station that included a 58-story office tower, eventually completed in 1973, but part of the 1950s masterplan. In 1958, a public body was created to oversee the implementation of the La Défense district, intended to become the main tall buildings zone in the Paris area. Both projects, the Maine-Montparnasse urban renewal project and the La Défense district, were government initiatives and although all the tall buildings have been erected by the private sector, the public sector devised the masterplans.

In 1990, Europe again made its mark on the tall building scene with the completion of the 912-foot MesseTurm, developed in Frankfurt, Germany by New York-based Tishman Speyer Properties and designed by Murphy/Jahn. In 1991, the 774-foot One Canada Square at Canary Wharf, developed in London by Toronto-based Olympia & York and designed by Cesar Pelli & Associates, was completed.

World's tallest buildings in 1966

		City	Country	Year	Stories	Feet	Meters	Use
1	Empire State Building	New York	USA	1931	102	1250	381	Office
2	Chrysler Building	New York	USA	1930	77	1046	319	Office
3	Cities Service Building (now American International Building)	New York	USA	1932	67	952	290	Office
4	40 Wall Street (now Trump Building)	New York	USA	1930	70	927	283	Office
5	RCA Building (now GE Building)	New York	USA	1930	70	850	259	Office
6	One Chase Manhattan Plaza	New York	USA	1961	60	813	248	Office
7	Pan Am Building (now MetLife Building)	New York	USA	1963	59	808	246	Office
8	Woolworth Building	New York	USA	1913	57	792	241	Office
9	Moscow State University	Moscow	USSR	1953	36	787	240	Educational
10	Palace of Culture and Science	Warsaw	Poland	1955	42	758	231	Educational

The 10 world's tallest buildings in 1966 look much like the ones of 1956, with two major new entries: the Pan Am Building and One Chase Manhattan Plaza, the first major building completed in downtown New York since the 1930s.

Source: G. Binder/Buildings & Data SA

Conceptual super-skyscrapers

Between the mid-1970s and the early 1990s, when few super-tall buildings were actually built, a number of super-tall projects were designed.

It appears that there is a correlation between periods of inactivity in the building of super-tall projects, and the creative design of new projects. One such example is Frank Lloyd Wright's Mile High Illinois project, designed in 1956 with a proposed height of one mile.

In the late 1970s, architect Robert Sobel of Emery Roth & Sons, and engineer Nat W. Krahl designed a 500-story concept tower. This theoretical project proposed for Houston was made from sixteen 200-foot sided triangular bundled tubes, arranged in an 800-foot equilateral triangle. The perimeter tubes drop off at different heights while some of the tubes in the proposal could be interrupted within the building in order to decrease the built volume when reaching the sky and also as an opportunity to create atriums within the tower. A single tube would have reached the full height of the 500-story, mile-high project. Such a project with its adjoining plaza would have covered 16 typical city blocks, which are actually rather small in Houston at 250 by 250 feet.

In the early 1980s, Harry Weese designed a 2500-foot, 210-story, mixed-use tower for Chicago, comprising seven 30-story stacked modules.

Television City, a project envisioned by architect Murphy/Jahn and developer Donald J. Trump along the Hudson River in New York, was another super-tall project announced in 1985. The project, developed over a 40.5-hectare site, comprised a series of six residential towers, a taller tower for NBC broadcast purposes, and a 150-story, 1670-foot building as the project centerpiece. Unlike most of the super-tall projects in the United States—completed or only dreamed—that are usually stand-alone towers, the Television City project was envisioned in a similar way to contemporary projects in Asia and in the Middle East such as the Petronas Towers, the International Commerce Center in Hong Kong, and the Burj Dubai, which are the centerpieces of larger projects comprising several buildings arranged in a landscaped park.

Almost twenty years ago, structural engineer William LeMessurier—Citicorp Center in New York is one of his most famous achievements—said of his own scheme for a 207-story Erewhon Center super-tall building, 'There is no likelihood of it ever being built … because there's no site I could imagine where it would make sense'. (*Discover*, September 1988)

In 1989, developer Miglin-Beitler unveiled a 1999-foot-high, 125-story tower for Chicago, designed by Cesar Pelli & Associates with associate architect HKS. The same year, Norman Foster unveiled his design for the 2756-foot-high Millennium Tower in Tokyo, wrapped in a helical structure integrated with the tapering building form. Also designed in 1989 was Jean Nouvel et Associés' 1397-foot Tour sans fins for La Défense in Paris. The tower was envisioned as having no visible extremities,

Super-tall concept study, Houston, Texas, USA, architect Robert Sobel of Emery Roth & Sons and engineer Nat W. Krahl, c 1979, 500 stories
Photography: courtesy Robert Sobel

descending several levels underground like a crater; on the other end, the building shaft was to grow increasingly lighter until it became transparent at the top, merging with the clouds.

The 1980s and 1990s witnessed a series of Japanese conceptual super-high-rise designs such as DIB 200 (DIB for Dynamic Intelligent Building), a 200-story 2625-foot mixed-use project designed by Kajima Corporation. X-Seed 4000, a circular pyramid-like structure designed by Taisei was intended to welcome 700,000 people and was scheduled to be built over a period of about 30 years. The project, with a total height of 13,123 feet (4000 meters) would have had residences up to 6562 feet. A final mention in this brief series of unbuilt super-skyscrapers, is of another Japanese project that was heavily inspired by the Sobel/Krahl 500-story tower designed years before and described above. Seen positively, such emulation would appear as an endorsement that such a dream (or nightmare for some) is achievable.

A new world's tallest

Returning to the United States, in New York, the 60-story, flat-roofed One Chase Manhattan Plaza broke away from the romantic imagery of the New York skyline, until then dominated by the early spire-topped towers at the tip of the island. Soon after the completion of One Chase Manhattan Plaza, plans were underway for what was to become a World Trade Center. The project was an initiative of the Port Authority of New York & New Jersey. For the first time in the United States, a super-tall skyscraper was initiated by the public sector and not by a private developer or company. And for the first time since 1931, there was a serious contender for the title of the world's tallest building. Originally planned as 1350 feet tall, just 100 feet more than the Empire State Building, and eventually 1362 and 1368 feet tall, the 110-story twin towers completed in 1972–1973 held the world's tallest building title for a short time until the completion of the Sears Tower in 1974. The innovative WTC plans by Minoru Yamaski and Associates, with associate architect Emery Roth & Sons and structural engineers Skilling and Robertson, allowed for a tower offering large, column-free floor plates. In the structural framing system of the towers, the exterior walls, comprising steels columns occurring at 3 ½-foot intervals, carried the vertical loads, resisted lateral wind loads, and eliminated the need for interior columns.

1970s and 1980s super-tall buildings

The first of the 1970s cycle of super-tall buildings was the 100-story, mixed-use, 1127-foot John Hancock Center in Chicago, designed by Bruce Graham and Fazlur Khan of Skidmore, Owings & Merrill. Completed in 1970, this project was the first 'mixed-use' super-tall building. In 1973, the 83-story, 1136-foot Standard Oil Building (now Aon Center) designed by Edward Durell Stone and the Perkins + Will Partnership topped the John Hancock Center by just 9 feet. In 1974, the 110-story, 1450-foot Sears Tower, designed by Bruce Graham and Fazlur Khan of Skidmore, Owings & Merrill, became the new world's tallest building, surpassing the World Trade Center by 82 feet. The Sears Tower is an example of the bundled-tube structural system, providing large column-free spaces and 70-foot clear spans. To reduce shear stress, the structure has diagonal bracing only on the two mechanical levels before each setback.

The next super-tall buildings series appeared in the booming city of Houston in the early 1980s: in 1982, the 75-story, 993-foot Texas Commerce Tower (now JP Morgan Chase Tower) developed by Gerald D Hines Interests and designed by I.M. Pei & Partners with 3/D International opened, followed shortly after in 1983, by the 71-story, 992-foot Allied Bank Plaza (now Wells Fargo Plaza) designed by Richard Keating of Skidmore, Owings & Merrill. Surprisingly, the developer and architect of Allied Bank Plaza did not attempt to top the earlier completed Texas Commerce Tower, but since they were under

construction simultaneously for some time, the final height of Texas Commerce Tower was not known to the Allied Bank Plaza team.

Among the last completed American super-tall buildings of this decade was the Library Tower (now US Bank Tower), a 73-story, 1018-foot tower completed in 1989 in Los Angeles and designed by Pei Cobb Freed & Partners with Ellerbe Becket as associate architect. It topped the 62-story United California Bank Building (now Aon Center), designed by Charles Luckman Associates, which, at 858 feet, had been the city's tallest building since 1974.

Architecture as corporate identity

Projects like the 61-story AT&T Corporate Center and the 110-story Sears Tower in Chicago; the 70-story Bank of China Tower in Hong Kong, or even the 50-story RepublicBank Center (now Bank of America Center) in Houston have the same real estate design philosophy even if their architecture, technology, and means of development vary. In contrast to the Sears Tower and Bank of China, which were developed and owned (at least in the early years of Sears Tower) by the companies putting their name on the building, RepublicBank Center, scheduled to become the headquarters of the RepublicBank in Houston, was the work of famous high-rise building developer Gerald D. Hines Interests and not the company whose name was on the door. In the public's mind, these buildings represent the companies they advertise as a whole, not the many tenants they also house.

In the examples mentioned above, the companies used the lower portion of the buildings in a most logical way: these large corporations need large floor plates while the upper speculative levels were scheduled for possible future company expansion. In many cases, the company vacated the building well before any expansion occurred, as in the case of Sears, and the building was leased to outside tenants. The upper levels provided a variety of lettable space, in some cases with more than the usual four corners, an amenity that was highly marketable, especially in the 1980s. The upper part of the building, with more offices close to a window, achieved higher rents than if the main occupant had taken over the upper levels. The reduced size of the upper levels also reduced the overall investment necessary to build such headquarters towers. In many cases, such as One Chase Manhattan Plaza in New York, the AT&T Corporate Center in Chicago, and the Bank of China Tower, the owner companies used only the lower levels for their own staff, retaining the top level for upscale conference and dining rooms. The prestige of height …

Thus, for decades the tallest skyscrapers promoted the companies that occupied them. Early examples include the Chrysler Building, the Cities Service Building, the RCA Building, the Woolworth Building, and the Metropolitan Life Insurance

Company Tower, all located in New York. In the 1960s, also in New York, the Pan Am Building was probably more famous because of its name, recalling the imagery of the jet age, than because of the building itself. One Chase Manhattan Plaza introduced with panache the plaza feature associated with building naming and corporate marketing. In the next decade, Chicago's Sears Tower became the world's tallest advertising totem for Sears, Roebuck and Co. On the west coast, the United California Bank put its logo atop its 62-story building in Los Angeles, while in San Francisco, the Transamerica Corporation, a huge conglomerate, named its 853-foot pyramidal headquarters 'Transamerica Pyramid', distributing 'Pyramid Facts' leaflets in the lobby while using the company logo in the form of the building in all kinds of advertising. 'The Power of the Pyramid[sm]' was even created as a company-wide marketing motto.

What's in a name? Today, the Sears Tower is no longer owned or occupied by Sears, Roebuck and Co. but is still officially called the Sears Tower. The Pan Am Building in New York, not owned by Pan American Airways since 1979, was eventually renamed MetLife in the early 1990s but still remains as the Pan Am Building in popular parlance. Although the Transamerica Pyramid is no longer the headquarters of Transamerica Corporation, (the company retains a small presence as a tenant) it still uses the building's image as its registered trademark logo and the Transamerica Pyramid name has remained, as it seems to be part of the building.

1990: the super-tall building arrives in Asia

The turn of the 1990s decade, and architect I.M. Pei, were both catalysts for the growth of tall buildings in Asia. Although tall buildings had begun to be built throughout Asia in the 1960s, especially in Hong Kong, there were very few real high-rise towers in that part of the world. There were a few significant towers in Tokyo, and in Hong Kong, such as the 52-story, 586-foot Connaught Center (now Jardine House), notable for its round windows, and the twin 52-story Exchange Square both designed by P&T Group, completed in 1973 and 1985, respectively. These locations were more remarkable for their density than the height of the buildings, but that was soon to change.

In Hong Kong in 1989, the 70-story, 1205-foot Bank of China Tower, a major super-tall building milestone designed by I.M. Pei & Partners, was the first real Asian initiative toward super-tall buildings. The project, formally opened in May 1990, was developed and owned by the Bank of China. Apart from being a headquarters building, it was also a political statement from the Chinese government that was to recover sovereignty over Hong Kong a few years later in 1997. Who could have imagined that the two spires atop the building would have such influence over the appearance of most, if not all, of the super-tall towers completed since? Of the eight buildings taller than the Pei project and completed after the Bank of China, only one does not have the now-usual spire: the 88-story Two International Finance Centre, which was completed not far away in Hong Kong. And even that one—although flat roofed—has a type of short crowning spire.

World's tallest buildings in 1976

		City	Country	Year	Stories	Feet	Meters	Use
1	Sears Tower	Chicago	USA	1974	110	1450	442	Office
2	One World Trade Center	New York	USA	1972	110	1368	417	Office
3	Two World Trade Center	New York	USA	1973	110	1362	415	Office
4	Empire State Building	New York	USA	1931	102	1250	381	Office
5	Standard Oil (now Aon Center)	Chicago	USA	1973	83	1136	346	Office
6	John Hancock Center	Chicago	USA	1970	100	1127	344	Mixed-use
7	Chrysler Building	New York	USA	1930	77	1046	319	Office
8	First Canadian Place	Toronto	Canada	1975	72	978	298	Office
9	American International Building (originally Cities Service Building)	New York	USA	1932	67	952	290	Office
10	40 Wall Street (now Trump Building)	New York	USA	1930	70	927	283	Office

The 10 world's tallest buildings in 1976 include, for the first time since the 1930s, a series of new super-tall buildings with three buildings taller than the Empire State Building, the world's tallest for more than 40 years. Chicago makes its mark with a mixed-use skyscraper appearing for the first time in the list: the John Hancock Center, with the world's highest apartment at over 1000 feet. Buildings are all located in North America.

Source: G. Binder/Buildings & Data SA

Taipei 101, Taipei, Taiwan, C.Y. Lee & Partners Architects/Planners, 2004, 101 stories
Photography: Courtesy C.Y. Lee & Partners Architects/Planners

In 1998, the 88-story Petronas Towers (also known as Petronas Twin Towers) in Kuala Lumpur, then the world's tallest building, carried the name of an oil company that was at the time relatively unknown in the Western world. But the goal in this case was different. The Petronas Towers was a project initiated by the prime minister of Malaysia with the aim of putting his country on the world map. And it worked, because if few still know the Petronas brand, many more are aware of the Petronas Towers' position, until recently, as the world's tallest towers, and their location.

Taipei, through the 101-story Taipei 101 designed by C.Y Lee & Partners, also wanted to express its economic success through high-rise architecture with the current world's tallest building. These two Asian projects have introduced a type of geographical marketing through super-tall buildings. Both projects feature a regionalist contextual approach to architectural style. Taipei 101, as the current world's tallest building, is of course also a political statement in the context of the history of Taipei.

The Kuala Lumpur and Taipei projects can be seen as exceptionally super-tall projects designed to promote a city or a country. This promotion has been successful, as the projects have been repeatedly published in the international press. In a similar way, the Jin Mao Tower in Shanghai brought attention to a country that was dramatically evolving from traditional Chinese construction to high-rise buildings, both commercial and residential. This evolution began in Shanghai and Shenzhen and moved to Beijing; Shanghai took on the role of the next Asian financial center through its Pudong zone, which has one of the most dynamic clusters of tall buildings built anywhere on earth. However, this rush to build has, in some cases, ignored the reality of economics and China has experienced a high number of empty tall buildings upon completion, and in some of the early examples, also some poorly built or designed buildings.

Approaching the turn of the first decade of the new millennium, the super-tall building is becoming an advertising board for society at large, rather than for the large corporation. This evolution is also linked to the fact that most of the super-tall projects now under progress are mixed-use towers, while the history of this building type has been mostly related to single-use office buildings. In the same way as tall office buildings need major tenants (such as in the case of RepublicBank in Houston) in order to secure an economically viable project, the mixed-use building is another way to achieve such a goal: hotels, for example, responding to the increasing demands of the tourism and travel industries, have proved to be a valuable major tenant, securing the viability of a project's construction.

1995: the emergence of the Middle East

1995 was a milestone year for Middle East high-rise structures, with the announcement of the world's tallest hospitality building in Dubai: the 1053-foot Chicago Beach Hotel, known since its completion as the Burj Al Arab. The hotel, designed by WS Atkins, is located offshore on a manmade island and features a dramatic 600-foot atrium. Until the 1990s, tall buildings in the Middle East were mainly found in Cairo, Egypt, and in Israel, with a series a moderately tall buildings completed since the mid-1960s and one 801-foot mixed-use tower completed in Ramat Gan near Tel-Aviv in 2001.

In Dubai, the Burj Al Arab was soon followed by the twin 1164-foot and 1014-foot Emirates Towers (now the Jumeirah Emirates Towers). Dubai was definitely establishing itself as a location where sky-high living was becoming a way of life, with the manifest support of Sheikh Mohammed bin Rashid Al Maktoum, then Crown Prince of Dubai and now its ruler. The example of the Malaysian prime minister's initiative to promote the Petronas Towers as a symbol of Malaysia also applied to Dubai, which rapidly became a new place to be visited by foreign tourists with hotels such as the Burj Al Arab and the Emirates Towers being destinations on their own.

Shortly after, a succession of other super-tall projects were announced, among them, the next world's tallest building: the more than 2300-foot mixed-use Burj Dubai, designed by Adrian Smith, Consulting Design Partner at Skidmore, Owings & Merrill. Nestled in a landscaped park, Burj Dubai will be the crown jewel of a larger, urban mixed-use ensemble.

Burj Dubai, Dubai, United Arab Emirates, Adrian Smith, Consulting Design Partner, Skidmore, Owings & Merrill, 2009, more than 150 stories
Photography: Courtesy Skidmore, Owings & Merrill LLP

World's tallest buildings in 1986

		City	Country	Year	Stories	Feet	Meters	Use
1	Sears Tower	Chicago	USA	1974	110	1450	442	Office
2	One World Trade Center	New York	USA	1972	110	1368	417	Office
3	Two World Trade Center	New York	USA	1973	110	1362	415	Office
4	Empire State Building	New York	USA	1931	102	1250	381	Office
5	Standard Oil (now Aon Center)	Chicago	USA	1973	83	1136	346	Office
6	John Hancock Center	Chicago	USA	1970	100	1127	344	Mixed-use
7	Chrysler Building	New York	USA	1930	77	1046	319	Office
8	Texas Commerce Tower (now JP Morgan Chase Tower)	Houston	USA	1982	75	993	303	Office
9	Allied Bank Plaza (now Wells Fargo Plaza)	Houston	USA	1983	71	992	302	Office
10	First Canadian Place	Toronto	Canada	1975	72	978	298	Office

The 10 world's tallest buildings in 1986 include newly built projects in Houston following a recent boom in the local economy.

Source: G. Binder/Buildings & Data SA

Super-tall mixed-use towers under construction in the Middle East and Asia

Dubai's tall buildings philosophy has been exported to other parts of the Middle East: Dubai International Properties has currently under construction the Dubai Towers in Doha, Qatar, a 1460-foot mixed-use tower designed by Hazel WS Wong of RMJM Dubai. The 86-story project will comprise office, hospitality, residential, and retail space and will create a strong statement for Doha, rising high above the Arabian Gulf. In Istanbul, the same developer plans to build a duo of super-tall twisted towers, designed by Skidmore, Owings & Merrill.

In the meantime, Asia continues to produce buildings such as the long-awaited 1614-foot 101-story Shanghai World Financial Center in Shanghai, designed by Kohn Pedersen Fox Associates comprising office, hotel and entertainment venues, and the 1608-foot 118-story International Commerce Center in Kowloon, Hong Kong, also designed by Kohn Pedersen Fox Associates and comprising offices, a hotel, retail, and entertainment venues in addition to an airport express rail link. Along with its neighbor, the Jin Mao Tower, the Shanghai World Financial Center will be the apex of Pudong, promoting Shanghai as the place to do business in the 21st century. The 118-story Hong Kong project will create, with the 88-story Two International Finance Center, an entry portal into the city with the effect of a virtual bridge over the bay, in the same way as the Golden Gate Bridge creates a sense of arrival to first-time visitors to San Francisco. The International Commerce Center is part of Union Square, a larger ensemble comprising housing, office, hotels, retail, and a landscaped park as well as cultural activities. The project was conceived as a transportation hub connecting the Kowloon area to Chep Lap Kok Airport; super-tall buildings in Hong Kong are no longer mono-purpose office projects.

Other Asian super-tall mixed-use towers are expected to create new lifestyles in South Korea. In Busan, the 107-story Lotte World II Tower designed by Parker Durrant International will provide office, hospitality, and retail space; in New Songdo City, the 65-story, 1001-foot Northeast Asia Trade Tower, designed by Kohn Pedersen Fox Associates, will become one of the most diverse mixed-use super-tall buildings ever designed, comprising office, residential, hospitality, and retail space.

The United States today

In the United States, tall buildings over 1000 feet are again under construction for the first time in almost 15 years. In Chicago, the construction of Trump Chicago International Hotel & Tower is now in progress. The 1361-foot, 92-story project, designed by Adrian Smith of Skidmore, Owings & Merrill, will also provide a mix of uses comprising retail, hotel, and residential but no office space—the first tower above 1000 feet to be built in the United States without office space. Without 9/11, this project could have been expected to become the tallest in the country; but for obvious reasons, Donald J. Trump chose not to add a further 100 feet to achieve that distinction.

Construction of another mixed-use tower in Chicago began in 2006. Waterview Tower, a 90-story, 1050-foot tower designed by Thomas Hoepf and Edward Wilkas of Teng Associates will also include a hotel and residences but again no offices. Since the completion of the John Hancock Center in 1970, Chicago is the city in the United States where mixed-use high-rise buildings have been the most widely accepted.

The United States' current crop of office buildings appear to be of a size compatible with the needs of the market, and not the ego-fuelled examples of the past. New tall buildings of note in

World's tallest buildings in 1996

		City	Country	Year	Stories	Feet	Meters	Use
1	Sears Tower	Chicago	USA	1974	110	1450	442	Office
2	One World Trade Center	New York	USA	1972	110	1368	417	Office
3	Two World Trade Center	New York	USA	1973	110	1362	415	Office
4	Empire State Building	New York	USA	1931	102	1250	381	Office
5	Central Plaza	Hong Kong	China *	1992	78	1227	374	Office
6	Bank of China Tower	Hong Kong	China *	1989	70	1205	367	Office
7	Amoco Building (now Aon Center)	Chicago	USA	1973	83	1136	346	Office
8	John Hancock Center	Chicago	USA	1970	100	1127	344	Mixed-use
9	Chrysler Building	New York	USA	1930	77	1046	319	Office
10	NationsBank Plaza (now Bank of America Plaza)	Atlanta	USA	1992	57	1039	317	Office

*Hong Kong was to return to China in 1997.

The 10 world's tallest buildings in 1996 include Asian projects for the first time, including one project not designed by an American-based architect, Central Plaza, designed by Ng Chun Man & Associates, now Dennis Lau & Ng Chun Man.

Source: G. Binder/Buildings & Data SA

New York include the 1046-foot New York Times Tower, designed by Renzo Piano Building Workshop and FXFOWLE Architects, and not far away, the 1200-foot Bank of America Tower designed by Cook+Fox Architects with Adamson Associates as associate architect. The name of each project says it all—a response to a demand. Such was not the case when the World Trade Center was built decades ago. The former WTC site in New York is scheduled to accommodate in the future the second-tallest building in North America at 1368 feet or the tallest at 1776 feet, if its antenna is included.

Current activity in Europe

With a series of projects in design and under construction in Europe, the Old Continent may in the coming years present skylines that in some places could not have been imagined even 10 years ago. London has several projects scheduled to become city landmarks, including the 1017-foot Shard at London Bridge designed by Renzo Piano Building Workshop, and the 945-foot Bishopsgate Tower, designed by Kohn Pedersen Fox Associates. The city of Moscow is undergoing tremendous change with a number of recently completed projects such as the residential 866-foot Triumph-Palace designed by Tromos, and with the construction of several super-tall mixed-use projects including the Moscow International Business Center designed by Swanke Hayden Connell Architects, Capital City by NBBJ, and the tallest of them all at 1471 feet, Federation Tower, designed by Peter Schweger/ASP Schweger Assoziierte and Sergei Tchoban/nps tchoban voss. The Moscow-City development, where most of the current Moscow super-tall buildings are located, is an initiative of the city authorities, and some of the Moscow projects are financed by state-owned banks. These political gestures are reminiscent of several Asian projects.

At the time of writing, a new super-tall mixed-use tower has just been announced for Moscow City in Moscow: the 118-story 1969-foot project designed by Foster and Partners could become Europe's tallest building, surpassing the United States for the first time since 1930.

In Paris, EPAD, the public body responsible for regulating the development of La Défense, the tall buildings district on the outskirts of Paris, has a plan that would allow, in 15 years, the construction or reconstruction of more than 9 million square feet of office space. The proposal includes a 1300-foot tower, which will be the subject of an international architectural competition. A recent brochure states, *'Even though projects that combine formal innovation with 'conquering the sky' flourish in America, Asia and also in Europe, it is inconceivable that La Défense should stay trapped under the current ceiling of 200 metres. International competition blueprints for the next towers will break the taboos about high-rise and will put La Défense on the international skyline!*

Moscow City Tower, Moscow, Russia, Foster and Partners, 2006 (design unveiled), 118 stories
Rendering: Courtesy Foster and Partners

This will be affirmed by the construction of an office tower of at least 400 metres high, which will stimulate both eye and spirit alike. This will be the Signal tower, whose silhouette will be an impressive exclamation mark in the ongoing commentary of La Défense'. (La Défense 2015/Le sens de l'avenir, EPAD, Paris, 2006). Although the tall building represented modernity in Europe from the 1960s until the early 1970s, its height generally remained modest on the Old Continent. The quotation from the La Défense brochure is perhaps the first in Europe to suggest that super-tall buildings can help to define a city and have an impact on its economic potential in a competitive global economy.

Built more than a century ago, the Eiffel Tower has defined the height of most of the super-tall buildings, ever since the race began with the Chrysler Building surpassing the Parisian tower by a small margin. It appears that 'Old Europe' would like to be on the international skyline scene again.

Conclusions

The super-tall skyscraper, once considered a North American (mainly American) product, is now an Asian product with the most examples currently under construction in the Middle East. Even if mainly built in Asia, many tall buildings architects are based in the United States—Pelli Clarke Pelli Architects, Kohn Pedersen Fox Associates, and Skidmore, Owings & Merrill, are some such examples.

While in the past, super-tall buildings were mainly office towers, many of the super-tall buildings currently or soon to be under construction are multi-purpose buildings; most of the super-tall towers, such as the 90-story 23 Marina or the 107-story Princess Tower in Dubai, are residential-only buildings. This has as much to do with the current market, which is not favorable for building office space in many areas of the world, but which displays an unprecedented demand for high-rise residences. Only time will confirm if this is the way of the future, or, as was the case in the early 1970s in Chicago and New York, it is a limited experience. It looks as if the pace of building such projects and the emulation in so many locations is becoming unstoppable. Even Moscow, Russia has several super-tall, mixed-use projects currently under construction, of which the tallest, Federation Tower, is 1471 feet high; London should follow soon with a series of tall projects.

Corporate or cultural totems?

For almost a century—with the exception of the 1950s Stalinist high-rises in Moscow, the tallest skyscrapers bore the names of the private companies that occupied them. Previously noted examples in the United States include the Woolworth Building, the Chrysler Building, the Pan Am Building, the Transamerica Pyramid, and the Sears Tower.

There are few famous such examples outside the North America, and it was not until 1986, with the Hongkong and Shanghai Banking Corporation Headquarters building and later the 70-story Bank of China Tower in Hong Kong, that the same effect was achieved on another continent. In 1998, the 88-story Petronas Towers in Kuala Lumpur propelled the tall building into another role envisioned by the prime minister of Malaysia—that of promoting an entire nation. The Taipei 101 initiative can also be put in the same category, expressing success and prosperity through high-rise architecture. These two Asian projects have introduced a type of regionalistic marketing through super-tall buildings. In parallel with Asia, the Middle East has also put its mark on the world map through super-tall architecture. Hotels such the Burj Al Arab and the Jumeirah Emirates Towers have become destinations in their own right and Dubai has created a strong image for tourism. In the same vein, the next world's tallest building is simply called 'Burj Dubai' (the 'Dubai Tower') promoting the city as a whole. All these projects would not have been developed the way they are without the support of Sheikh Mohammed bin Rashid Al Maktoum, then Crown Prince of Dubai and now its ruler.

At the turn of the new millennium the super-tall tower is becoming an advertising board for the society at large and no longer only for the large corporations as was the case in the past.

The race to the sky

In New York City in the 1930s, there was fierce competition between the developers of first 40 Wall Street and the Chrysler Building, and later the Empire State Building, to build the world's tallest building. Forty years later, the race to the sky struck again, this time in Chicago: the 1127-foot John Hancock Center was completed in 1970, followed by the 1136-foot

World's tallest buildings in 2006

		City	Country	Year	Stories	Feet	Meters	Use
1	Taipei 101	Taipei	Taiwan	2004	101	1667	508	Office
2	Petronas Towers 1	Kuala Lumpur	Malaysia	1998	88	1483	452	Office
3	Petronas Towers 2	Kuala Lumpur	Malaysia	1998	88	1483	452	Office
4	Sears Tower	Chicago	USA	1974	110	1450	442	Office
5	Jin Mao Tower	Shanghai	China	1999	88	1380	421	Mixed-use
6	Two International Finance Center	Hong Kong	China	2003	88	1362	415	Office
7	CITIC Plaza	Guangzhou	China	1997	80	1280	390	Office
8	Shun Hing Square	Shenzhen	China	1996	80	1260	384	Office
9	Empire State Building	New York	USA	1931	102	1250	381	Office
10	Central Plaza	Hong Kong	China	1992	78	1227	374	Office

The 10 world's tallest buildings in 2006 show for the first time the predominance of Asia over North America. The trend would have been the same even with the inclusion of the World Trade Center, which disappeared from the list in 2001.

Source: G. Binder/Buildings & Data SA

Standard Oil Building (now Aon Center) in 1973, both then topped by the Sears Tower in 1974 at 1450 feet, which also surpassed the 1368-foot World Trade Center in New York.

With the Burj Dubai announced at over 2300 feet but with no exact height, we return to the Chrysler era when the spire was assembled inside the building in secrecy to ensure that the record was achieved (albeit for a short time). The announced 2300 feet of the Burj Dubai is hopefully far enough ahead of the rest of the pack for it to be the world's tallest for some time.

It is perhaps appropriate to explain here that, although every effort has been made throughout this book to record correct height figures, these figures no longer make a lot of sense—if they ever did make sense—since the spires put atop I.M. Pei's Bank of China in Hong Kong seem to have skewed the whole height matter ever since. Prior to that, only the Chrysler Building had a spire included in the 'official' overall height and the spire was obviously part of the design, even if the reason for this design was to increase the height. Since the early 1990s, most super-tall projects completed include spires in order to reach taller overall height records. Perhaps the several flat-roofed super-tall skyscrapers recently designed by Kohn Pedersen Fox Associates, such as the Shanghai World Financial Center and the International Commerce Center in China, and the Northeast Asia Trade Tower in South Korea, will be the the beginning of a trend away from the spire and its influence over height.

'And so Sears Tower will hold its height record in perpetuity,' wrote Paul Gapp, architecture critic, in 1980 (*Chicago Tribune*, September 14, 1980). Gapp was summarizing factors against tall buildings, such as the large plazas associated with tall buildings, supposedly disliked by the public, and the 'growing public distaste' for such buildings as well as the lack of need in the future for tall platforms needed for telecommunication because of cable technology and satellites. Gapp appeared to be right for almost 20 years but obviously, there is still a need for elevated platforms to house broadcast telecommunication antennas and the super-tall building seems to be more popular today than ever before.

Northeast Asia Trade Tower, New Songdo City, South Korea,
Kohn Pedersen Fox Associates, 2009, 65 stories
Rendering: 3D-Win, Korea

Three cycles of construction of super-tall skyscrapers can be identified: the late 1920s to early 1930s; the early 1970s; and most recently the mid-1990s to 2010. From a product originally located in one location only (the United States of America), mono-use (office), designed according to a single style only, (Art-Deco first, Modernism in the 1970s) it has evolved to the point where super-tall skyscrapers are now found on every continent with the exception of Africa, with a current predominance in Asia. Super-tall buildings currently in progress are characterized by their mixed-use or residential nature, and their style, which is driven more by the personality of their architects than by the style currently in vogue.

When Gapp predicted the end of the super-tall skyscraper in the early 1980s, so-called Postmodernism was at its peak in terms of media coverage, with the Johnson/Burgee-designed AT&T Building published widely and Modernism presented until then as a unique way to reflect modernity. The fact that a large number of super-tall skyscrapers are under progress does not mean that they are the answer to people's needs in terms of living together, but obviously seems to mean that they are more and more widely accepted, having been adopted in so many places for different uses. Perhaps the fact that super-tall buildings are used by different categories of occupants, for office, housing, and hotel purposes, helps their wide acceptance, since they are no longer seen as intrusive corporate symbols in people's lives. The symbol of the few is now becoming the symbol of the masses, representing an entire city, region or country.

Integration into urban ensembles

Many of today's super-tall buildings are part of larger mixed-used urban developments. The Petronas Towers in Kuala Lumpur, the Jin Mao Tower and the Shanghai World Financial Center in Shanghai, or the International Commerce Center in Hong Kong, are all part of larger urban projects comprising a newly built landscaped park. Many of the new super-tall projects are also mixed-use towers—the 65-story Northeast Asia Trade Tower in Songdo New City, South Korea epitomizes this new trend of super-tall projects comprising office, residential, hotel and retail space. In the previous super-tall construction cycles of the 1930s and the 1970s, the buildings were isolated objects, such as the Empire State Building, or Sears Tower. While some were integrated into the city urban fabric, they were usually not part of an overall urban/real estate plan—a notable exception is the RCA Building (now GE Building) in New York City, part of the Rockefeller Center. Of course, there are still individual and mono-functional super-tall buildings (usually residential ones) under progress now, but more than ever projects are being designed as part of larger mixed-use urban ensembles.

Back to the future?

Perhaps an aspect of the future may include expandable tall buildings. The BlueCross BlueShield of Illinois Headquarters Building, designed by Lohan Associates, (now Goettsch Partners) was completed in Chicago in 1997 and planned in a period not favorable for speculative projects. The project was therefore built to answer the current needs of the occupant, with no more space than immediately necessary. The design allowed the vertical expansion of the building in a second phase. The project already completed comprises 32 stories and 1.4 million square feet, but it has been designed to expand to 54 stories with a capacity of 2.3 million square feet. The solution is achieved by moving the elevator banks, conventionally located in the central core, to a five-bay glazed atrium in the back of the building. Banks of elevators for future expansions are added to the unoccupied bays and existing operations are uninterrupted.

World's tallest buildings scheduled to be completed by 2010

		City	Country	Year	Stories	Feet	Meters	Use
1	Burj Dubai	Dubai	UAE	2009	150+	2300+	700+	Mixed-use
2	Lotte World II Tower	Busan	South Korea	2008	103	1673	510	Mixed-use
3	Taipei 101	Taipei	Taiwan	2004	101	1667	508	Office
4	Shanghai World Financial Center	Shanghai	China	2007	101	1614	492	Mixed-use
5	International Commerce Center	Hong Kong	China	2010	118	1608	490	Mixed-use
6	Abraj Al Bait Hotel	Makkah	Saudi Arabia	2008	76	1591	485	Hotel
7	Petronas Towers 1	Kuala Lumpur	Malaysia	1998	88	1483	452	Office
8	Petronas Towers 2	Kuala Lumpur	Malaysia	1998	88	1483	452	Office
9	Nanjing Greenland Financial Center	Nanjing	China	2008	66	1476	450	Mixed-use
10	Federation Tower	Moscow	Russia	2007	93	1471	448	Mixed-use

The 10 world's tallest buildings expected to be completed by 2010 present a dominant Asia with no American projects, for the first time since the creation of the skyscraper in the United States. At the same time, a European high-rise building is again in the top 10 list, again located in the eastern part of the continent. We also note that whatever the zone, for the first time in the history of the skyscraper, the mixed-use tall building dominates the office building. Along with the dominance of the mixed-use building, the trend of building names that are not associated with corporations, already evident in 2006, is confirmed.

Source: G. Binder/Buildings & Data SA

Each new skyscraper breaking any height record induces the next taller skyscraper, which in turn is expected to break the next record. Instead of trying to speculate about the future of the super-tall high-rise city, perhaps we can have a brief look at Richard Rummell's 1911 drawing, *Future New York*, or *The City of the Future* as envisioned by architect Francisco Mujica in 1928, both visions integrating horizontal circulation in a vertical city.

Could it be that, considering the proliferation of super-tall buildings currently in progress, these imaginary utopias of yesterday may perhaps be tomorrow's reality?

Georges Binder
Managing Director
Buildings & Data SA
Brussels, Belgium, 2006

Future New York, *a romantic future vision of New York City*
by Richard Rummell, 1911
Reproduced from King's Views of New York, *Manhattan Post Card Company, New York, 1926, Coll. G. Binder/Buildings & Data SA*

BlueCross BlueShield of Illinois Headquarters Building, Chicago, Illinois, USA, Lohan Associates (now Goettsch Partners) and Goettsch Partners for the future expansion, 1997, 32 stories (and 54 stories after a future expansion) Rendering: Courtesy Goettsch Partners

The City of the Future: Hundred Story City in Neo-American Style, *by Francisco Mujica, Architect, 1928. A 1011.6-foot 100-story city with the 20 lower levels for office use and the residential levels above.*
Reproduced from Francisco Mujica, History of the Skyscraper, *Archaeology & Architecture Press, Paris/New York, 1929*

Completed Buildings

TAIPEI 101

TAIPEI 101 was a joint effort between the government of Taiwan and the private sector, with the aim of increasing Taiwan's global profile by constructing the world's tallest building.

Located in the Xin Yi New District, TAIPEI 101 is the largest engineering project in the history of Taiwan. The design is based on the Chinese number 8, a numeral representing prosperity in Chinese culture. The design is based on eight-floor interlocking structural units, a rhythmic aesthetic new to skyscraper design. Inclining 7 degrees inwards, the structure increases in size as it gets higher. Although the floor plates increase within each structural unit, the three sections are identical in size. Wind effects usually created on the surface of high-rise buildings are minimized by the building's W-shaped corners.

The section employs a mega structure system for disaster and wind damage prevention, and is designed to withstand the effects of a grade 17 typhoon. Built in a highly active earthquake zone, the building's seismic-proof equipment includes 800 tons of wind resistance and seismic-proof wind damper, which automatically calculates the shaking magnitude, and self-adjusts the building's movement. A safety escape path is provided on each floor of the building, with a fire safety holding area on each floor, fire-protection shelter rooms and outdoor shelter balconies on every eighth floor. The triple accident protection segregation system, smoke control system and life escape system provide the most comprehensive and rapid accident prevention and emergency escape methods.

The two observatory shuttle elevators in TAIPEI 101 are the fastest in the world, traveling upwards at 3312 feet per minute and downwards at 1969 feet per minute.

TAIPEI 101 employs cutting-edge infrastructure, to supply world-class facilities and technical services for business tenants. It is equipped with dual communication channels comprised of a fiber optic backbone, microwave and satellite communication backups. The 24/7 global communication system enables financial operations to keep pace with the world and enjoy non-stop quality communication. An advanced information security system prevents hacking or information leakage from the broadband network .

With its balance of traditional cultural elements and cutting-edge technology, TAIPEI 101 is the benchmark for tall buildings around the world.

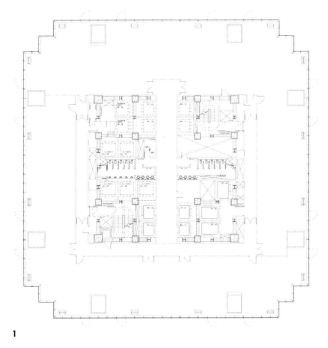

1

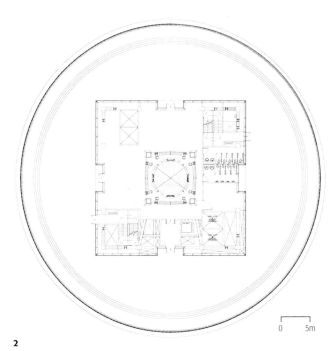

2

0   5m

1   Typical office floor plan
2   91st floor plan
3   Aerial view

3

Location Taipei, Taiwan

Completion date 2004

Architect C.Y. Lee & Partners Architects/Planners

Client Taipei Financial Center Corp.

Structural engineer Thornton-Tomasetti Engineers; Evergreen Consulting Engineering, Inc.

Wind damper consultant Motioneering Inc.

Services engineer Lehr Associates; Continental Engineering Consultants, Inc.

Vertical transportation consultant Lerch, Bates & Associates Inc.

Landscape architect Genius Luci

Contractor Kumagai Gumi; Taiwan Kumagai; RSEA Engineering; Ta-You-Wei Construction

Developer Taipei Financial Center Corp.

Project manager Turner International SA

Height 1667 ft/508 m

Above-ground stories 101

Basements 5

Full mechanical levels 92–100

Use Mixed: office, shopping mall

Site area 325,781 sq ft/30,277 sq m

Area of above-ground building 4,438,500 sq ft/412,500 sq m (total)

Area of typical floor plate 30,235–46,268 sq ft/2810–4300 sq m (low zone); 26,900–35,562 sq ft/2500–3305 sq m (mid zone); 28,460–38,413 sq ft/2645–3570 sq m (high zone)

Basic planning module 5 ft/1.5 m

Number of parking spaces 1839 (car); 2990 (motorcycle)

Principal structural materials Steel

Other materials Glass curtainwall, stone wall base

4

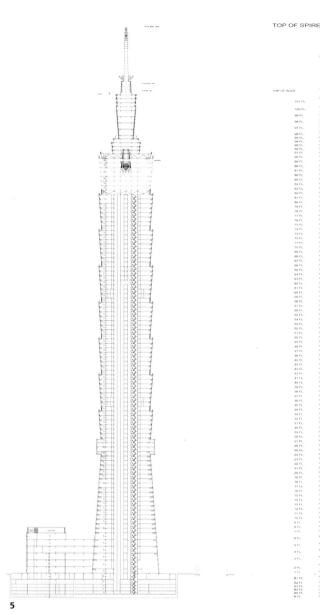

TOP OF SPIRE

5

4   Shopping mall
5   Building section
6   Taipei's new icon
Opposite:
    Façade detail

Photography: Taipei Financial Center Corp.

6

Petronas Towers

An international competition was held to select a master plan for the 100-acre site, selected by the Malaysian government to be developed into a new 'city within a city'. Based on the winning scheme by Klages, Carter, Vail and Partners, further improvements were made by the City Mayor and his planning team, KLCCB and its consultants.

Approximately half of the site is devoted to public parks and gardens, surrounded by 18 million square feet of commercial, retail, hotel, recreational and residential development. Phase One of the Kuala Lumpur City Centre development comprises more than 10.7 million square feet of mixed-use development, which includes the twin 88-story Petronas Towers; two other office towers; 1.5 million square feet of retail/entertainment facilities; and 2.7 million square feet of below-grade parking and service facilities. Public functions include a Petroleum Discovery Centre, an art gallery, the Dewan Petronas Filharmonik concert hall, and a multimedia conference center. A multi-story shopping and entertainment galleria connects the office towers at the base, integrating the entire complex.

The two Petronas Towers are connected by a skybridge at the sky lobby levels (41st and 42nd floors). Organized around this interchange of the circulation system are shared facilities such as the conference center, Upper Surau (prayer room), and the executive dining room.

The lobby core walls are finished in light-colored Malaysian woods within a stainless steel grid. The lobby marble floor pattern is derived from popular Malaysian 'Pandan' weaving and bertam palm wall matting patterns. A continuous wooden screen wall shields the perimeter of the lobby wall, reinforcing the sense of the tropical locale and optimizing the use of Malaysian crafts.

The crescent-shaped mall of the retail/entertainment complex has 1.5 million square feet of retail, food and entertainment facilities located on six levels. Arcades and canopies at street level enhance pedestrian comfort, evoking the 'five-foot way' commonly found in traditional shop houses.

The towers express traditional Malaysia, but they also express the new Malaysia: a rapidly industrializing country with a dynamic economy.

In 2004, the Petronas Towers were awarded the Aga Khan Award for Architecture.

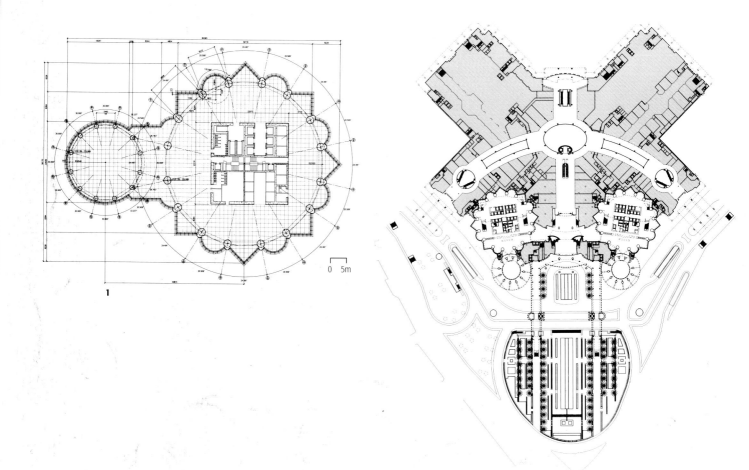

1

0 5m

Location Kuala Lumpur, Malaysia

Completion date 1998

Architect Cesar Pelli & Associates (now Pelli Clarke Pelli Architects)

Associate architect Adamson Associates

Architect of record KLCC Berhad Architectural Division

Client Kuala Lumpur City Centre Sendirian Berhad; Kuala Lumpur City Centre Berhad

Structural engineer Thornton-Tomasetti Engineers; Ranhill Bersekutu Sdn. Bhd.

Mechanical engineer Flack + Kurtz; KTA Tenaga Sdn. Bhd.

Vertical transportation consultant Katz Drago Company, Inc.

Landscape architect Balmori Associates

Contractor Tower 1: MMC Engineering & Construction Co. Ltd.; Ho Hup Construction Sdn. Bhd.; Hazama Corporation; JA Jones Construction Co. Ltd.; Mitsubishi Corporation

Contractor Tower 2 and Skybridge: Samsung Engineering & Construction Co. Ltd.; Kukdong Engineering & Construction Co. Ltd.; Syarikat Jasatera Sdn. Bhd. JV

Developer Kuala Lumpur City Centre Sendirian Berhad; Kuala Lumpur City Centre Berhad

Project management consultant Lehrer McGovern Malaysia

Height 1483 ft/452 m

Above-ground stories 88

Basements 4

Above-ground useable levels 88

Mechanical levels and level numbers

Use Office, retail, performing arts center, public space, gallery

Site area more than 100 acres/40 ha

Area of above-ground building 2,300,000 sq ft/213,670 sq m (towers)

Area of typical floor plate Lower floors: 28,239 sq ft/2623 sq m; upper floors: 22,490–10,000 sq ft/2089–929 sq m

Number of parking spaces 5000

Principal structural materials A core and cylindrical tube frame system constructed entirely of cast-in-place high-strength concrete (up to Grade 80); floor framing at tower levels are concrete fill all of conventional strength on composite steel floor deck and composite rolled steel framing; clad in unitized stainless steel and glass curtain wall.

1   Floor plan
2   Ground level plan
3   Night view of towers from west
4   Elevation

Photography: Jeff Goldberg/Esto

3

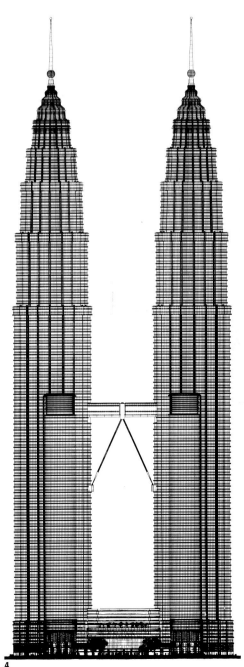

4

Sears Tower

For 22 years, Sears Tower was the tallest building in the world. Still the tallest building in the western hemisphere, it boasts the tallest occupiable floor and the tallest skyscraper roof in the world. It is also the largest private office building, with some 3.7 million square feet of office space.

The Sears Tower is the quintessential example of the revolutionary bundled-tube structural system, providing large, virtually column-free spaces and 70-foot clear spans. As the building climbs upward, the tubes begin to drop off, and the wind forces on the building are reduced. The square tubes measure 75 x 75 feet with perimeter columns spaced at 15 feet on center. At the base, nine tubes rise to the 49th floor. Two tubes drop off at the 50th and 66th floors, and three at the 90th floor, allowing the last two tubes to rise to the building's 110-story top. To reduce shear stress, the structure has diagonal bracing only on the two levels (mechanical floors) before each setback. The 222,500-ton building is supported by 114 caissons that reach bedrock.

The exterior skin of the building is an expression of the structural skeleton inside, with the fireproof frame sheathed in black aluminum and glare-reducing bronze-tinted glass. The exterior skin is maintained with yearly check-ups and six window-washing machines.

The Sears Tower's 104-cab elevator system divides the building into three separate zones, with sky lobbies in between at levels 33–34 and levels 66–67. Twenty-eight double-deck express shuttle elevators serve the sky lobbies, and 63 single-deck elevators provide intra-zonal travel; there are also six freight elevators. Two express elevators take 61 seconds to reach the 1353-foot-high Skydeck on level 103 from lower level 2, traveling at 1600 feet per minute.

A description of Sears Tower would not be complete without mentioning 'Universe', a 55-foot-wide, 33-foot-tall bright colored mobile, designed by Alexander Calder, that is located in the main lobby.

1   A rectangular promontory, 75 x 150 feet, rises from floors 90–109
2   Floor plan, floors 66–89; these floors are in a cruciform shape after setbacks of the northeast and southwest modules
3   Floor plan, floors 50–65; at the 49th floor, two of the nine 75-foot-square modules terminate, changing the tower's shape to a Z-form from the 50th to 6th floors
4   Floor plan, floors 1–49; the base of the Tower is a 225-foot square
5   General view

Photography: Courtesy Skidmore, Owings & Merrill LLP

Floor plans reproduced from original Sears Tower leasing brochure, Coll. G Binder/Buildings & Data SA

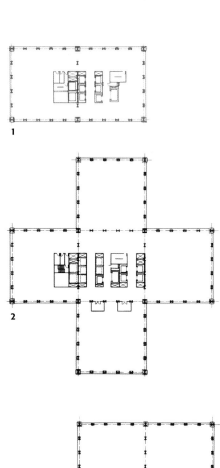

1

2

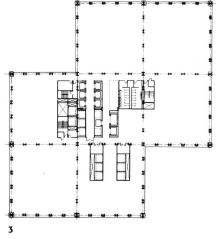

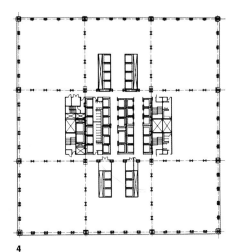

3

4

Location Chicago, Illinois, USA

Completion date 1974

Architect Skidmore, Owings & Merrill LLP, Bruce Graham, Design Partner

Client Sears, Roebuck and Co.

Structural engineer Fazlur Khan of Skidmore, Owings & Merrill LLP

Mechanical and electrical engineer Jaros, Baum & Bolles

Interior planners Saphier, Lerner, Schindler, Inc.

Project developer consultant Cushman & Wakefield, Inc.

General contractor Morse Diesel International

Height 1450 ft/442 m; 1725 ft/526 m (including antennas)

Above-ground stories 110

Basements 4

Mechanical levels 29–33, 64–66, 88–90, 104–109

Use Office, retail, conference center (levels 33 and 99), observatory (level 103)

Site area 2.96 acres/1.12 ha (plaza area 80,000 sq ft/7432 sq m)

Area of above-ground building 4,560,000 sq ft/423,624 sq m (gross); 3,810,000 sq ft/353,949 sq m (rentable)

Area of typical floor plates (approx) Floors 1–49: 50,000 sq ft/4645 sq m; floors 50–65: 39,000 sq ft/3623 sq m; floors 66–89: 29,000 sq ft/2694 sq m; floors 90–109: 11,000 sq ft /1022 sq m

Number of parking spaces 160 below grade

Principal structural materials Steel

Other materials Black duranodic aluminum

Jin Mao Tower

Located in the Pudong District in the city's Lujiazui Finance and Trade Zone, the project is a 3-million-square-foot multi-use development incorporating office, hotel, retail, service amenities and parking. The 88-story tower houses hotel and office space, with a 555-room Grand Hyatt Hotel in the top 38 stories affording impressive views of the city and the surrounding region. Jin Mao's six-story podium houses hotel function areas, a conference and exhibition center, a cinema auditorium and a 226,000-square-foot retail galleria. The base of the tower is surrounded by a landscaped courtyard with a reflecting pool and seating, offering visitors a peaceful retreat from Shanghai's busy street activity.

In addition to the tower and podium, Jin Mao incorporates three below-grade levels with a total area of 615,000 square feet. These levels accommodate parking for 993 cars and 1000 bicycles; hotel service facilities; additional retail space; a food court; an observatory elevator lobby; and building systems equipment areas including electrical transformers and switchgear, a sewage treatment plant, a domestic water plant, a boiler room and a chiller plant.

The building systems design integrates intelligent building features that provide life safety, security and comfort; high levels of energy efficiency; ease of building maintenance, operation and control; and technologically advanced communications systems. Advanced structural engineering concepts employed in the design of the tower protect it from the typhoon winds and earthquakes typical of the area.

The tower recalls historic Chinese pagoda forms, with setbacks that create a rhythmic pattern. Its metal and glass curtain wall reflects the constantly changing skies, while at night the tower shaft and crown are illuminated. At 1381 feet, the tower and its spire are a significant addition to the Shanghai skyline. Jin Mao is the tallest building in China and the centerpiece of Shanghai.

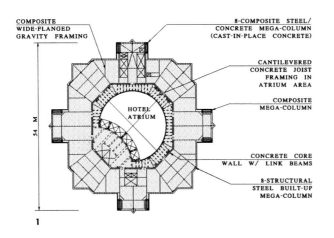

1

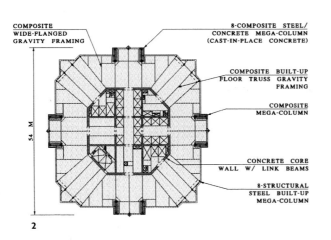

2

3

1 Typical hotel framing plan
2 Typical office framing plan
3 Detail of curved glass wall
4 View at dusk
5 Section

Photography: Courtesy Skidmore, Owings & Merrill LLP

4

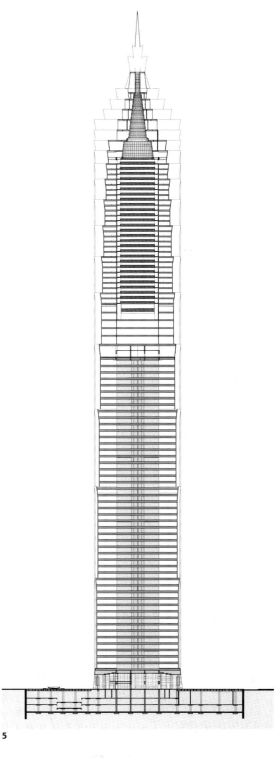

5

Location Shanghai, China

Completion date 1998

Architect Skidmore, Owings & Merrill LLP, Adrian Smith, Design Partner

Associate architect The Shanghai Institute of Architectural Design & Research (SIADR); East China Architectural Design & Research Institute Co. Ltd. (ECADI)

Client China Jin Mao Group Co.

Developer China Shanghai Foreign Trade Company

Structural engineer Skidmore, Owings & Merrill LLP

Mechanical engineer Skidmore, Owings & Merrill LLP

Vertical transportation consultant Edgett Williams Consulting Group

Contractor Shanghai Jin Mao Contractor (SJMC)

Project manager Zhang Guan Lin, Chairman; Zhu Qi Hong, Director; Ruan Zhen Ji, Deputy Director

Height 1380 ft/420.5 m

Above-ground stories 88 plus 4 penthouse levels

Basements 3

Above-ground useable levels 86

Mechanical levels Partial floors at 2 and 2 Mez; full levels 50 and 51, and full levels at penthouse 1–4

Use Office, hotel, retail

Site area 5.8 acres/2.36 ha

Area of above-ground building 3,000,000 sq ft/278,700 sq m

Area of typical floor plate 29,180 sq ft/2711 sq m (level 3) –15,480 sq ft/1438 sq m (level 88)

Basic planning module 5 ft/1.5 m

Number of parking spaces 993 (car); 1000 (bicycle)

Principal structural materials Reinforced concrete core, steel floor framing with concrete fill on metal deck; steel and composite (steel and concrete) mega-columns

Other materials Anodized aluminum, high performance insulating glass and stainless steel custom curtain wall

Two International Finance Centre

Hong Kong, CHINA

This project reflects the importance of Hong Kong as a world financial center and is an integral part of a large complex of buildings that includes the new air terminal station, which offers express service to the new Chek Lap Kok Airport.

Two International Finance Centre is part of Phase One of the Hong Kong Central Station Development. The development also includes One International Finance Centre, a 689-foot tower; the new air terminal station; and a four-story, 545,000-square-foot retail podium with a public roof garden. Future phases of the development will include a hotel and serviced apartments.

Two International Finance Centre occupies one of the most beautiful urban sites in the world. It is located adjacent to the narrowest crossing of Victoria Harbour, marking a new gateway to the City. The design of the northeast tower is in the tradition of true skyscrapers, with a simple, strong, and memorable presence. It is a great pylon or obelisk in the scale of the city and the Harbour. It has a centric form that tapers with well-proportioned setbacks, expressing a vertical ascending movement. The massing of the tower becomes more sculptural near the top, enhancing this upward thrust. It culminates in a sculptural crown that celebrates the height of the tower. The surface articulation of the curtainwall reinforces the verticality of the design. The curtainwall is clad in lightly reflective glass panels and silver pearl-colored mullions. The tower glows warmly against the backdrop of the Peak and the City.

The top of Two International Finance Centre is designed as a welcoming gesture to the City. Its open design brings the blue of the sky into the tower's crown, partially dematerializing the building form as it reaches its highest point. When lit at night, the sculptured tower top is a shimmering beacon by Victoria Harbor. Two International Finance Centre is confident of its presence and in harmony with the natural beauty of its physical setting—a fitting new symbol for a city known as the 'Pearl of the Orient'.

2

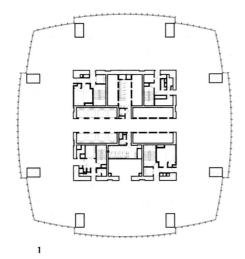

1

1   *Typical floor plan, levels 19–32*
2   *View from Victoria Harbour*
3   *Elevation*
Photography: Tim Griffith/Esto

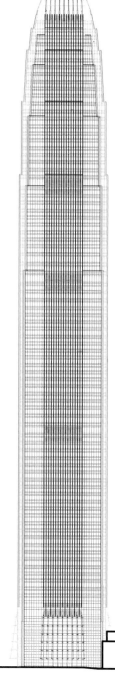

3

Location Hong Kong, China

Completion date 2003

Architect Cesar Pelli & Associates (now Pelli Clarke Pelli Architects)

Architect of record Rocco Design Ltd

Client MTR Corporation

Developer IFC Development Ltd

Development consortium Sun Hung Kai Properties, Henderson Land Development Co. Ltd., Towngas, Sun Chung Estate Co. Ltd.

Structural engineer Ove Arup & Partners

Landscape architect Urbis Limited

Contractor E Man-Sanfield JV Construction Ltd.

Height 1378 ft/420 m

Above-ground stories 88

Basements 4-level parking garage, 2-level train station below grade

Above-ground useable levels 88

Mechanical levels 9

Refuge levels 4

Use Office

Site area 430,000 sq ft/39,947 sq m

Area of above-ground building 3,400,000 sq ft/315,860 sq m

Area of typical floor plate 22,981–24,282 sq ft/2135–2256 sq m (lettable area)

Basic planning module 5 ft/1.5 m

Number of parking spaces 1800

Principal structural materials Concrete and steel core with unitized stainless steel, aluminum and glass curtain wall

CITIC Plaza

CITIC Plaza (originally Sky Central Plaza) was both the tallest reinforced concrete building in the world and the tallest building in China at the time of its completion in 1995.

The development, comprising an 80-story office tower, two blocks of serviced apartments and a shopping center is the centerpiece of a new business district developed in the Tien Ho neighbourhood of Guangzhou.

The complex is at the center of a 2.5-mile-long axis of gardens and boulevards stretching between Guangzhou East Station, Guangzhou's main railway station, in the north and Haxinsha Island in the Pearl River to the south.

The symmetry of the CITIC Plaza development complements the formality of the axis, which is itself perfectly symmetrical. The complex is the first sight that meets visitors to the city upon emerging from the main railway station. The project has become an emblem of the city of Guangzhou.

1   Cross section
2   View from south
3   Office tower grand floor entrance lobby
4   Office tower, typical floor plan (levels 9–17)
5   Office tower entrance lobby
6   Serviced apartment tower, typical floor plan

Photography: Frankie FY Wong

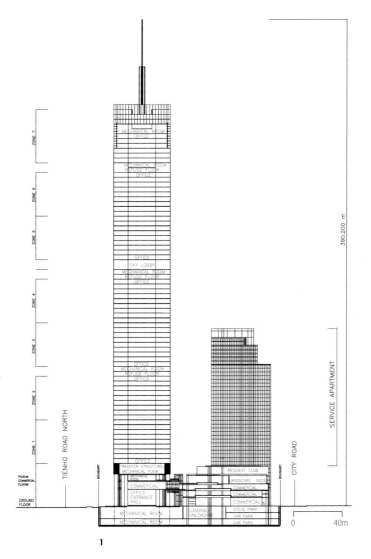

1

2

3

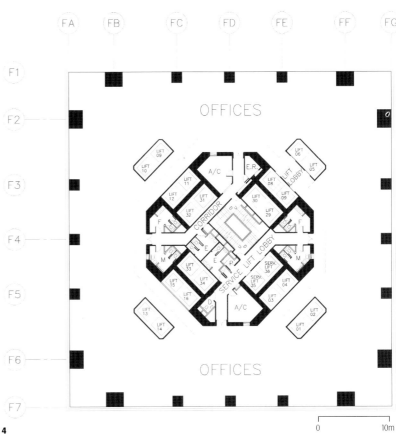

4

5

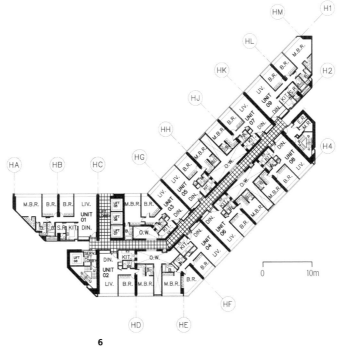

6

Location Guangzhou, China

Completion date 1997

Architect Dennis Lau & Ng Chun Man Architects & Engineers (HK) Ltd

Developer Kumagai SMC Development (Guangzhou) Ltd

Structural engineer Maunsell Consultants Asia Ltd, Hong Kong

Mechanical engineer Associated Consulting Engineers, Hong Kong

Contractor Kumagai Gammon Joint Venture

Height 1280 ft/390.2 m to top of tower mast; 1056 ft/322 m to top of roof

Above-ground stories 80

Use Office, residential

Site area 250,052 sq ft/23,239 sq m

Area of above-ground building 1,579,008 sq ft/146,748 sq m (office tower); 754,706 sq ft/70,140 sq m (residential towers); 389,469 sq ft/36,196 sq m (retail)

Area of typical floor plate 23,564 sq ft/2190 sq m

Principal structural materials Reinforced concrete

Cost US$286 M

Shun Hing Square

The rooftop rotating laser signals the tower as the icon of Shenzhen, a city with 12 million residents in China, just north of Hong Kong. The tower highlights a complex aligned on an east–west axis, also containing an executive apartment annex and shopping center. The 1260-foot tower's silhouette resembles a pair of pens, symbolizing the Chinese and foreign joint venture. Architect KY Cheung was responsible for the master plan, architectural and interior design of the project, originally known as the Di Wang Commercial Building.

The 1992 international design competition winner was designed and completed within 40 months. It occupies a narrow 985-foot-long triangular site on Shen Nan Road, the city's east–west spine. The tower and the wedge-shaped annex are juxtaposed in a 'T' formation to respect mutual sightlines. Placing the rectangular tower perpendicular to the road ensures that its main façades dominate the entire city.

A rectangular tower plan readily accommodates an efficient array of 1076-square-foot office modules to meet market demand. Another consideration is to adopt the maximum net

21,520-square-foot fire compartment size per floor. Consequently this design creates the extreme width to height ratio at over 1:8 in a typhoon and earthquake design zone.

From a distance, simple horizontal and vertical patterns articulate the building skins, recalling the orthogonal strokes of ancient 'Li' script calligraphy. Up close, the colors and materials of the towers and the podium diversify, revealing further layers of individual details to enrich the pedestrian experience. A palette of green and earthen tones with accent colors resonates with indigenous sub-tropical flora.

A fountain of fortune for good *fengshui* faces the 95-foot-high A-frame lobby gate, dramatically revealing the tower's steel structure. The canted prisms at the top complement the red crest of the annex and nod figuratively to the cityscape below.

The annex cradles a mid-air swimming pool in a 72-foot-wide opening in between the well-disguised twin towers, allowing sunlight and views to penetrate the 328-foot-long boulevard façade and brighten the otherwise looming northern wall. It captures the imagination of passersby as a modern reinterpretation of 'grotesque' hollowed stones in classic Chinese gardens.

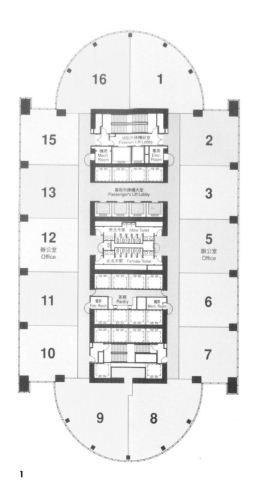

1

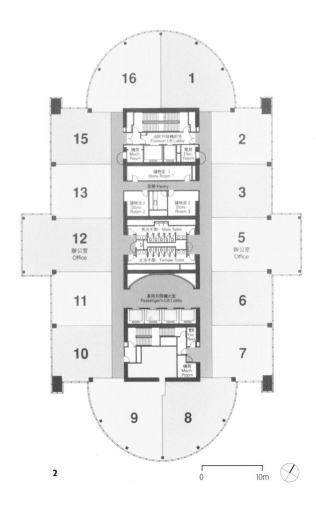

2

0   10m

Location Shenzhen, China

Completion date 1996

Architect KY Cheung, AIA; American Design Associates Ltd, Hong Kong

Associate architect The Second Architectural Design Institute of Shenzhen, PRC

Client Karbony Investment LTD (an associated company of Kumagai Gumi (HK) Limited)

Structural engineer Maunsell Consultants Asia Ltd, Hong Kong; Nippon Steel Corporation, Tokyo, Japan (with Leslie E. Robertson, RLLP, NY, USA, as consulting structural engineers)

Mechanical engineer Associated Consulting Engineers, Hong Kong

Vertical transportation consultant Associated Consulting Engineers, Hong Kong

Landscape architect American Design Associates Ltd, Hong Kong

Contractor Kumagai Gumi (HK) Limited, Hong Kong

Project manager Kumagai Gumi (HK) Limited, Hong Kong

Height 1260 ft/384 m to top of twin antennae; 1066 ft/325 m to top of curtain wall

Above-ground stories 80

Basements 3

Above-ground useable levels 69 (note: not all levels are labelled or are accessible by elevators. The final floor number label system in the elevators skips many numbers, including mechanical floors.)

Mechanical levels 12

Use Office

Site area 201,578 sq ft/18,734 sq m

Area of above-ground building 1,485,687 sq ft/138,075 sq m

Area of typical floor plate 22,596 sq ft/2100 sq m

Basic planning module 1076 sq ft/100 sq m (office module)

Number of parking spaces 868

Principal structural materials Concrete-filled square steel tube columns and steel beams with reinforced concrete core, and curtain wall

Other materials Stone

Cost RMB230 M

3

4

5

1   Office tower floor plan, floors 1–11
2   Office tower floor plan, floors 60–66
3   General view
4   Entry detail
5   Interior detail

Photography: Karbony Investment Ltd

Empire State Building

The Empire State Building, completed in 1931, remained for 41 years the tallest building in the world. Today it remains in the top 10 tallest buildings, and is an internationally known landmark; probably the most famous building ever built, attracting many millions of visitors from all over the world each year.

During planning and construction, the design changed 16 times, but despite this, construction was completed in just over 18 months. Three thousand workers were on the job daily; the building set a record at the time for speed of construction. In addition to 60,000 tons of steel, the building was finished with 200,000 cubic feet of Indiana limestone and granite, 10 million bricks, and 730 tons of aluminum and stainless steel.

The main shaft of the building rises 85 floors above the setbacks that were required by the 1916 New York City zoning law. The structure is a standard riveted steel frame with simple portal bracing. The girders are riveted throughout their depth to the columns and beams. The façade is granite, with chrome-nickel chips and Indiana limestone with stainless steel mullions. The three-story lobby, considered a true work of art, is covered in marble from France, Germany, and Belgium.

The lighting atop the Empire State Building has changed throughout the years. The first light to shine was a searchlight beacon that proclaimed the election of Franklin D Roosevelt as President in 1932. In 1956, revolving synchronized beacons called 'freedom lights' were installed, and could be seen from as far away as 300 miles. Today, colored lights celebrate holidays and other events with various lighting combinations.

1

2

1,3&5   *General views*
   2   *Spire detail*
   4   *Empire State Building depicted in 1930s postcard*

Photography: Wayne La Bar (1,2); Helene Alonso (3,5);
© The Skyscraper Museum (4)

3

4

5

Location New York, New York, USA
Completion date 1931
Architect Shreve, Lamb & Harmon Architects
Client John J Raskob
Structural engineer HG Balcom
Contractor Starrett Brothers and Ekin
Height 1250 ft/381 m to 102nd floor observatory; 1472 ft/
448 m to top of antennae

Above-ground stories 102
Use Office
Site area 79,288 sq ft/7366 sq m
Area of above-ground building 2,200,000 sq ft/204,380 sq m
Principal structural materials Steel
Other materials Indiana limestone, granite, brick, marble
Cost (including land) US$40,948,900

Central Plaza

Central Plaza is a 78-story office tower located beside Hong Kong Harbour in Wanchai. At the time of its completion (1992) it was the tallest building in Hong Kong and the tallest reinforced concrete building in the world outside North America.

The building plan form of a triangle with rebated corners maximizes views of the Harbour from the tower. The roof of the tower is treated as a positive architectural feature with a strong pyramidal form surmounted by a 197-foot-tall mast. At night the tower is illuminated by gold-colored neon-accent lighting built into the façade and various changing colors of floodlighting.

Central Plaza's tower stands on a 100-foot-high podium. The tower itself consists of three sections: the base or podium forming the main entrance and public circulation spaces; the tower consisting of 67 office floors, a sky lobby at the 46th floor; and the tower top consisting of six mechanical plant floors culminating at the 75th floor. The apparent triangular shape is not truly triangular as all three corners are truncated, to provide more workable internal space, and to avoid the negative connotations of sharp corners, in keeping with Feng Shui principles.

The façade is clad in insulated glass of three different colors. Gold and silver coating is used in a vertical and horizontal pattern and is juxtaposed with a ceramic painted pattern glass to create the classical and shimmering image.

The building, in line with the premium sector of the international office market, offers substantial leisure and recreation facilities for tenants, including a swimming pool, gymnasium, health club, and café-bar.

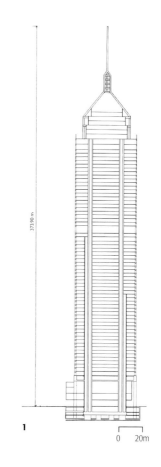

373.90 m

1

0   20m

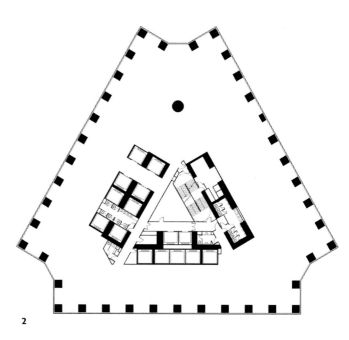

2

Location Hong Kong, China

Completion date 1992

Architect Ng Chun Man & Associates Architects & Engineers, now Dennis Lau & Ng Chun Man Architects & Engineers (HK) Ltd

Developers Sun Hung Kai Properties; Sino Land Co Ltd; Ryoden Property Development Co Ltd

Structural engineer Ove Arup & Partners HK Ltd, Hong Kong

Mechanical engineer Associated Consulting Engineers, Hong Kong

Contractor Manloze Ltd

Height 1227 ft/374 m to top of tower mast; 1015 ft/309.4 m to top of roof

Above-ground stories 78

Mechanical levels 6

Use Office

Site area 77,795 sq ft/7230 sq m

Area of above-ground building 1,400,306 sq ft/130,140 sq m

Area of typical floor plate 24,000 sq ft/2230 sq m

Number of parking spaces 237

Principal structural materials Reinforced concrete

Other materials Exterior: curtain wall and natural granite cladding; interior: natural granite and sandstone cladding

Cost US$141 M

3

4

5

1   Cross section
2   Typical floor plan, low zone
3   View from southeast
4   Escalators to upper level of entrance lobby
5   Evening view

Photography: Frankie FY Wong

Bank of China Tower

The Bank of China Tower, acclaimed for its unusual geometric design, has been likened to a 'glittering tower of diamonds' and is one of the most outstanding achievements in modern architecture. The architect designed it with the elegant poise of the bamboo shoot in mind—'advancing with every stage of growth.' The building was topped out on the 8th day of the 8th month in 1988—the luckiest day of the century, according to the Chinese.

When the Bank of China was completed, it was the tallest building in Asia and was the first building outside the United States to break the 1000-foot mark. For the first time, a mega-structure composed of a pure space-truss was used to support the weight of a skyscraper. The mega-structural steelwork is expressed externally by naturally anodized panels that form part of the curtain wall.

The Bank of China was engineered on the principle that a single eccentricity in a column will cause bending; but two or more lines of eccentricity, joined by a uniform shear force mechanism, will counteract and therefore eliminate the bending. The five composite columns of the system support the braced frame of structural steel that spans them. The centroid, shape and position of these columns change as they move down the building—the source of eccentricity. Because the concrete 'glues' the steel to itself, bending is eliminated.

The podium is sheathed in light granite, which allowed the base to appear rooted to the ground. The geometry changes from a square base to four triangles, then begins to drop quadrants—the first triangle at the 25th floor, the second at the 38th floor, and the third at the 51st floor. The geometric changes, ultimately resulting in a single spire, produce a multifaceted façade of angles and profiles that reflect the light and seem almost crystalline in composition. The silver reflective glass is glazed in a low-maintenance dry gasket system, and the curtain wall is a unitized design assembled off-site under factory conditions. This enabled close quality control of all aspects of the frame assembly, which includes more than 10,000 pieces.

1   Typical floor plan, floors 51–66
2   Typical floor plan, floors 38–50
3   Typical floor plan, floors 20–37
4   Hong Kong skyline view
5   View to top of tower
6   Axonometric

Photography: Courtesy Pei Cobb Freed & Partners (4);
Ian Lambot/arcaid.co.uk (5)

Plans reproduced from original leasing brochure, Coll. G Binder/Buildings & Data SA

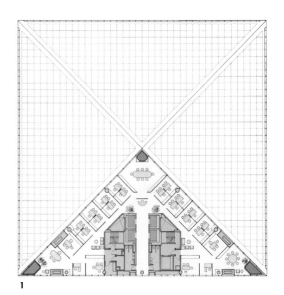

1

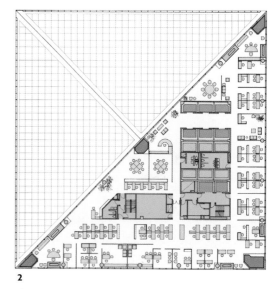

2

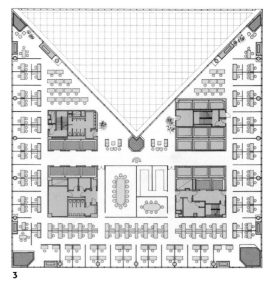

3

4

5

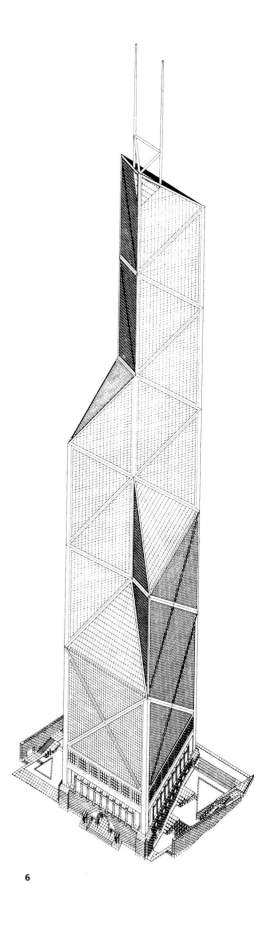

6

Location Hong Kong, China

Completion date 1989

Architect I.M. Pei & Partners

Associate architect Wong/King & Lee

Client Bank of China

Structural engineer Leslie E Robertson Associates; Valentine, Laurie, and Davies

Mechanical engineer Jaros Baum and Bolles; Associated Consulting Engineers

Lighting consultant Fisher-Marantz

Acoustical consultant Cerami and Associates

General contractor Kumagai Gumi

Height 1205.4 ft/367.4 m

Above-ground stories 70

Basements 2

Use Office

Area of above-ground building 1,452,600 sq ft/135,000 sq m

Area of typical floor plate 29,000 sq ft (ground floor) – 7265 sq ft (70th floor)/2695–675 sq m

Basic planning module 4.36 ft/1.33 m

Number of parking spaces 370

Principal structural materials Composite steel and concrete floor slabs; columns braced by steel diagonals

Other materials Anodized finish aluminum, granite

Jumeirah Emirates Towers

A major landmark in Dubai's thriving central business district, Jumeirah Emirates Towers (originally Emirates Towers) is a symbol of the city's growing prominence. The twin silver-gray metal and glass towers rise from a stepped granite base. At night, lighting effects reinforce the drama of the unique soaring forms.

Flanking each tower at its base is a low curvilinear structure, designed in a form reminiscent of massive shifting sand dunes, which houses parking for 1800 cars and service elements. Connecting the two towers is Boulevard at Jumeirah Emirates Towers, a two-story retail development with walkways lined by skylit courtyards, high-end retail shops, restaurants, and cafés.

Equilateral triangles in plan, the towers are inspired by Islamic geometric themes, and the triangular pattern is visible at various levels of detail throughout the project, from the tower roofs, triangular skylights and canopy structures with their repeating positive-negative patterns in ceramic fritted glass, to various interior and exterior paving patterns. Balancing the rigid geometry are the soft curves of the base structure's north and south granite-clad walls, a large cascading waterfall in front of the hotel entrance and the gentle lines of the retail mall's precision-cut paving pattern.

The 1164-foot, 52-story office tower has a spacious lobby formed by circular floor plates, creating an eight-story-high drum of clear glass. The triangular geometry of the tower above is made apparent at the drum levels by the three structural legs that straddle these circular floors. The 16 elevators, travelling at speeds of up to 7 meters per second, are divided into four banks serving respective zones of the tower. A typical floor plate provides 14,354 square feet of gross floor area and is designed to provide maximum efficiency with a minimum number of columns.

The 52-story hotel tower rises to a height of 1014 feet. Above the eight-story atrium are 400 luxurious guestrooms and suites served by four glass-enclosed elevators and organized around a 31-story glazed atrium facing the waters of the Gulf. An exclusive restaurant is located on the penthouse level, offering dramatic views of the coastline.

1   Typical low-rise office floor plan (floors 10–23)
2   Typical hotel floor plan
3–6   General views

Photography: Courtesy Jumeirah

Plans reproduced from *Cities in the Third Millennium*, Council on Tall Buildings and Urban Habitat/CTBUH Sixth World Congress, Melbourne, Australia, Spon Press, London/New York, 2001

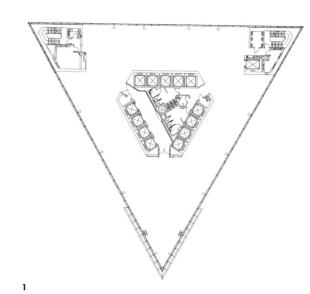

1

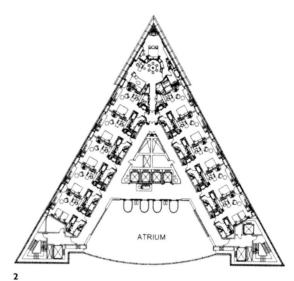

ATRIUM

2

3

4

5

6

Location Dubai, United Arab Emirates

Completion date 2000

Lead consultant Hyder Consulting Middle East Ltd

Architect NORR Group Consultants International (design architect Hazel WS Wong)

Client The Office of HH General Sheikh Mohammed bin Rashid Al Maktoum, Crown Prince of Dubai

Structural engineer Hyder Consulting Pty Ltd.

Mechanical engineer Donald Smith Seymour Rooley

Mechanical design The Mitchell Partnership

Contractor BESIX and SsangYong Engineering & Construction Co. Ltd. (hotel); Nasa Multiplex LLC (offices)

Project manager Turner International

Height 1014.1 ft/309.1 m (hotel); 1164 ft/354.8 m (offices)

Above-ground stories Hotel: 52 above 2-level podium; offices: 52 above 1-level podium

Basements 1 (semi-grounded)

Use Office, hotel, retail

Site area 1,818,440 sq ft/169,000 sq m

Area of above-ground building 1,507,000 sq ft/140,000 sq m; hotel: 541,873 sq ft/50,360 sq m; offices: 737,060 sq ft/68,500 sq m

Area of typical floor plate 14,354 sq ft/1334 sq m

Basic planning module 5 ft/1.5 m

Number of parking spaces 2500

Principal structural materials Concrete (hotel); mixed (offices)

Other materials Brazilian Kinawa granite, aluminum panels, glass

T&C Tower

The 85-story T&C Tower is a landmark of Taiwan, built with a distinct, traditional Chinese flavor. Its symbolic blossom flower is a typical Chinese building idiom, and denotes wealth and prestige.

The podium base of the high-rise is raised higher than other similar buildings, making way for a tunnel underneath. The architecture is in keeping with considerations of weather, topography, and aesthetics, as well as reflecting ancient Chinese principles of geomancy.

Internally, the building is constructed around eight separate cores, allowing easy access to and through the building's facilities, including, commercial, hotel, and office space. Each of these four areas of the building are also independent, each with its own entrance that extends upward toward the sky lobby. The building gains its basic vertical structure from the eight elevator shafts and horizontally from the mechanical floor. The overall spatial structure is created by piling a pagoda-style tower atop two elevated podiums. The core of the three units is designed as a high atrium, which facilitates the entry of sunlight, and allows greater communication between the office units. The elevated podium, while serving a crucial structural function, also allows the wind to pass through, reducing wind pressure.

1 General view
2 Floor plans, top to bottom: B2 food court, B1 retail, 1st floor
3 Night context view
4 Typical hotel floor plan
Photography: Courtesy C.Y. Lee & Partners Architects/Planners

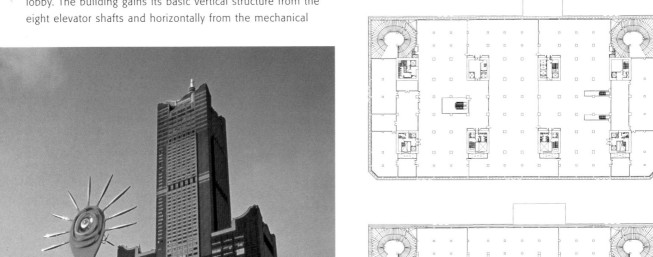

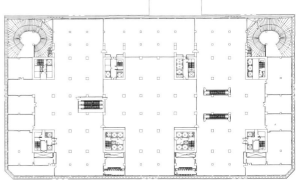

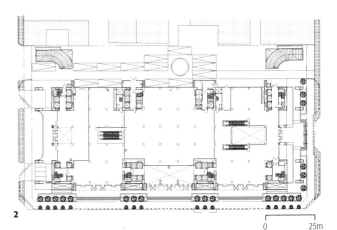

1

2

0   25m

3

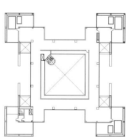

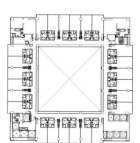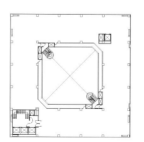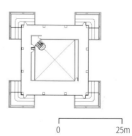

4

0   25m

Location Kaohsiung, Taiwan

Completion date 1998

Architect C.Y. Lee & Partners Architects/Planners

Associate architect HOK Architects

Client Tuntex Group

Developer Chien Tai Cement Corporation; Tuntex Group

Structural engineer Evergreen Consulting Engineering, Inc.; TY Lin International

Mechanical engineer Continental Engineering Corporation; William Tao Associates

Vertical transportation consultant Lerch Bates & Associates Inc.

Landscape architect HOK Architects

Construction consulting services Turner International

Contractor Chien Tai Cement Corporation; Tuntex Group

Project manager Tuntex Group

Height 1140 ft/348 m

Above-ground stories 85

Basements 5

Mechanical levels 36, 57, 71, 78–85

Use Mixed: department store, office, hotel, entertainment, serviced apartments

Site area 129,120 sq ft/12,000 sq m

Area of above-ground building 3,296,326 sq ft/306,350 sq m

Area of typical floor plate 66,787 sq ft/6207 sq m (retail); 41,415 sq ft/3849 sq m (office); 17,593 sq ft/1635 sq m

Number of parking spaces 1151

Principal structural materials Steel, reinforced concrete

Other materials Glass curtain wall, stone wall base

Aon Center

This pristine tower, originally known as the Standard Oil Building, is square in plan, measuring 194 feet on each side with 15-foot cutouts at the four corners. Each floor plate covers approximately 33,000 square feet. The slender steel structure was originally clad in white Carrara marble, with its strong vertical emphasis making it seem even taller. Each side of the building has 15 vertical bands of black windows, recessed between triangular white piers.

Until the completion of the Sears Tower in 1974, the building (originally known as Standard Oil Building, then Amoco Building) was Chicago's tallest building and world's tallest marble-clad structure. It remains the tallest building in the world without any major antennae, spires, or finials at the top. The tower design is based on an innovative tubular structural system in which closely spaced peripheral columns form a hollow tube. Five-foot v-shaped sections, part of the building frame, absorb wind loads. The system permits a column-free interior and totally flexible floor planning between the service core and the exterior walls.

The perimeter of v-shaped steel columns also houses the piping and utility lines, eliminating the need for interior column chases that so often rob buildings of valuable office space. Double-deck elevator cabs also conserve office footage by minimizing shaft space. Single-deck elevators service the lower levels.

The building underwent extensive renovation in 1990–1992 when its marble veneer required total replacement. Due to its high sensitivity to heat and cold, the original Italian marble panels had bowed and expanded unevenly. Twenty years after it was built, the Carrara marble facing was replaced by 2-inch-thick Mt Airy granite panels. All 43,000 panels were replaced at the cost of about $80 million.

Part of the redevelopment also included the upper and lower plaza areas, and a new two-story arched vestibule serving as a main entrance to the building. The upper plaza combines a landscaped sitting area with garden sculptures. The lower plaza features a 197-foot-long waterfall, and a sunken garden which can function as a stage for various performances.

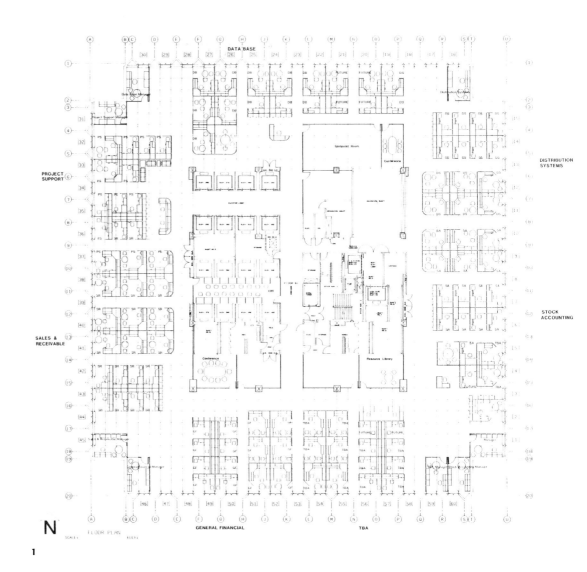

2

1   *Typical floor plan*
2   *General view*
3   *Plaza view*
4   *Façade detail*

Photography: Courtesy Perkins+Will

3

4

Location Chicago, Illinois, USA

Completion date 1973

Architects Edward Durell Stone & Associates;
The Perkins+Will Corporation (in joint venture)

Client Standard Oil Realty Corporation

Structural engineer Perkins+Will Engineering Division

Mechanical engineer Cosentini Associates

Vertical transportation contractor Otis Elevator Company

Contractor Turner Construction Company

Height 1136 ft/346 m

Above-ground stories 83

Above-ground useable levels 80

Mechanical levels and level numbers 5: levels 5, 27, 28, 81, 82

Use Office

Area of above-ground building 2,500,000 sq ft/232,250 sq m

Area of typical floor plate 33,000 sq ft/3066 sq m

Number of parking spaces 679 below grade

Principal structural materials Steel

Other materials Granite, aluminum, concrete

Cost US$120 M

The Center

The Center was the third-tallest building in Hong Kong at the time of completion (1998).

The project is an urban renewal development located in the middle of an existing city block. Screened by existing buildings on much of the site perimeter, the building offers several new public spaces including a major pedestrian plaza, tranquil pockets of green space, and an open concourse at the upper ground floor. The tower stands in the ornamental ponds that form part of the public open space. A viewing platform, bar and restaurant are located at the mid-level of the tower.

The building has a steel structure and a full range of state-of-the-art fittings and equipment including raised floors featuring under-floor air-conditioning, Hong Kong's first automatic gondola, and built-in external wall lighting.

The star-shaped plan of the typical floors has the effect both of diminishing the bulk of the very large superstructure and increasing the amount of naturally lit office space at the perimeter.

The highly permeable ground floor space offers convenient new pedestrian rights of way between the busy Queen's and Des Voeux Roads Central.

1

2

1   Projecting bay
2   Entrance from Queen's Road Central
3   Evening view, showing built-in feature lighting
4   Typical floor plan
5   External corner

Photography: Frankie FY Wong

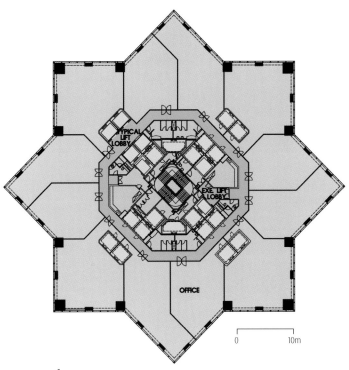

4

3

5

Location Hong Kong, China

Completion date 1998

Architect Dennis Lau & Ng Chun Man Architects & Engineers (HK) Ltd

Developer Cheung Kong (Holdings) Ltd; Land Development Corp (now Urban Renewal Authority)

Structural engineer Maunsell Consultants Asia Ltd, Hong Kong

Geotechnical engineer Maunsell Geotechnical Services Ltd, Hong Kong

Building services engineer Associated Consulting Engineer, Hong Kong

Contractor Paul Y – ITC Construction Ltd

Height 1135 ft/346 m to top of tower mast; 991 ft/302 m to top of roof

Above-ground stories 73

Use Office

Site area 94,860 sq ft/8816 sq m

Area of above-ground building 1,399,144 sq ft/130,032 sq m

Area of typical floor plate up to 26,000 sq ft/2415 sq m

Number of parking spaces 402

Principal structural materials Steel

Other materials Glass, stainless steel, granite

Cost US$385 M

John Hancock Center

The John Hancock Center is located on North Michigan Avenue, along Chicago's 'Magnificent Mile'. With 100 floors, it accommodates office, residential, retail and parking, and a public observation deck on the 94th floor. A panoramic restaurant is on the 95th and 96th floors. Offices occupy levels 13–41; apartments are located on floors 46–93, and a parking garage for 1200 cars is on floors 6–12. Only 50 percent of the site is covered by the building, leaving the rest as open space.

The 705 apartments within the building range from serviced apartments to four-bedroom luxury residences. Additional facilities include restaurants, health clubs, a swimming pool, and an ice skating rink, in effect completing a vertical city-within-a-city. The building is topped by television transmitters.

In order to reach its height of 1127 feet, this colossal tower of 384 million pounds was designed to rest on large caissons that extend down to bedrock. One of the caissons reached 191 feet below ground, the deepest ever sunk in Chicago. This job required a custom-made drilling rig, the most powerful ever devised.

The tapering shaft rises from 40,000 square feet at the base to 18,000 square feet at the summit. This tapered form provides structural stability as well as space efficiency. The exterior columns and spandrel beams create a steel tube that is reinforced by the clearly articulated diagonal bracing and structural floors that meet those diagonals and corner columns. The overall result is a very simple and highly efficient structural system.

John Hancock Center's distinctive cross-bracing eliminates the need for inner support beams, greatly increasing the usable floor area. The innovative structure is also quite economical, since it required only half the steel that would have been used for a building with traditional interior columns. The steel structure is clad in black aluminum accented with tinted bronze glare-reducing glass and bronze-colored aluminum window frames. Remodeled in 1995, the lobby features rich travertine marble and textured limestone surfaces.

The John Hancock Center was only the third building in the world to be more than 1000 feet tall, and the first outside of New York. The first two were the Chrysler Building in 1930 and the Empire State Building in 1931.

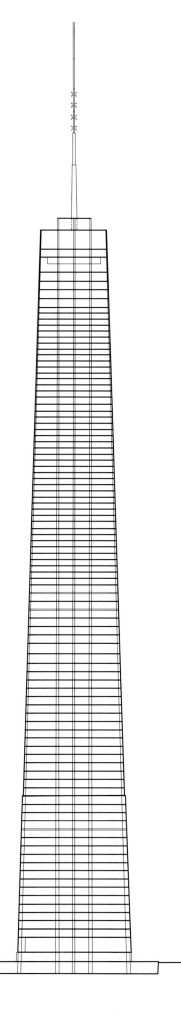

1

1   Elevation
2   John Hancock Center, with Water Tower in foreground
3   View from Lake Michigan

Photography: Courtesy Skidmore, Owings & Merrill LLC

2

3

Location Chicago, Illinois, USA
Completion date 1970
Architect Bruce Graham of Skidmore, Owings & Merrill LLP
Initial developer Jerry Wolman
Client John Hancock Mutual Life Insurance Company
Structural engineer Fazlur Khan of Skidmore, Owings & Merrill LLP
Structural consultants Weidlinger Associates; Amman & Whitney

Mechanical engineer Skidmore, Owings & Merrill LLP
Project manager Richard Lenke of Skidmore, Owings & Merrill LLP
Contractor Tishman Construction Company
Height 1127 ft/343.5 m (1453 ft/443 m including antennas)
Above-ground stories 100
Basements 1
Above-ground useable levels 95
Mechanical levels 16–17 (mechanical and offices), 42–43, 98–99, 100

Use Office, residential, retail
Site area 104,000 sq ft/9662 sq m
Area of above-ground building 2,834,699 sq ft/263,343 sq m
Area of typical floor plate 50,000 sq ft/4645 sq m (at base) – 16,000 sq ft/1486 sq m (at summit)
Number of parking spaces 1200
Principal structural materials Steel, metal, stone
Other materials Black aluminum, glass

Q1

Q1 is an 80-story glass residential tower, comprising 526 apartments, a rooftop observation deck, retail precinct, and associated recreation facilities.

The ground level layout includes a wide pedestrian pathway taking the visitor from the public plaza on the northwest, through the retail arcade, lobby and water features to the east. The double-volume lobby links the water features to the inside, and connects through the void to the level-two facilities above. The perimeter podium roof form provides cover to the podium areas, while still allowing views of the tower. The podium is a glazed retail precinct at the base of the tower. The ground plane area around the tower incorporates a porte-cochere, main entrance foyer, a large pool, and beach club. A series of ribbons wrap concentrically around the tower form and hover above the entry plaza area, providing cover and shading. The result is an open-air galleria-like shopping precinct under the glazed ribbon structure and a curved retail façade to the street edges.

The tower is an unconventional concrete frame structure, which connects 'outrigger' columns on the building perimeter to the core through concrete blade walls. The glass curtain wall provides a weatherproof insulated skin, incorporating white spandrel glass to reinforce the curvature of the tower form. The podium ribbon roofs are clad in Alpolic panels with a glass roof framed with structural steel. The tower roof crown is a steel framed structure, providing support for the roof glazing and the roof spire. The spire provides an effective lightning conductor, which has operated a number of times since the building's completion.

This building was conceived in the Sydney Olympic year 2000, and drew inspiration from the Olympic Torch and the Sydney Opera House. The objective was to produce a sculptural form reminiscent of these Australian icons, and a glass skin facilitated this expression. The upswept roof form and spire strongly reference the shape of the torch and provide a dramatic crown to the tower.

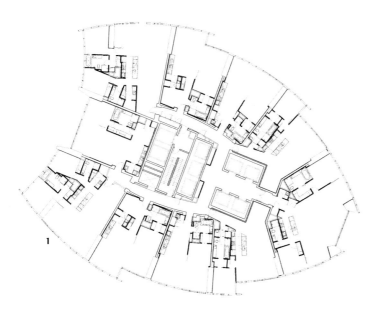

1   Floor plan
2   Context view of Q1 on Surfers Paradise beach
Opposite:
     Q1's sculptural form, seen from the pool

Photography: Russell Shakespeare

2

Location Surfers Paradise, Queensland, Australia
Completion date 2005
Design architect Sunland Design Group
Design architect (tower podium) Innovarchi
Documentation architect The Buchan Group
Client Q1 Joint Venture
Developer Surfers Paradise Beach Resort Pty Ltd
Structural engineer (concept) ARUP
Structural engineer (design and documentation) Whaley Consulting Group
Mechanical engineer Lincolne Scott Australia

Vertical transportation consultant Transportation Design Consultants Pty Ltd
Landscape architects Imagine Design Pty Ltd; Urban Smash Pty Ltd; Sunland Design Group
Contractor Sunland Constructions
Project manager Sunland Group Limited
Height 1058 ft/322.5 m (including spire)
Above-ground stories 79
Basements 2
Above-ground useable levels 75
Mechanical levels and level numbers 9: levels B1, B2, 38, 40, 41, 75, 76, 79

Use Residential, observation deck, retail in separate podium
Site area 134,500 sq ft/12,500 sq m
Area of above-ground building 1,156,700 sq ft/107,500 sq m
Area of typical floor plate 14,547 sq ft/1352 sq m
Basic planning module 3.9 ft/1.2 m (curtain wall grid)
Number of parking spaces 837
Principal structural materials Reinforced concrete, structural steel
Other materials Glass curtain wall, non load-bearing blockwork, Alpolic metal cladding
Cost AUD$255 M

Burj Al Arab

Dubai's Burj Al Arab is located offshore on a manmade island in the Arabian Gulf. The tallest all-suite hotel in the world at 1053 feet, it forms the centerpiece of Atkins' design for the world-class Chicago Beach Resort Development that includes the Jumeirah Beach Resort, the Wild Wadi aqua park and the Beit Al Bahar Villas.

The design for the hotel resembles the spinnaker sail of a J-Class yacht and reflects the seafaring heritage of Dubai. By a combination of innovative and efficient structural design, complemented by and integrated with dramatic architecture, the resulting unique building is now globally recognized as an icon of Dubai.

Extending up to the underside of the 26th duplex floor level, reaching to almost 600 feet, the dramatic and glittering atrium is the tallest of its kind in the world and addresses the space that is the core of the Burj Al Arab. It is flanked on two sides by the balconies of hotel suites and on the third side by a sail-shaped geometric membrane of PTFE-coated fiberglass. Internally, the 202 luxury duplex bedroom suites are the height of opulence.

As well as providing a natural light source and insulating the atrium space, the membrane also acts as a 'canvas' for the myriad lighting effects generated by the luminaries concealed in the main access bridge that project onto the front face to highlight the hotel at night. The membrane also provides a screen for the long-range 'light cannon' projectors that operate from the mainland to cast pictorial images onto the Burj.

A further sense of interior luxury is provided by a circular atrium water feature, composed of 24 white fiber-optically lit water arches with a central 165-foot-high jet and a two-story-high tropical aquarium extending to a 'submerged' restaurant, which contrasts with the elevated sky view restaurant, offering panoramic views of the city and Arabian Gulf.

State-of-the-art technology is prevalent throughout the hotel from the electromechanical design to the guest and operational interfaces and the amazing water and flame feature at the main entrance.

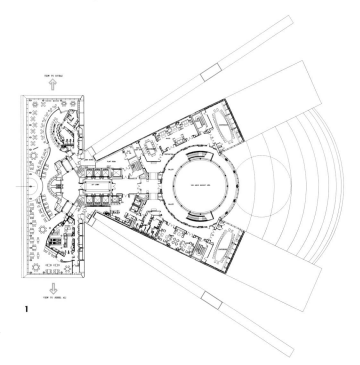

1

1   27th floor plan – Sky restaurant
2   Innovative structure with a dramatic architecture
3   The Burj Al Arab (the Arabian Tower) is the tallest hotel
    in the world

Photography: Courtesy Jumeirah (2); Courtesy Atkins (3)

Location Dubai, United Arab Emirates

Completion date 1999

Architect Atkins

Structural engineer Atkins

Mechanical engineer Atkins

Project manager Atkins

Vertical transportation consultant Dunbar Boardman
Associates

Landscape architect Al Khatib Cracknell

Contractor Al Habtoor Murray & Roberts

Height 1053 ft/321 m

Above-ground stories 52 [25 duplex floors = 50 conventional
floor levels (from 1st to underside of 26th (duplex) floor) +
26th and 27th floors containing ball room and the Skyview
(Al Muntaha) restaurant. Total of 52 'levels' (excluding ground
which is also double-level).]

Basements 3

Above-ground useable levels 59

Mechanical levels and level numbers 3: levels 8, 16, 28

Use Hotel

Site area 54,445 sq ft/5060 sq m

Area of above-ground building 1,291,200 sq ft/120,000 sq m

Area of typical floor plate 21,520 sq ft/2000 sq m

Basic planning module 26 ft/8 m

Number of parking spaces 380

Principal structural materials Steel, curtain wall, reinforced
concrete

Other materials Aluminum cladding, Teflon-covered glass fiber
fabric wall

Chrysler Building

The Chrysler Building is recognized as New York City's greatest display of Art Deco architecture. Following automobile tycoon WP Chrysler's purchase of the 39,456-square-foot site, construction of the 77-story building began in 1928 and was completed in May 1930.

At the time of completion, the Chrysler Building was the world's tallest structure with a height of 1046 feet. Four months later, that distinction was claimed by the Empire State Building.

Lobby walls three stories high rise from the ground level and are the first prominent display of the Art Deco interior and façade. Its walls and floor are covered in materials from around the world: a dark green Norwegian granite proscenium-like entrance; blue marble from Belgium; red marble from Morocco; and Sienna travertine from Germany. The ceiling fresco by Edward Trumbull depicts a view of the Chrysler Building, several airplanes of the period, and scenes from the assembly line at the Chrysler automobile plant.

The four elevator banks contain 30 passenger elevators, of which no two are alike. Each elevator door displays a modernistic use of wood veneer on steel. The interiors are faced with a wide variety of woods: Japanese ash, American walnut, Oriental walnut, English gray hardwood, dye ebonised wood, and curly maple.

Above the 30th level, the façade's Art Deco style is exemplified by a frieze of hubcaps with protrusions of steel and car fenders. The tower's corners at this level have protruding steel decorations of winged radiator caps. Just above the 60th level are four corners with steel American eagle gargoyles.

At the 72nd level, six stainless steel arcs begin. Each arc, one surmounted by another, is complemented by triangular windows. The overall effect is one of shimmering sunbursts, culminating in a stainless steel needlepoint spire. The spire alone adds 187 feet to the height. The actual materials used in the arc and spire structures are platinum-colored, non-magnetic, non-tarnishing Nirosta chrome-nickel steel, which was bolted onto wooden forms.

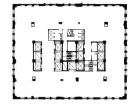

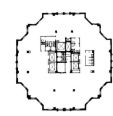

1

2

3

4

5

6

1   *Typical floor plans*
2   *Period postcard featuring Chrysler Building*
3   *Façade detail*
4&6   *Art Deco spire detail*
5   *General view*

Photography: © The Skyscraper Museum (2); Tony Morales © Liberty Science Center (3,4); Coll. G Binder/Buildings & Data SA (5); Douglas Mason (6)

Location New York, New York, USA
Completion date 1930
Architect William Van Alen
Owner Tishman Speyer Properties
Structural engineer Ralph Squire & Sons
Services engineer Louis TM Ralston
Contractor Fred T Ley & Co Inc.
Developer WP Chrysler

Height 1046 ft/319 m
Above-ground stories 77
Use Office
Site area 39,456 sq ft/3665.5 sq m
Area of above-ground building 1,040,000 sq ft/96,616 sq m
Principal structural materials Steel
Other materials Brick

Bank of America Plaza

Previously known as the NationsBank Plaza, this building is located between Peachtree and West Peachtree at North Avenue, Atlanta. The site is narrow, with full frontage along North Avenue at the crest of a hill. The neighborhood south of the site is primarily commercial, while to the north it is primarily high-density residential. The shape of the site and location suggested that the new tower be placed centrally on the North Avenue block front and flanked on either side by landscaped parks. This urban design solution at a key point in the city enables the differing neighborhood characters to blend.

A three-level building stretches from the tower to West Peachtree Street and contains a branch bank that opens onto the lobby, a restaurant, retail shop, conference center, and health club. The north wall is of reflective glass, visually doubling the size of the park in front of it.

Four levels of parking are provided, below grade, over most of the site. Three vehicular access points lead into the garage from each bordering street. A rapid-transit stop is located at one corner of the site. Pedestrians enter this end through a mirrored-glass gallery to approach the tower. They can also walk through parks at either side and enter directly into the tower lobby.

The tower is square in plan and sits diagonally across the site, facing the border streets at 45-degree angles and providing undisturbed views in all directions. It employs a 'super-column' type structural scheme. Two large columns, 8 feet square at the base, located at each tower face and at each corner of the central core, act as both vertical support and wind bracing.

This system eliminates costly interior columns and provides maximum tenant space utilization and design flexibility. The tower curtain wall starts 12 feet above the lobby floor, offering unobstructed views to the exterior on all sides.

A large spire constructed of closely spaced tubes tops the tower and encloses the cooling tower, elevator penthouses and other mechanical equipment. At night, the spire is illuminated internally, adding a softly glowing beacon to the Atlanta skyline.

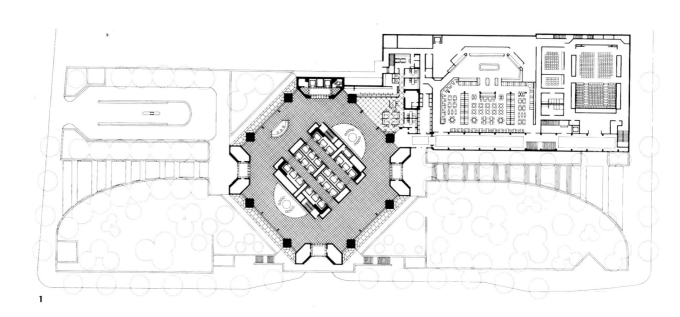

1

1　Ground floor plan
2　The spire becomes a softly glowing beacon at night
3　General view
4　Arcade joining three-level building to tower
Photography: Courtesy Kevin Roche John Dinkeloo and Associates LLC

2

3

4

Location Atlanta, Georgia, USA

Completion date 1992

Architect Kevin Roche John Dinkeloo and Associates LLC

Client Citizen and Southern Bank, NationsBank (now Bank of America)

Developer Cousins Properties Incorporated

Structural engineer CBM Engineers

Mechanical engineer Newcomb & Boyd; Environmental Systems Design

Vertical transportation consultant Ray Hahn

Landscape architect Gibbs Landscaping

Contractor Beers Construction Company

Project manager Jim Overton, Thomas Cousins

Height 1039 ft/317 m (including spire)

Above-ground stories 57

Basements 4

Above-ground useable levels 55 office levels

Mechanical levels and level numbers 2: floors 56, 57

Use Office, bank, restaurant, retail

Site area 158,911 sq ft/14,763 sq m

Area of above-ground building 1,760,000 sq ft/163,504 sq m

Gross area of typical floor plate 32,000 sq ft/2973 sq m

Basic planning module 5 ft/1.5 m

Number of parking spaces 1250 below grade

Principal structural materials Structural steel, concrete

Other materials Glass and granite curtain wall, aluminum cage for mechanical spire

Cost US$115.8 M

US Bank Tower

US Bank Tower (previously First Interstate World Center, and Library Tower) came into being in 1990, partly because its neighbor, the 1926 Los Angeles Central Library, had been gutted by fire and was scheduled for demolition.
Its air rights were sold to First Interstate World Center, allowing the library to be restored and modernized, and enabling the tower to rise to 75 stories.

The architects took many design cues for the tower from the nearby library. The tower's base and shaft are simplified with very little ornament. The top of the tower, however, is sheathed in a multi-faceted glass crown, which is illuminated after dark.

Located just 26 miles from the San Andreas fault, the structure of the building was designed to withstand an earthquake with a magnitude of 8.3 on the Richter scale. The structure needed to be not only flexible enough to absorb the forces of an earthquake, but also stiff enough to resist the enormous wind forces on a building of this height. A moment-resisting steel frame on the exterior perimeter of the tower (designed for

ductility against seismic loading) and a rigid 74-square-foot steel core extend the full height of the building, together providing lateral support against the load.

The tower is organized by a simple geometry of an overlapped circle and square, with the circle emerging beneath the crown as the dominant geometrical form. The curved colonnade of structural piers at street level, each encased in translucent envelopes of green tinted glass, serves a variety of functions. The sweeping curve softens the impact of the enormous structure on the site, allowing the building at ground level to defer to the library across the street. The colonnade creates a feeling of transparency and openness at grade level, welcoming passersby. These articulations provide the tower with a subtle privacy at street level, while the setbacks in the façade and distinctive crown create a memorable image for the building in the Los Angeles skyline.

Another element on the site is the Bunker Hill steps, a monumental stairway with a fountain and cascading waterway. The steps serve as a pedestrian link between the tower and the office and retail complexes nearby.

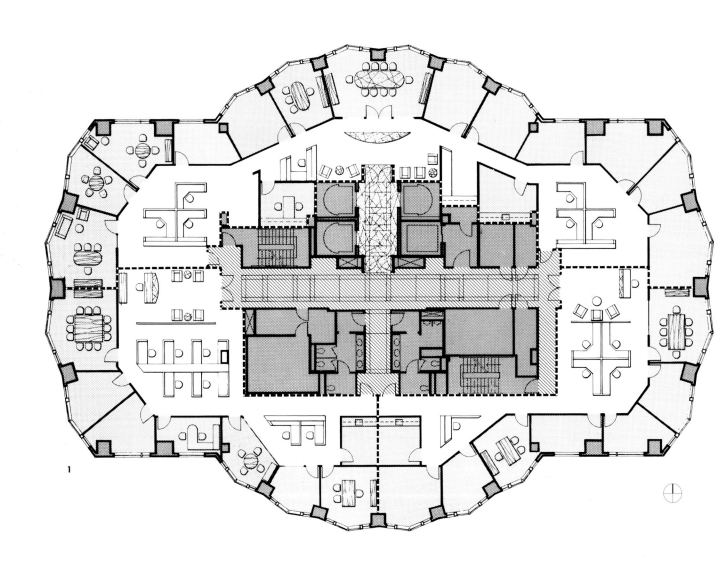

1

2

1   Typical high-rise floor plan
2–4   General views

Photography: Terry Wilkenson, courtesy Ellerbe Becket

Plan reproduced from Maguire Thomas Partners leaflet,
Coll. G Binder/Buildings & Data SA

3

4

Location Los Angeles, California, USA
Completion date 1989
Architect Pei Cobb Freed & Partners (Henry N Cobb and
Harold Fredenburgh)
Associate architect Ellerbe Becket
Developer Maguire Thomas Partners
Structural engineer CBM Engineers Inc.

Mechanical engineer James A Knowles and Associates
Electrical engineer Levine/Seegal Associates
Landscape architect Lawrence Halprin & Associates
Contractor Turner Construction Co.
Height 1018 ft/310 m
Above-ground stories 73
Basements 2

Use Office
Area of above-ground building 1,432,607 sq ft/133,089 sq m
Area of typical floor plate 23,000 sq ft/2137 sq m (rentable
area, levels 33–45)
Principal structural materials Mixed
Other materials Granite

Menara Telekom

The movement to make Asia the world's fastest growing telecommunications market prompted Telekom Malaysia to build a new corporate headquarters to reflect its role as the provider of high technology for the third millennium.

The inspiration behind the new headquarters building involved combining the technological needs and high-tech nature of Telekom Malaysia with a functional, yet organic workplace that would be an impressive symbol for TM employees and Malaysia as a whole.

The shape of the tower, which echoes the beauty of an unfurling leaf, was strongly influenced by the work of Malaysian sculptor and painter, Latiff Mohidin, and his sketch of bamboo shooting up from the earth. This organic nature had to be balanced against the technical aspects of construction and planning efficiency. Repetitive elements for the façade and floor plates and tight core planning achieved that balance.

The structural support systems use the most advanced construction technology and engineering techniques and materials. The typical office floors are supported by perimeter columns and long span beams extending 56 feet between the two edges, resulting in open, column-free space for maximum office planning flexibility. The floor-to-floor height is a generous 13 feet.

The system uses post-tensioned concrete beams and slabs with high-strength concrete columns. A feature of this structural system is an 18.7-foot-deep x 7.8-foot-wide concrete transfer beam at the second floor level, which shifts the entire 77 floors of building column loads to a 39.4-foot span, opening up the main entrance levels to dramatic expanses of glass and maximum daylight.

A key element of the design is the inclusion of large, open-air terraced gardens scaling the heights of the tower and providing natural shade on the eastern and western façades and a general "greening" of the building. Every third level in the tower, alternating from east to west, has direct access to a skygarden, thus creating the sense of a series of low-rise, vertically stacked neighborhoods.

An auditorium and exhibition complex occupies a separate structure within the site, with its own entry and identity. The 1500-seat theater will not only accommodate Telekom's AGM, but will also offer Kuala Lumpur a venue for major international cultural events, conferences and seminars.

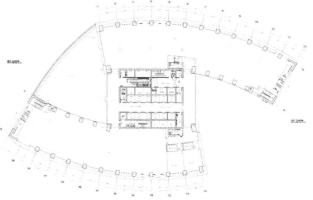

3

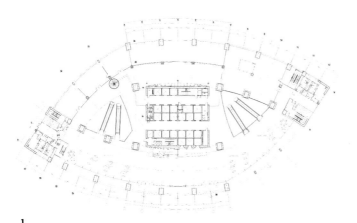

1

2

1 Ground floor plan
2 Typical floor plan zone 1
3 Interior view of main lobby
4 Tower at night
5 South elevation
6 Façade detail

Photography: Hlin Ho

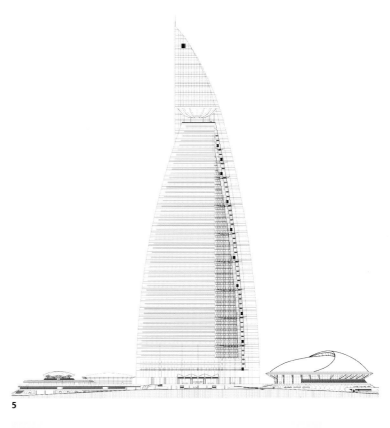

5

4

6

Location Kuala Lumpur, Malaysia
Completion date 2003
Architect Hijjas Kasturi Associates Sdn
Client Telekom Malaysia
Structural engineer Ranhil Bersekutu
Mechanical engineer Zainuddin Nair & Ven Associates; Maunsell NVOF Bhd
Project manager Hasmi-Bucknall JV

Vertical transportation consultant Schindler
Landscape architect Perfect Scale Sdn Bhd
Contractor Daewoo; Peremba JV
Height 1017 ft/310 m
Above-ground stories 55 above 4-level carpark podium
Above-ground useable levels 52
Mechanical levels 3
Use Office tower and mixed-use podium

Site area 7.59 acres/3.08 ha
Area of above-ground building 1,666,326 sq ft/154,863 sq m (tower)
Basic planning module 5 ft/1.5 m
Number of parking spaces 1700 car/300 motorcycle
Principal structural materials Steel, reinforced concrete
Other materials Aluminum and glass curtain wall, copper cladding
Cost RM 600 M

Baiyoke Sky Hotel

The success of the earlier Baiyoke Tower I initiated the Baiyoke Tower II project in 1988. The project, now known as Baiyoke Sky Hotel, has the silhouette of the first Baiyoke Tower I at its base but stands taller, with its massive concrete base of red sandstone set into 184-foot-deep pilings, giving the image of natural sandstone rising from the earth.

The glittering gold color, a Thai/oriental element symbolizing wealth, defines the top silhouette of Baiyoke Tower I that points upward to the top of Baiyoke Sky Hotel; a suggestion of continuous prosperity. Both towers are located in the heart of Pratunam, a long-established wholesale garment market of Bangkok. The surrounding sites are mostly low-rise, high-density shophouses of the old business sectors, with which the two towers have smoothly blended.

The tower's program includes a 673-room hotel; garment center (basement to 4th levels); car park (5th to 14th levels); convention center (18th level); hotel lobby (18th level); swimming pool (20th level); hotel rooms (22nd to 74th levels); multifunction rooms (75th level); observation deck (77th level); restaurants (76th, 78th and 79th levels); roof-top bar (83rd level); and sky walk revolving roof deck (84th level).

The 88-story hotel remains today Thailand's tallest building.

1   Floor plan: levels 74–80
2   Day view of Baiyoke Sky Hotel
3   Swimming pool on 20th floor
4   General view at night
Photography: Courtesy Baiyoke Sky Hotel

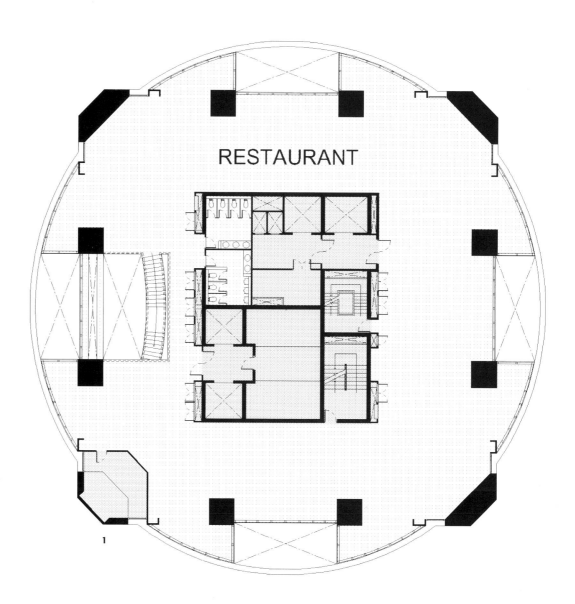

RESTAURANT

1

2

3

4

Location Bangkok, Thailand

Completion date 1999

Architect Plan Architect Co. Ltd, Plan Associates Co. Ltd, Plan Studio Co. Ltd

Client Land Development Co. Ltd

Developer Land Development Co. Ltd, Baiyoke Group of Hotels

Structural engineer Arun Chaiseri Consulting Engineers Co. Ltd

Mechanical engineer W. and Associates Consultant Co. Ltd

Construction management Project Planning Service Co. Ltd

Interiors Bent Severin & Associates Co. Ltd; Leo International Design Co. Ltd

Contractor Concrete Constructions (Thailand) Co. Ltd

Height 1014 ft/309 m (excluding antenna)

Above-ground stories 88

Basements 2

Use Hotel, commercial

Site area 68,864 sq ft/6400 sq m

Area of building 1,926,040 sq ft/179,000 sq m

Number of parking spaces 900

Principal structural materials Reinforced concrete

AT&T Corporate Center
at Franklin Center

This 61-story tower of more than 1.5 million square feet, is a modern rendition of the American skyscraper of an earlier epoch. The tower sits upon a highly articulated five-story granite base with bronze-accented entries and storefronts, reinforcing the building's vital connection to the urban and commercial fabric of Chicago's Loop district, and providing a generous amount of retail space and a friendly dialog with the pedestrian. The building changes color as it rises, from deep red at the ground floor to a lighter red facing between the second and the fifth floor, to a lighter rose for the tower above. Recessed spandrels and accent pieces are a deep green granite with a decorative abstract pattern.

A five-foot setback at the 30th, 45th, and 49 floors reinforces the termination of elevator banks, while a special setback at the 15th floor refers to the prevailing building line of Chicago's early skyscrapers, all of them defining a strong silhouette against the skyline.

The lobby spaces of the ground floor are designed as a series of grand-scale rooms finished in oak and a variegated palette of marbles. The main three-story lobby off Monroe Street, 48 feet high, follows the tradition of European great halls, rich in detailing and the use of elegant marble, gold leaf, bronze, and oak wood trim. Three custom-made chandeliers illuminate the lobby, which leads to a five-story atrium at mid-block, opening onto the Franklin Street lobby.

Similar motifs are reflected in the two ground floor elevator lobbies, as well as in the skylobbies on the 29th and 44th floors, featuring 1930s Art Deco details on the walls, floor and lighting. The top of the building is crowned by four spires embellished with fins and open metalwork, gently tapering as they rise 130 feet above the rooftop.

In 1992 the 61-story tower was complemented by an adjoining second tower, the 36-story 927,192-square-foot USG Building, as planned in the original overall project. Together, the buildings are known as the Franklin Center.

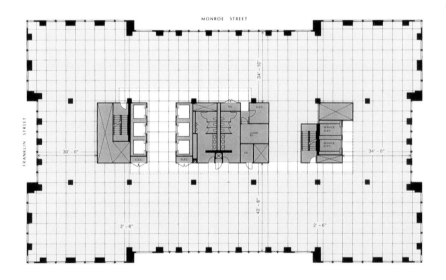

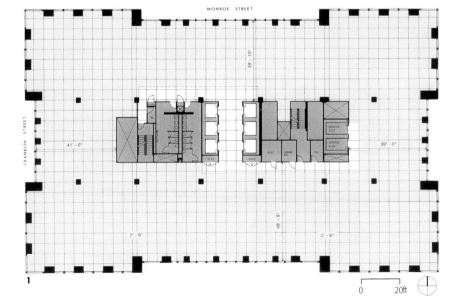

1   Typical tower floor plan (levels 45–60)
1   Typical high-rise floor plan (levels 30–43)
2   General view
3   Section showing the vertical transportation system with the sky lobbies at levels 29 and 44

Photography: Hedrich-Blessing, courtesy Skidmore, Owings and Merrill LLP

Plans reproduced from original AT&T Corporate Center leasing brochure, Coll. G Binder/Buildings & Data SA

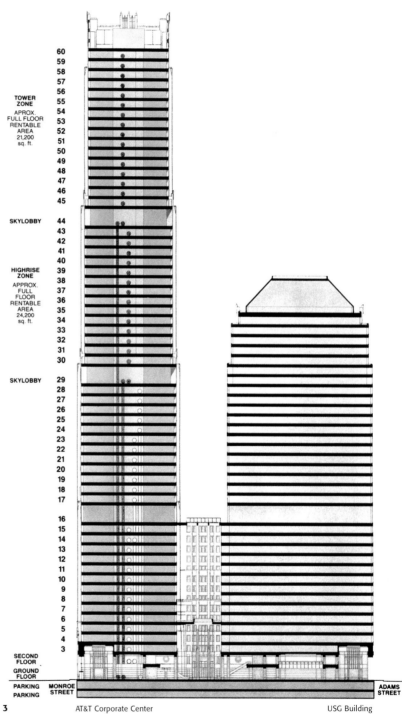

	60
	59
	58
	57
	56
TOWER ZONE	55
APROX. FULL FLOOR RENTABLE AREA 21,200 sq. ft.	54
	53
	52
	51
	50
	49
	48
	47
	46
	45
SKYLOBBY	44
	43
	42
	41
	40
HIGHRISE ZONE	39
APROX. FULL FLOOR RENTABLE AREA 24,200 sq. ft.	38
	37
	36
	35
	34
	33
	32
	31
	30
SKYLOBBY	29
	28
	27
	26
	25
	24
	23
	22
	21
	20
	19
	18
	17
	16
	15
	14
	13
	12
	11
	10
	9
	8
	7
	6
	5
	4
	3
SECOND FLOOR	
GROUND FLOOR	
PARKING	MONROE STREET
PARKING	

ADAMS STREET

3   AT&T Corporate Center   USG Building

Location Chicago, Illinois, USA

Completion date 1989

Architect Adrian D Smith, FAIA, Design Partner, Skidmore, Owings & Merrill LLP

Client AT&T; Stein & Company

Structural engineer Skidmore, Owings & Merrill LLP

Mechanical engineer Skidmore, Owings & Merrill LLP

Project manager Mike Oppenheim Associates

Lighting consultants Jules Fisher & Paul Marantz

General contractor Mayfair Construction; Blount Brothers

Height 1007 ft/306.9 m

Above-ground stories 61

Basements 2

Mechanical levels and level numbers 1: level 61

Above-ground useable levels 60

Use Office, retail

Area of above-ground building 1,547,200 sq ft/143,735 sq m

Area of typical floor plate 21,000–24,000 sq ft/1951–2230 sq m

Basic planning module 5 ft/1.5 m

Principal structural materials Composite structure, with a poured-in-place concrete exterior tube, steel columns at the core, steel horizontal members

Other materials Granite, marble, white oak

Two Prudential Plaza

This distinctive 64-story structure, clad in red and gray granite and reflective glass, is part of the Prudential Plaza redevelopment project. This includes One Prudential Plaza, a renovated 41-story tower built in 1955, a public plaza and a five-level underground parking garage for 600 cars. It is situated at the center of a major underground walkway system connecting directly to the Illinois Central Railroad. An exterior arcade creates a new base at the lower three stories with a colonnade wrapped around both the existing and the new towers, joining the two tall buildings.

Two Prudential Plaza soars 920 feet to the beginning of its 75-foot spire, and at the time of completion was the world's second-tallest reinforced concrete building. Prudential requested that this tower be designed to recall One Prudential Plaza in color and vertical expression. The building's north and south facades display gable-shaped recesses with skylights at the 42nd and 52nd floors. The one-acre terraced and landscaped plaza features fountains, waterfalls, and flowers, and provides an inviting outdoor setting for tenants, visitors, and passersby.

Floor plans range from 22,500 square feet at the low-rise portion of the building to 15,500 square feet in the high-rise portion, reflecting the building's geometry of multiple, cantilevered corners, providing prime office space with corner offices.

Concrete was chosen because of its scheduling and economic advantages, ease of installation of the granite skin, and above all, for its rigidity. In this windy city, the limiting-sway requirement (9 inches at the top of a structure) could be achieved only through the use of high-strength concrete with superplasticizers. This high-strength concrete also diminished the size of the columns, thus allowing more rentable floor space with fewer columns, and provided natural fireproofing, one of the great advantages of concrete.

The building's shape at the top, with its succession of layered chevrons in its graceful transition from the shaft to the spire, has been widely compared to the Chrysler Building.

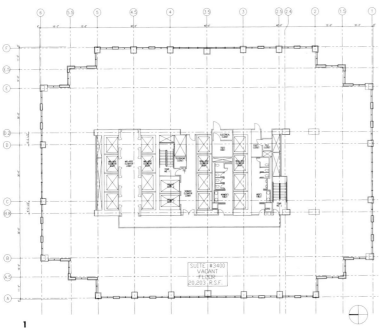

1

1   *Typical floor plan, floor 34*
2   *Evening views of Prudential Plaza*
3   *Two Prudential Plaza*

Photography: James Steinkamp © Steinkamp/Ballogg Chicago (2);
Scott McDonald © Hedrich-Blessing (3)

2

Location Chicago, Illinois, USA
Completion date 1990
Architect Loebl Schlossman & Hackl
Developer The Prudential Property Company
Structural engineer CBM Engineers Inc.
Services engineer Environmental System Design Inc.
Vertical transportation consultant John J Urbikas & Associates, Inc.

Contractor Turner Construction Company
Project manager Garrison Associates Inc.
Height 995 ft/303 m
Above-ground stories 64
Use Office
Area of above-ground building 1,200,000 sq ft/111,480 sq m
Area of typical floor plate 15,500 sq ft/1440 sq m (high-rise) – 22,500 sq ft/2090 sq m (low-rise)

Number of parking spaces 608 in 5-level, below-street parking garage
Principal structural materials Concrete
Other materials Red and gray granite, reflective glass

JPMorgan Chase Tower

Upon completion in 1981, this 75-story tower (originally the Texas Commerce Tower) was the tallest building in Houston, the sixth tallest in the United States, the tallest granite-clad building in the world, and the tallest composite concrete and steel building ever erected. The tower, however, is only part of a 2.2-million-square-foot complex that includes a one-acre public plaza, a linked 2000-car garage with retail and athletic facilities, and a shopping concourse that interconnects with Houston's pedestrian tunnel system.

Clad in pale gray polished granite, stainless steel, and gray glass, the tower departs from the classic four-sided box with one corner of the tower sheared off at a 45-degree angle to produce a slender five-sided structure. The front façade is an 85-foot column-free span of butt-jointed glass and stainless steel that offers panoramic views of the entire west side of Houston. Loads normally carried by corner columns are transferred back to the tower's structural core—one that introduced the elevator 'sky lobby' for the first time outside New York and Chicago.

While the form and the shape of the tower were determined by skyline considerations, siting was a conscious attempt at urban space creation. Set back into a corner, the tower leaves open two-thirds of the full-block site to create a public plaza that offsets the tower's mass and forms a common setting for the buildings that surround it. The plaza is paved with rose and gray flamed granite and is bordered on each side by landscaped gardens. Its focal point is the Joan Miro sculpture, 'Personage and Birds'.

The plaza's paving extends into the five-story main lobby and is repeated in the 13-foot-high sky lobby on the 60th floor. Both lobbies have interior walls of polished gray granite.

1

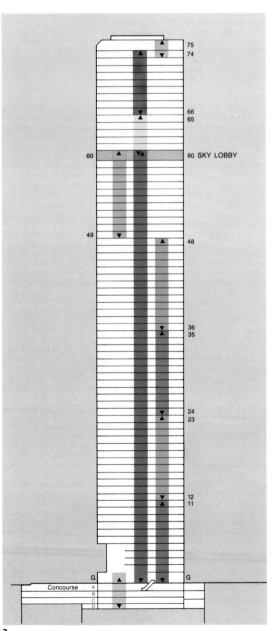

2

1&3   *General view*
2   *Elevator schematic*
4   *Typical floor plans, floors 15–23 and 28–35*

Photography: Georges Binder, courtesy Buildings & Data SA (1);
Courtesy Gerald D Hines Interests (3)
Plans reproduced from original leasing brochure, Coll. G Binder/Buildings & Data SA

3

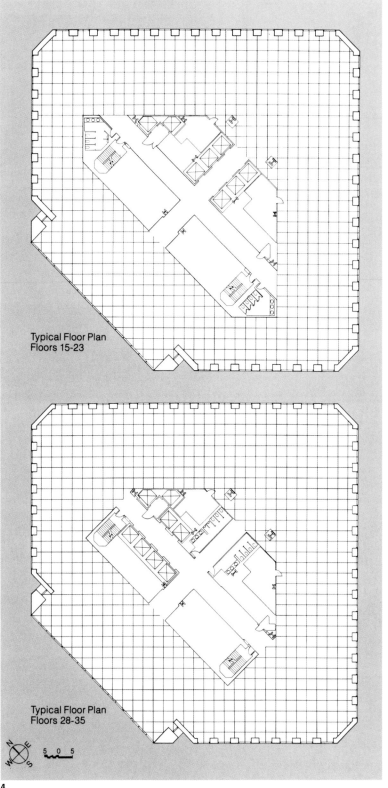

Typical Floor Plan
Floors 15-23

Typical Floor Plan
Floors 28-35

4

Location Houston, Texas, USA

Completion date 1982

Architect I.M. Pei & Partners

Associate architect 3D/International

Client Gerald D Hines Interests; Texas Commerce Bank; United Energy Resources

Developer Gerald D Hines Interests

Structural engineer CBM Engineers Inc.

Mechanical engineer I.A. Naman + Associates, Inc.

Contractor Turner Construction Company

Height 993.3 ft/302.7 m

Above-ground stories 75

Basements 4

Use Office

Site area 62,500 sq ft/5806 sq m

Goss building area 2,054,000 sq ft/190,817 sq m

Area of typical floor plate 22,500 sq ft/2090 sq m (rentable area)

Number of parking spaces 192 (plus 2000 spaces in seperate building)

Principal structural materials Steel, concrete

Other materials Gray granite cladding, glass, stainless steel

Wells Fargo Plaza

Houston, Texas, USA

This 71-story tower (previously known as First Interstate Plaza and originally as Allied Bank Tower) is located at the center of downtown Houston. The tower is sited so that its flat sides are in alignment with neighboring façades, unifying the buildings and the skyline. The semi-curved form was achieved by juxtaposing two quarter-cylinder shafts, which are offset by one bay. The combination of planes and curves results in the constant interplay of sunlight on the tower's surface and also reduces the building's substantial mass.

In contrast to the surrounding dark granite high-rises, this building is light and fluid, with its upper 70 stories clad in an uninterrupted skin of reflective green glass. At grade, the building is sheathed in polished black granite with a 5-foot stainless steel band capping the junction of the granite and glass. This use of rich materials and careful detailing also provides a human-scaled sense of entry to the building.

Approximately 65 percent of users enter the building through Houston's downtown pedestrian tunnel system, which protects against the city's infamous heat, rain, and humidity. As the tunnel enters the building, it becomes a glass corridor, bisecting a sunken plaza that provides views and sunlight to the underground path.

Double-deck express elevators shuttle passengers to sky-lobbies on floors 34–35 and 58–59, where they transfer to local elevators. This arrangement keeps the core to a manageable size—there are 27 elevator shafts running 56 cabs.

The lower sky-lobby incorporates horizontal trusses tying together the bundled-type structural systems in each half of the plan. These structural elements are prominent in the two-floor public space, and are clad in white paneled wood casings rather than a high-tech material.

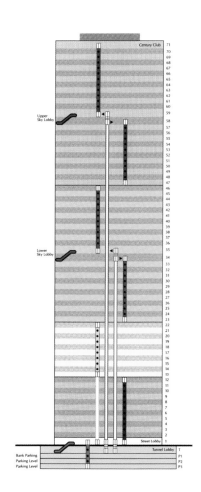

Legend (diagram 1):
- Floors 47-71
- Floors 23-46
- Floors 13-22
- Floors 2-12
- Tunnel Level through P3

1

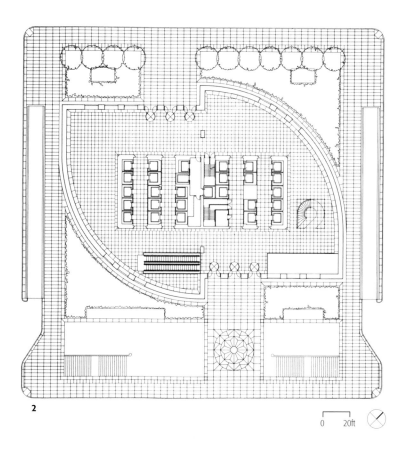

2

0   20ft

1   Section diagram plan explaining the vertical transportation system. 22 double-deck express elevators provide direct access from street and tunnel levels to the lower and upper sky-lobbies located at levels 34–35 and at levels 58–59. The lower sky-lobbies serve as transfer levels to floors 23–46 while the upper sky-lobbies serve as transfer levels to floors 47–71.
2   Ground floor plan
3   North view

Photography: Nick Merrick/Hedrich-Blessing, courtesy Keating/Khang Architecture

Section diagram reproduced from First Interstate Bank Plaza leaflet, Coll. G Binder/Buildings & Data SA

4

Location Houston, Texas, USA

Completion date 1983

Architect Skidmore, Owings & Merrill LLP; Partner in charge: Edward Charles Bassett; Design partner: Richard Keating

Associate architect Lloyd Jones Brewer & Associates, Inc.

Client Century Development Corporation

Structural engineer Skidmore, Owings & Merrill LLP

Mechanical engineer I.A. Naman + Associates, Inc.

Acoustical consultant Vito Cerami Acoustical Consultants

Lighting consultants Claude R. Engle

Fountain Richard Chaix

Contractor Miner-Turner J.V.

Height 992 ft/302 m

Above-ground stories 71

Basements 4

Above-ground useable levels 71

Mechanical levels 1 penthouse level; 1 basement level

Use Office

Site area 62,500 sq ft/5806 sq m

Area of above-ground building 1,721,242 sq ft/159,903 sq m

Area of typical floor plate (approx) 25,000 sq ft/2323 sq m

Basic planning module 5 ft/1.5 m

Number of parking spaces 426 below grade

Principal structural materials Trussed steel tube

Other materials Green reflective glass and stainless steel curtain wall, black granite

Kingdom Centre

The Kingdom Centre occupies a site of more than 1 million square feet in the heart of Riyadh's retail district. The three principal elements of the project, the tower, the east podium, and the west podium have a gross built-up area of almost 2 million square feet, plus more than 1.2 million square feet of parking space for up to 3000 cars.

Unlike most podium and tower assemblages, where the tower rises from the podium roof, the Kingdom Tower actually rises from ground level, with the two podiums flanking it. This gives the tower an individual identity at the arrival apron, while still giving the impression from a distance of a tower resting on a single podium.

The east podium accommodates a shopping mall, and the west podium accommodates a wedding hall/banquet facility, conference hall and sports facilities. The upper third of the total tower height comprises a monumental inverted parabolic arch spanned by an enclosed observation bridge.

The deliberate use of butt-jointed glazing on the tower, coupled with the vast amount of space around it gives the tower an enhanced scale, adding to its monumental character. The absence of scale-relating elements such as mullions and transoms or floor lines gives the tower, which is relatively small by global standards, the awe-inspiring scale and iconic quality inherent in very tall buildings.

In contrast to typical high-rise construction in western countries, the substructure and greater part of the superstructure of the tower is designed as a reinforced concrete frame. The top third of the tower is constructed in tubular steel frame, triangulated for stability against lateral wind forces. The connections between the reinforced concrete lower frame and the steel structure above incorporate specially designed high-strength steel anchor bars extending two stories in height. The tower foundations comprise a reinforced concrete mat bearing on rock.

The building uses silver reflective glass, concrete, granite and brushed aluminum. These materials, combined with variations in the reflection of the sky on the curved glass form, give the tower an unusually rich visual character.

1   Typical floor plans
2–4 General views of Kingdom Centre
5   Detail of inverted parabolic arch
Photography: Courtesy Ellerbe Becket

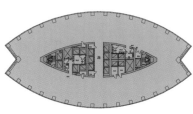

LEVELS 1-6 TYPICAL PLAN
OFFICES

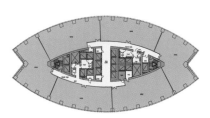

LEVELS 7-13 TYPICAL PLAN
OFFICES

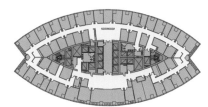

LEVEL 14 PLAN
BUSINESS CENTER

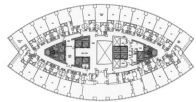

LEVEL 22 PLAN
HOTEL

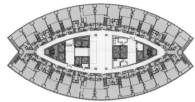

LEVEL 24 PLAN
APARTMENTS

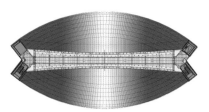

OBSERVATION DECK LEVEL
+286 M. ABOVE GROUND LEVEL

1

2

3

4

5

Location Riyadh, Saudi Arabia	**Landscape architect** Ellerbe Becket	**Use** Mixed: office, hotel, residential, retail
Completion date 2002	**Contractor** El-Seif Engineering Company	**Site area** 23 acres/9.3 ha
Architect Consortium of Ellerbe Becket and Omrania & Associates	**Construction manager** Saudi Arabian Bechtel Co.	**Area of above-ground building** 3,300,000 sq ft/306,570 sq m
Client HRH Prince Alwaleed Bin Talal Bin Abdulaziz Alsaud (Kingdom Holding Company)	**Height** 992 ft/302 m	**Number of parking spaces** 3000
	Above-ground stories 32	**Principal structural materials** Reinforced concrete, steel
Structural engineer Ove Arup & Partners	**Basements** 3	**Other materials** Glass, granite, brushed aluminum
Mechanical engineer Ellerbe Becket	**Above-ground useable levels** 30	**Cost** SAR 1.7 billion
	Mechanical levels 4	

Eureka Tower

Melbourne, Victoria, AUSTRALIA

Towering above Melbourne's Southbank precinct, Eureka Tower offers 360-degree views and easy access to the city and surrounding arts and dining precincts. It is a dramatic new architectural addition to the Melbourne skyline and complements the city's unique character and reputation for architectural achievement.

Eureka Tower's striking sculptural profile, luxury finishes, environmentally sound design and premium services and facilities are unlike any other residential development in Melbourne. Facilities and services include a 24-hour concierge, sophisticated security systems and around-the-clock security personnel, a 25-meter pool, two saunas, gymnasium, a private cinema and an outdoor terrace. Apartments are in a variety of configurations of one, two and three bedrooms, and summit levels 82–87 include luxury penthouses. On level 88, the observation deck will be the highest public vantage point in the Southern Hemisphere, at 935 feet above ground. At ground level, an open landscaped plaza accommodates retail outlets and restaurants.

The tower was designed with abundant environmental and energy-saving features.

The internalised mass concrete structure stabilizes the internal thermal environment and double-glazed, high-performance glass minimizes heat gain and loss, reducing energy use. The maximization of glazed areas increases natural light infiltration, reducing the use of artificial lighting. The curtain wall skin that envelops the structure is insulated with spandrels, minimizing thermal loss, and openable windows provide fresh air, reducing the need for mechanical ventilation. Materials were selected with consideration for life cycle, and waste minimization. Low-emission products were used whenever possible, as were natural materials (stone flooring and benchtops, wool carpets), and plantation timbers.

1   Sky Rise apartment configuration, levels 66–80
2   Sky Rise apartment configuration, levels 56–64
3   Premier Rise apartment configuration, levels 28–52
4   River Rise apartment configuration, levels 11–24
5   Tower seen from Yarra River
6   View from Melbourne's Royal Botanic Gardens
7   Canopy detail
8   General view

Photography: Angelo Marcina, courtesy Eureka Tower Pty Ltd
Plans: Courtesy Eureka Tower Pty Ltd

5

7

6

8

Location Melbourne, Victoria, Australia

Completion date 2006

Architect Fender Katsalidis Architects Pty Ltd

Client Eureka Tower Pty Ltd

Structural engineer Connell Mott MacDonald Pty Ltd

Mechanical engineer Norman Disney & Young Pty Ltd

Vertical transportation consultant Norman Disney & Young Pty Ltd

Landscape architect Tract Pty Ltd

Contractor Grocon Constructors Pty Ltd

Height of building 984.3 ft/300 m

Above-ground stories 92

Basements 1

Above-ground useable levels 89

Mechanical levels and level numbers 6: Levels 25, 53, 81, 90, 91, 92

Use Residential, retail, observation deck

Site area 52,724 sq ft/4900 sq m

Area of above-ground building 645,600 sq ft/60,000 sq m

Area of typical floor plate Levels 11–24, 26–52, 54–55: 15,322 sq ft/1424 sq m; levels 56–64: 10,760 sq ft/1000 sq m; levels 65–87: 6994 sq ft/650 sq m

Number of parking spaces 200 (basement); 580 (carpark decks)

Principal structural materials Off form reinforced concrete, curtain wall

Other materials Off form reinforced concrete shear walls, acoustic rated lightweight plasterboard wall panels, post tensioned reinforced concrete floors, powdercoated aluminium framed windows

Cost AUD$500 M

Commerzbank Headquarters

The Commerzbank was considered to be the world's first ecological office tower. The outcome of a limited international competition, the project explores the nature of the office environment, developing new ideas for its ecology and working patterns. Central to this concept is a reliance on natural systems of lighting and ventilation. Every office in the tower is daylit and has openable windows. External conditions permitting, this allows occupants to control their own environment for most of the year, resulting in energy consumption levels equivalent to half those of conventional office towers.

The plan form is triangular, comprising three 'petals'—the office floors—and a 'stem' formed by a full-height central atrium. Pairs of vertical masts enclose services and circulation cores in the corners of the plan and support eight-story Vierendeel beams, which in turn support clear-span office floors.

Four-story gardens are set at different levels on each of the three sides of the tower, forming a spiral of gardens around the building. As a result, on any level only two sides of the tower are filled with offices. The gardens become the visual and social focus for village-like clusters of offices. They play an ecological role, bringing daylight and fresh air into the central atrium, which acts as a natural ventilation chimney up the building for the inward-facing offices.

The gardens are also places to relax during refreshment breaks, bringing richness and humanity to the workplace. From the outside they give the building a sense of transparency and lightness.

The tower has a distinctive presence on the Frankfurt skyline but it is also anchored into the lower-scale city fabric. It rises from the center of a city block alongside the original Commerzbank building. Through restoration and sensitive rebuilding of the perimeter structures, the traditional scale of this block has been reinforced. The development at street level provides shops, car parking, apartments and a banking hall, and forges links between the Commerzbank and the broader community. At the heart of the scheme a public galleria with restaurants, cafés and spaces for social and cultural events forms a popular new route cutting across the site.

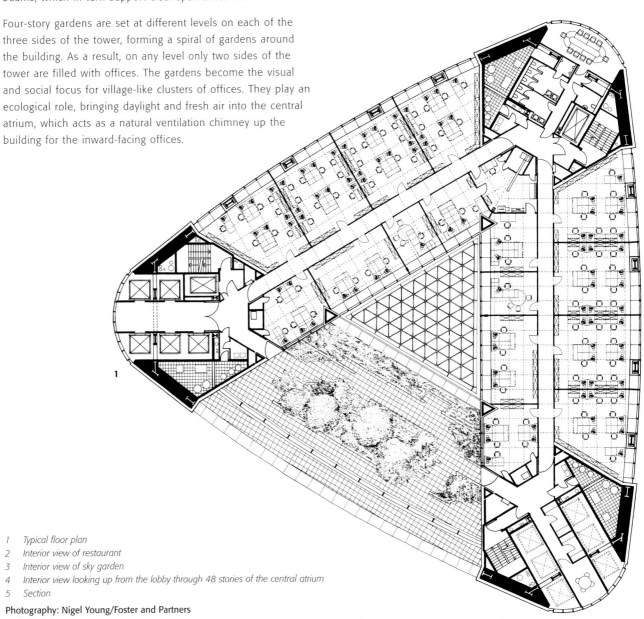

1

1   Typical floor plan
2   Interior view of restaurant
3   Interior view of sky garden
4   Interior view looking up from the lobby through 48 stories of the central atrium
5   Section

Photography: Nigel Young/Foster and Partners

2

3

4

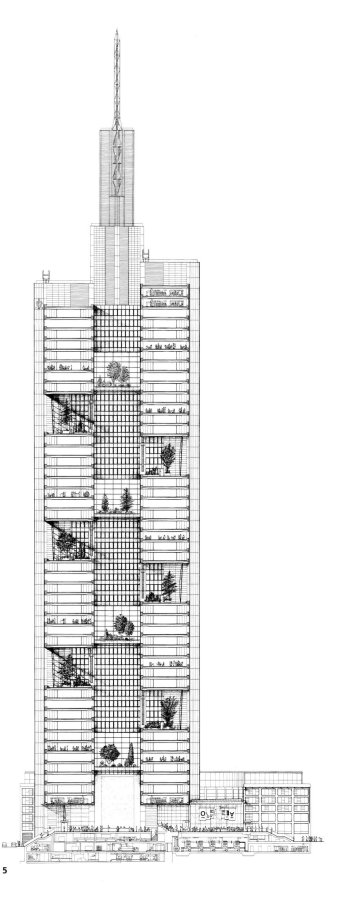

5

Location Frankfurt, Germany

Completion date 1997

Architect Foster and Partners

Client Commerzbank AG

Structural engineer Ove Arup & Partners; Krebs & Kiefer

Mechanical engineer J Roger Preston & Partners; Pettersen & Ahrends

Vertical transportation consultant Jappsen & Stangier

Landscape architect Sommerland and Partners

Contractor Nervus Gmbh

Project manager Nervus Gmbh

Height 980 ft/298.7 m (with aerial); 849 ft/258.7 m (without aerial)

Above-ground stories 51

Basements 2

Above-ground useable levels 3 entrance halls, 45 office floors

Use Office

Site area 1,299,119 sq ft/120,736 sq m

Area of above-ground building 920,012 sq ft/85,503 sq m (tower)

Number of parking spaces 300 cars, 200 bicycles

Principal structural materials Reinforced concrete, steel

First Canadian Place

The First Canadian Place tower dominates the downtown Toronto area. The 72-story structure rises to 978 feet above the city, making it Canada's tallest building. The structure resembles a modified cruciform with a 15-foot indentation at each corner. This arrangement allows for eight corner offices per floor. The 3.5-million-square-foot tower takes up less than half of the 7-acre site, with the remaining area dedicated to public use. Surrounding the tower is a three-level podium, creating an ideal space for shopping, entertainment, and recreational activities.

Italy's finest Carrara marble adds to the beauty of both the tower and podium. Each of the 72 floors of the tower offers 30,000 square feet of column-free space, allowing for flexibility in floor planning. All windows are double-glazed, tinted, and heat absorbing to eliminate heat and glare from the sun.

The tower is supported by a steel tubular frame. The structure consists of two tubes of vertical and horizontal steel, linked diagonally and horizontally. The inner tube typically surrounds the elevators and other core features, while the outer tube defines the external skin. Once the two tubes are linked, they work together to resist forces from wind and earthquakes.

The location and attractions of First Canadian Place draw thousands of people each day. It is connected to a vast underground network of walkways which link the lower levels of major hotels, offices, and transportation facilities in downtown Toronto. The 36-foot sidewalk around the tower is designed to prevent congestion during the midday rush. Extensive landscaping and protected promenades surround the complex.

First Canadian Place achieves a balance between an office tower and recreational area for those who visit the financial district of Toronto. The complex represents both design technology and space efficiency as well as aesthetic appeal and convenience.

1

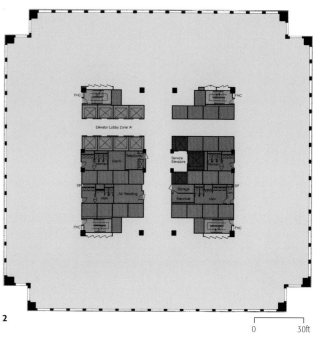

2

0   30ft

1   Exterior view of banking pavilion
2   Typical office floor plan
Opposite:
    General view of Canada's tallest building

Photography: Ian Leith (1); Fiona Spalding-Smith (opposite)

Location Toronto, Ontario, Canada
Completion date 1975
Architect Bregman + Hamann Architects
Design consultant Edward Durell Stone
Client Olympia & York Developments
Structural engineer M.S. Yolles & Partners
Mechanical engineer The ECE Group
Vertical transportation consultant Keith Jenkins & Associates

Contractor Olympia & York Developments
Height 978 ft/298 m
Above-ground stories 72
Basements 4
Above-ground useable levels 70
Mechanical levels and level numbers 2 double-height levels at top of building
Use Office, retail

Site area 223,556 sq ft/20,768 sq m
Area of above-ground building 3,498,610 sq ft/325,020 sq m
Area of typical floor plate 33,700 sq ft/3130 sq m
Basic planning module 5 ft/1.5 m
Number of parking spaces 1465
Principal structural materials Steel
Other materials Marble, glass
Cost $250 M

The Landmark Tower

The Landmark Tower is located in the Minato Mirai (literally, 'the harbor of the future') development, in Yokohama, Japan. Since its completion in 1993, the tower has become the symbol of the area, which also includes office and residential space, hotels, shopping centers, restaurants, convention centers, and public parks.

At 972 feet, the Landmark Tower is Japan's tallest building. Very tall buildings have long been a challenge in Japan, given its hundreds of earthquakes a year, and the advanced techniques necessary to protect buildings and the population from their devastating effects. The Landmark Tower has a flexible structure that absorbs the force of earthquakes, theoretically the same structure as that of the five-storied pagodas of Japanese temples, which have never collapsed, despite enduring many series of earthquakes. Structurally, the building is a tube within a tube. A composite system is used up to the ninth floor to increase lateral stiffness, boost compression strength, and add mass to resist overturning. The steel-framed tubes on the upper floors are tied together with braces. Two tuned active dampers are located at the 925-foot level, each equipped with a tuned spring system and a control system so they can act in two directions.

The tower's tapered form is clad in granite and contains 1.5 million square feet of office space on 52 floors. The Yokohama Royal Park Hotel occupies the upper 15 floors, making it the highest hotel in Japan. The top two floors have two restaurants and an observation deck on the 69th floor is reached by the world's second fastest elevator (traveling at 2460 feet per minute). On a clear day, Mount Fuji can be seen from the observation deck. A skylit swimming pool and health facilities are located at the base of the hotel portion of the tower.

1

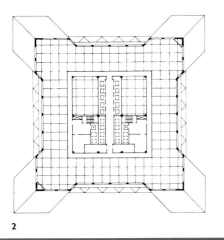

2

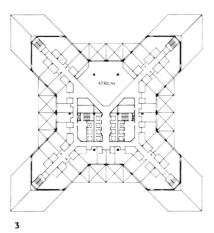

3

4

5

1   General view, night
2   Typical high-rise floor plan, levels 36–52
3   Typical hotel floor plan, levels 56–71
4   General view, day
5   Entrance

Photography: Courtesy The Stubbins Associates, Inc.

Location Yokohama, Japan
Completion date 1993
Design architect The Stubbins Associates, Inc.
Architect/engineer Mitsubishi Estate Architectural and Engineering Office
Client Mitsubishi Estate Company Ltd.
Structural engineer LeMessurier Consultants, Inc.
Services engineer Syska & Hennessy

Principal contractors Taisei Corporation and Shimizu Corporation
Height 972 ft/296 m
Above-ground stories 73
Basements 3
Use Offices, hotel, shopping mall
Area of above-ground building 4,220,976 sq ft/392,284 sq m (total), comprising: 1,750,103 sq ft/162,649 sq m (office); 952,583 sq ft/88,530 sq m (hotel); 778,497 sq ft/72,351 sq m (shopping mall); 651,905 sq ft/60,586 sq m (parking); 87,888 sq ft/8168 sq m (misc)

Number of parking spaces 1400
Principal structural materials Steel
Other materials Granite
Cost $1 billion

American International Building

When completed in 1932, this building of 67 stories above ground and three below was the third tallest building in the world; all three were located in Manhattan. Today considered a landmark building, it was the last of the great Art Deco structures built in lower Manhattan before World War II.

The American International Building was erected by Cities Services Company, known today as CITGO. At one time the owner of the building purchased another building on Wall Street, and built a bridge connecting this structure to the Wall Street building in order to gain the prestige of the Wall Street address. This connection was eventually demolished and the building could no longer claim its Wall Street address.

It is in this skyscraper that double-deck (serving two floors at a time) Otis elevators were first installed. This invention saved 24,000 square feet of office space, a precious commodity at this highly valued location, but the elevators were later removed due to their unpopularity.

While the building foundations were being excavated for this tall and narrow tower, steel mills in the midwest United States operated around the clock to produce the 24,000 tons of beams and girders needed for the skeleton. As the skeleton began to rise, other materials followed from around the world, including Indiana limestone for the exterior trimming, bricks for the tower shell enclosure, and miles of pipe and conduit wires and cables for the infrastructure. To decorate the elegant two-story lobby and the 66th-floor glass-enclosed observatory, ornamental materials were shipped from France, Italy and Spain. The American International Building was also among the first to make extensive use of aluminum on the exterior.

The 66th-floor observatory, perched high above the financial district, features a glass-enclosed solarium with terraces in all four directions and an inlaid compass in the polished stone floor. This elegant glass bubble is a private domain for executives of the American International Group, the owner of the building since 1976.

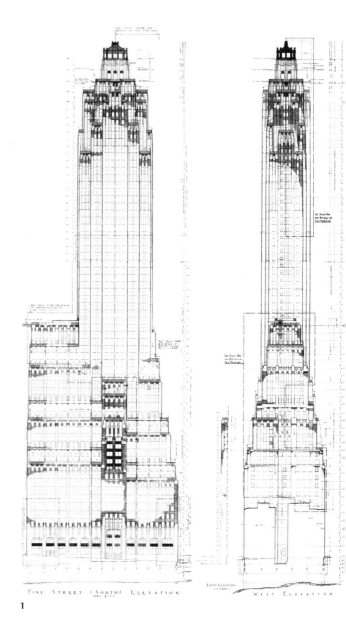

PINE STREET (SOUTH) ELEVATION   WEST ELEVATION

1

Location New York, New York, USA	**Above-ground stories** 67
Completion date 1932	**Basements** 3
Architect Clinton & Russell; Holton & George	**Use** Office
Owner American International Group	**Area of above-ground building** 865,000 sq ft/80,359 sq m
Engineer Taylor Fichter Steel Construction Inc.; Tenny & Dhems Inc. Consulting Engineers	**Principal structural materials** Steel
Contractor James Stewart & Co. Builders	**Other materials** Indiana limestone, brick, aluminum, marble
Height 952 ft/290 m	

2

3

4

5

6

1   *Original blueprint showing south elevation*
2&5 *General views*
3   *1930s postcard showing the newly finished building*
4   *Exterior detail*
6   *Elevator lobby*

Photography: Courtesy American International Realty Corp.
(2,4–6); © Skyscraper Museum (3)

Key Tower

On a corner site, Key Center (originally known as Society Center) faces both the Public Square and the Mall, defining and linking Cleveland's two most important historic downtown public spaces. Its presence at the northeast corner of the square completes the perimeter envelope of the space and creates a gateway to the mall on axis with the Terminal and BP America Towers. In combination with the other two towers, the 57-story tower locates Public Square on Cleveland's skyline and creates a landmark silhouette for the center of Cleveland.

The design of Key Center included rehabilitation of the historic Society for Savings bank (designed by Burnham and Root in 1889) and a 403-room convention hotel, which completes the full block development known as Key Center. The ornate public banking hall, designed by William Pretyman with allegorical murals by Walter Crane, is still in use today and remains substantially unchanged. The cleaning and repair of the bank's red sandstone exterior and the removal of a mid-century addition restored its original appearance.

Key Center is larger than the original bank, but the perception is of two polite and sympathetic urban neighbors. In response to the site, the tower was designed to feel like an independent building. Its narrower face stands next to the bank on Public Square, articulated in plan and section with setbacks that create a sympathetic 11-story base as a companion to the Society for Savings building. The Public Square façade is set a few feet behind that of the bank; its wide reveal separates the two, allowing the original building's mass and silhouette to be expressed.

Stone cladding, setbacks, material changes and surface treatments of the base respond to the scale and profile of the bank. Key Center is clad in Stony Creek granite, composite steel and concrete. The building top is composed of stainless steel.

1   Floor plan
2   View of Key Tower looking south
3   Contextual view of tower
4   Elevation

Photography: Hedrich-Blessing (2); Richard Payne, FAIA (3)

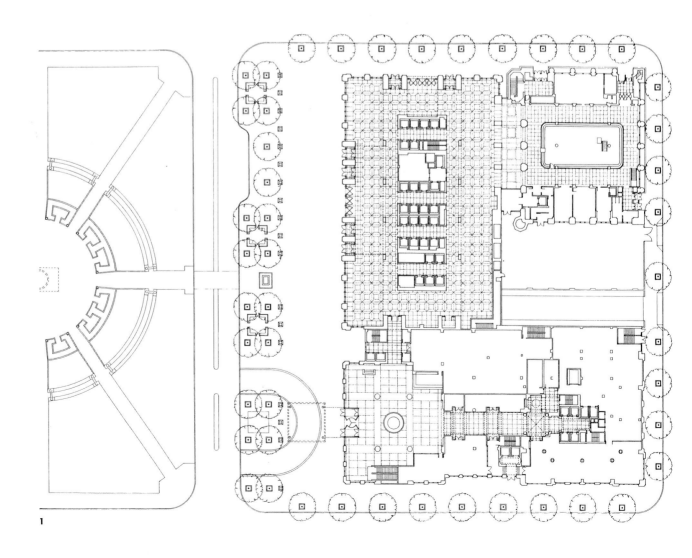

1

2

3

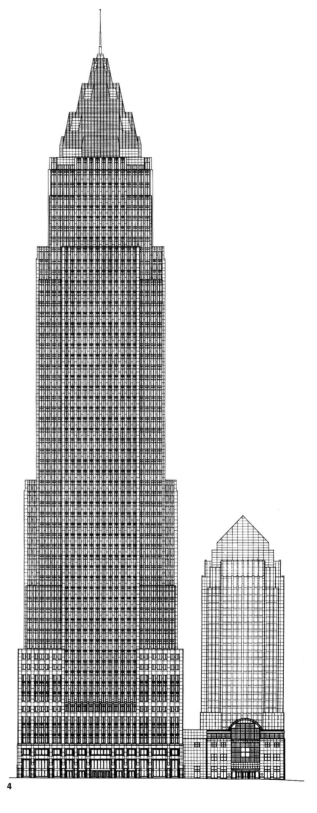

4

Location Cleveland, Ohio, USA

Completion date 1992

Architect Cesar Pelli & Associates (now Pelli Clarke Pelli Architects)

Associate architect Kendall/Heaton Associates, Inc.

Client The Richard and David Jacobs Group, Cleveland

Structural engineer Skilling Ward Magnusson Barkshire Inc.

Mechanical engineer Flack + Kurtz

Contractor Turner Construction Company

Height 950 ft/289.5 m to top of spire

Above-ground stories 57

Above-ground useable levels 57

Use Office with attached hotel and bank

Site area 150,718 sq ft/14,000 sq m

Area of above-ground building 1,371,143 sq ft/127,379 sq m

Area of typical floor plate 17,000–23,500 sq ft/1579–2183 sq m

Principal structural materials Composite steel and concrete

Other materials Stony Creek granite, aluminum curtainwall with stainless steel accents, stainless steel top

Plaza 66/Nanjing Xi Lu

Shanghai, CHINA

The program for Plaza 66/Nanjing Xi Lu called for a mix of retail, entertainment and extensive below-grade parking areas with more than one million square feet of office space in Tower I and 750,000 square feet in Tower II. The solution arranges a series of radially derived volumes—lozenge, cone, almond, and arc—in the manner of a collage. The elements closest to the ground match the scale of historic structures, and reflect the busy street life of Nanjing Xi Lu. The 500,000-square-foot, five-story retail podium is punctuated by two major interior public spaces. Enclosed within curved volumes, these two atriums are cradled by the tower walls.

1   View inside lantern
2   Roof plan
3   Skyline view of the project
4   Retail atrium interior
5   Entrance view

Photography: John Butlin (1,3); HG Esch (4,5)

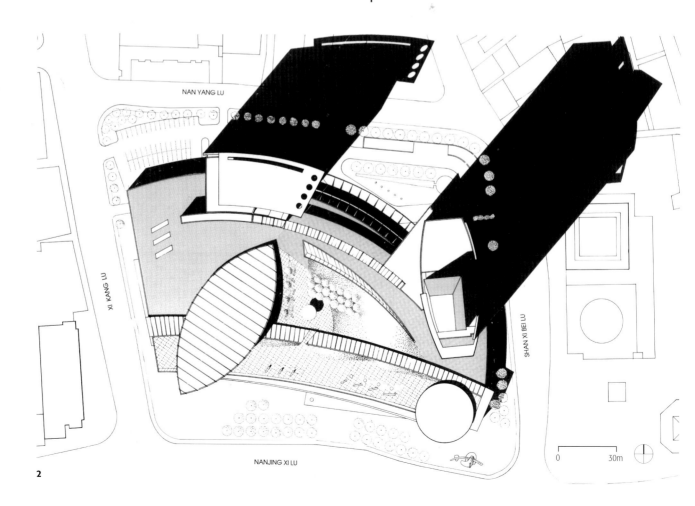

1

2

3

4

5

Location Shanghai, China
Completion date 2002 (Tower I); 2006 (Tower II)
Design architect Kohn Pedersen Fox Associates PC
Associate architect Frank CY Feng Architects & Associates, Ltd
Client Hang Lung Development Company, Ltd.
Structural engineer Thornton Tomasetti Engineers
Mechanical engineer Flack & Kurtz Consulting Engineers
Vertical transportation consultant John A Van Deusen & Associates, Inc.

Contractor Shanghai Construction Group
Project manager Dominic Dunn
Height 945 ft/288 m
Above-ground stories 66 in Tower I
Basements 3
Above-ground useable levels 49 in Tower I
Mechanical levels and level numbers Tower 1: 6, 7, 8, 24, 25, 39, 40, 54, 55, roof
Use Office, retail
Site area 2,300,639 sq ft/213,729 sq m

Area of above-ground building 1,509,832 sq ft/140,263 sq m
Area of typical floor plate 19,185 sq ft/1783 sq m
Basic planning module 3.9 ft/1.2 m
Number of parking spaces 572
Principal structural materials Reinforced concrete
Other materials Exterior: aluminum and glass curtainwall, stone-clad retail base; interior: terrazzo, plaster, wood, aluminum storefront
Cost US$320 M

One Liberty Place

One Liberty Place was the architects' response to their continuing quest to achieve synthesis between romantic yearnings of traditional skyscrapers and the display of modernist technological imagery. At the time of building, it represented a new beginning for the city of Philadelphia, with the establishment of a special high-rise zoning district.

The three-story retail podium represents the contextual, urban element within the cityscape. The tower integrates with the podium through the clear distinction of wall surfaces that either reach the ground or are set back. The tower is square with reentrant corners. A shift in plane between the building's shaft and the corners emphasizes the location of eight major columns that tie with outriggers to the building's braced central core at intermittent floor levels. The top of the building is a logical conclusion of the building's geometry. The single and repetitive use of the gable is the generator of this form. The multiple gables create a visual image not unlike the Chrysler Building in New York.

Varying surface treatments of stone and glass are supported in a structural, aluminum grid. From the stone-clad base, the amount of glass increases until the top is totally sheathed in synthetic glass—the abstracted historic form is rendered in a modern technological material.

Vertical stone piers accentuate the columns of the tower's shaft and, with horizontal stone bands at one-, two- or four-story intervals, form various decorative patterns and different scales. The multi-story lobby provides the spatial transition from the street to the workspaces on stacked office floors.

Tower gravity loads and lateral wind forces are carried primarily by a network consisting of a conventionally braced core with four major corner columns in alignment with eight perimeter 'super-columns' connected to the core by four-story 'outriggers' at three points in the tower. The outrigger/super-column tower structure permits great flexibility and openness for office space and particularly the ground floor retail area (only eight major columns and the core penetrate the retail area).

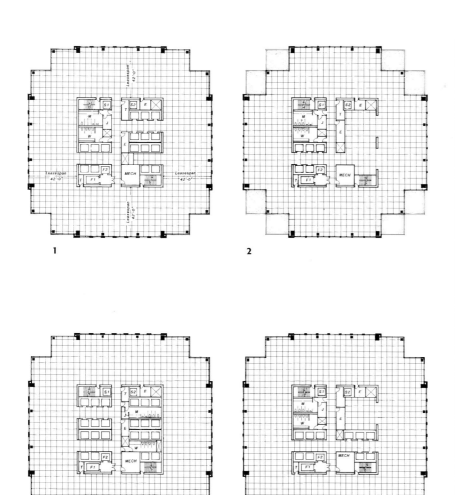

1

2

3

4

0   40ft

5

6

1 Midrise level floor plan, zone 2
2 Highrise level floor plan, zone 4
3 Lower level floor plan, zone 1
4 Midrise level floor plan, zone 3
5 General view at night
6 General view
7 Façade detail
8 Street level detail

Photography: Lawrence S Williams Photography

7

8

Location Philadelphia, Pennsylvania, USA
Completion date 1987
Architect Murphy/Jahn, Inc.
Client One Liberty Place Tower joint venture
Developer Rouse & Associates
Structural engineer Lev Zetlin Associates, Inc.
Mechanical and electrical engineer Flack & Kurtz

Vertical transportation consultant Katz Drago & Co, Inc.
Landscape architect Murphy/Jahn, Inc.
Contractor LF Driscoll Company; Huber, Hunt & Nichols, Inc.
Height 945 ft/288 m
Above-ground stories 62
Basements 2
Above-ground useable levels 61

Use Office
Site area approx 39,496 sq ft/3669 sq m
Area of above-ground building 1,334,896 sq ft/124,012 sq m
Principal structural materials Composite metal, concrete slab
Other materials Marble, granite, stainless steel

Tomorrow Square

Tomorrow Square comprises three major elements on a landscaped plaza. A high-rise tower with hotel and apartment space is joined to a low-rise podium with a retail galleria and conference center. An atrium links the tower and podium. Incorporating a comprehensive program of hotel, residential, and retail functions, Tomorrow Square creates a dramatic landmark on Shanghai's skyline.

Tomorrow Square's dynamic geometric form, created by the simple rotation of two squares, has a monolithic, futuristic quality. Two factors motivated the twist in the structure. The first influence was the building's orientation. The building's prestigious site is at the top of the curve on Nanjing Road, one of Shanghai's premier shopping streets. Therefore, the first 36 floors of the building are oriented perpendicular to the pedestrian and vehicular traffic on Nanjing Road, providing a welcoming and alluring street-level entrance. The site is also adjacent to People's Square and People's Park. So, in consideration of the park, the building's basic square plan is rotated by 45 degrees at the 37th floor, creating an inviting view for park visitors and hotel guests.

The twist is also an indication of the change of function at the tower's 37th level. The 60-story tower features 36 floors of Marriott executive apartments, topped by a 342-room JW Marriott Hotel. The aluminum and glass façade of the building's basic square plan reaches upward in a straight-forward, geometric progression, reflecting the change of function within via the 45-degree rotation at the tower's 37th level. A stunning panoramic city view welcomes guests upon arrival to the hotel lobby, situated on the 37th floor where the building twists.

The tallest hotel in the Puxi district, the tower elegantly rises from the street to a distinctive pinnacle that can be seen throughout the city. At the top, the building's façade continues skyward with the four individual sides angled toward one another but never touching, so as not to indicate finality, but rather a continuum of their inherent relationship. The result is an iconic, highly contemporary sculptural form.

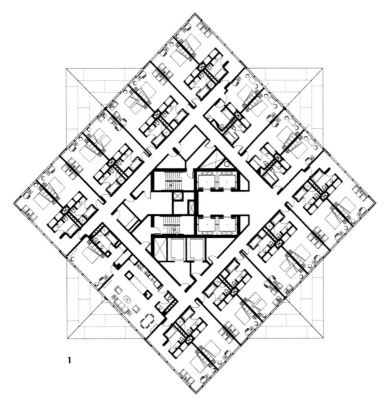

1

2

1   Typical hotel floor plan
2   Bird's-eye view
3   Tomorrow Square in the Shanghai skyline
4   Porte-cochere
5   Entry
Photography: Michael Portman (2,4,5); Courtesy JW Marriott (3)

3

4

5

Location Shanghai, China

Completion date 2003

Architect John Portman & Associates, Inc.

Local architect Shanghai Institute of Architectural Design & Research (SIADR)

Client Shanghai Tomorrow Square Co., Ltd.

Developer Shanghai Anlian Investment & Development Company

Structural engineer John Portman & Associates, Inc.; Shanghai Institute of Architectural Design & Research

Mechanical engineer Newcomb & Boyd Consultants and Engineers

Interior design Hirsch Bedner Associates

Vertical transportation consultant Lerch, Bates & Associates

Landscape architect Arnold Associates

Contractor Shanghai Construction Group General Company (main contractor); Shanghai No. 2 Construction Company (general constructor); Timalco International Pty Ltd. (façade contractor)

Height 935 ft/285 m

Above-ground stories 60

Basements 3

Above-ground useable levels 55

Mechanical levels and level numbers 5: levels 23, 36, 47, 59, 60

Use Hotel, residential, retail

Site area 125,505 sq ft/11,664 sq m

Area of above-ground building 1,002,326 sq ft/93,153 sq m

Area of typical floor plate 13,945 sq ft/1296 sq m

Basic planning module 5 ft/1.5 m

Number of parking spaces 380

Principal structural materials Reinforced concrete, structural steel, glass and aluminum façade cladding

Other materials Granite, glass

Columbia Center

Columbia Center is a six-sided tower with alternating straight and concave sides. As the building rises, two of the concave sides step back at the 43rd and 61st floors, to reveal the solitary partial ring, which rises to the top. In plan, the building can be described as three overlapping ring segments.

At the time of completion, it was the tallest building in the United States, west of the Mississippi, and is still the tallest building in the Pacific Northwest. Originally designed as a 1005-foot tower, the FAA requested that the building be shortened because of a flight path to SeaTac Airport. The same number of floors was retained by shortening the floor-to-floor height by 6 inches, allowing the building to reach its 943-foot height and comply with FAA requirements.

The excavation for the building's underground parking garage and foundation reached a depth of 135 feet, and measured 240 x 248 feet, almost an entire city block, the largest such undertaking in the city up to that time.

The tower is primarily made of steel, but is identified structurally as of mixed construction because the main loads of the building are supported by three composite steel and concrete columns. Constructed of clusters of wide flange columns embedded in concrete, these 8 x 12-foot columns are located at the corners of the building core. The slender tower top could have been prone to an uncomfortable level of sway in severe wind storms, so dampers were added to the core. The dampers consist of a steel plate sandwiched between two steel Ts, connected by a rubberized plastic material.

When opened on 2 March 1985 the building was known as the Columbia Center, and subsequently was changed to Columbia Seafirst Center. It became the Bank of America Tower on 27 September 1999, and once again was named Columbia Center on 21 November 2005.

Equity Office, in partnership with Zimmer Gunsul Frasca, recently completed a $5-million renovation of the tower's lobby and retail corridor to emphasize the building's role as a "vertical city" with customer and visitor amenities on three full floors. The renovation expanded the retail and restaurant mix, commissioned two original sculptures by prominent Northwest artists for the lobby, and lightened the space by adding light-toned wood and light-colored surfaces covered with translucent glass.

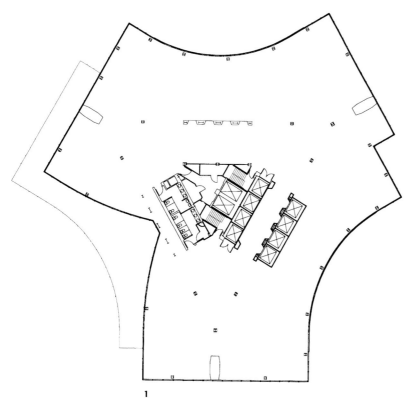

1

2

Location Seattle, Washington, USA
Completion date 1984
Architect Chester L Lindsay Architects
Developer Martin Selig
Structural engineer Skilling Ward Rogers Barkshire, Inc.
Mechanical engineer University Mechanical
Contractor Howard S Wright Construction
Height 933 ft/284 m

Above-ground stories 76
Use Office
Area of above-ground building 1,520,088 sq ft/141,216 sq m (rentable area)
Area of typical floor plate 13,400–23,500 sq ft/1245–2183 sq m (rentable area)
Principal structural materials Steel, concrete
Other materials Granite, glass

1   Mid-rise floor plan (floors 43–60)
2   Recently renovated entrance
3   View of building as it towers above Seattle
4   Section showing elevator plan

Photography: Courtesy Equity Office Properties (2); Courtesy Magnusson Klemencic Associates, Inc. (3)

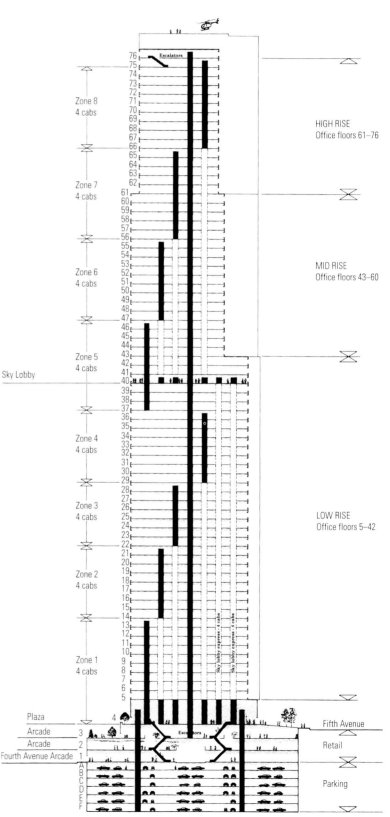

Zone 8
4 cabs

Zone 7
4 cabs

Zone 6
4 cabs

Zone 5
4 cabs

Sky Lobby

Zone 4
4 cabs

Zone 3
4 cabs

Zone 2
4 cabs

Zone 1
4 cabs

HIGH RISE
Office floors 61–76

MID RISE
Office floors 43–60

LOW RISE
Office floors 5–42

Escalators

Sky lobby express – 4 cabs
Sky lobby express – 4 cabs

Plaza
Arcade
Arcade
Fourth Avenue Arcade

Fifth Avenue
Retail

Parking

3

4

The Trump Building

The Trump Building is located at 40 Wall Street, within the midblock between William Street and Broad Street. Designed in 1928 and erected in the record time of less than one year, it was built during a period in history when rivalry in the race to 'reach the sky' was at its most intense. Its main rival in 1928 was the Chrysler Building, which had originally been announced at a height of 927 feet. Architect H Craig Severance, with partner Yasuo Matsui, set out to leapfrog Chrysler by adding an ornate pyramidal crown and Gothic spire to the 40 Wall Street building, then known as the Bank of Manhattan Trust Building. The massing of the building took advantage of the setback regulation mandated by the zoning law passed in New York in 1916.

40 Wall Street was completed in May 1930 with a height of 927 feet. But William Van Alen, architect of the Chrysler Building was not prepared to allow Severance to surpass him. Van Alen added a 185-foot spire, which, according to historians, was secretly assembled within Chrysler's crown, and raised into place just as the tower was finished. At 1046 feet, Chrysler tipped the balance in its favor, gaining the tallest building title briefly before it was overtaken by the Empire State Building.

Although 40 Wall Street dominated the lower Manhattan skyline, it was overtaken in 1932 by the 952-foot American International Building.

Irritated by Chrysler's victory, the architects of 40 Wall Street claimed in a newspaper article that their tower was actually taller, since its observation deck, 'the highest usable floor, was some 100 feet above Chrysler's.' Chrysler's top spire was purely ornamental and effectively inaccessible. 40 Wall Street's observation deck, while very cramped, was open free of charge during business hours, up until World War II.

In 1995 the Trump Organization acquired the building as a speculative venture. Donald J Trump announced a rehabilitation and conversion of the building, the 'crown jewel of Wall Street', to its original grandeur.

1

Location New York, New York, USA
Completion date 1930; restored 1997
Architect H Craig Severance in association with Yasuo Matsui
Consulting architect Shreve and Lamb
Developer Bank of Manhattan Trust Company
Owner The Trump Organization

Height 927 ft/283 m
Above-ground stories 72
Use Office
Area of above-ground building 903,000 sq ft/83,889 sq m
Principal structural materials Steel
Other materials Marble cladding

1   Archways in the upper banking hall
2   General view
3   Pyramidal crown
4   Ground floor elevator lobby
5   Period postcard of the building, known then as the Manhattan Trust Building

Photography: Courtesy The Trump Organization (1,4); Douglas Mason (2,3);
© The Skyscraper Museum (5)

3

4

2

5

Bank of America Plaza

Sheathed in silver reflective glass and outlined at night by emerald green argon gas lights, the 72-story Bank of America Plaza (formerly NationsBank Plaza and originally Interfirst Plaza) dominates the Dallas skyline.

Unlike many of the towers of the 1960s and 1970s that expressed their structure on the exterior, the Bank of America Plaza building is free from perimeter columns. This was achieved by an innovative structural system that supports the gravity loads of the entire building (including the core), and resists lateral forces.

The selection of window color was a subject of great debate. Ultimately, the more conservative silver reflective won because of its elegance and homogenous design. On typical floors, the windows in this glass skin extend from 8 inches above the floor to the ceiling. The glazing is an energy-efficient insulated glass which, combined with the reflective coating, serves to cut cooling costs.

Flexibility of interior design was another innovative feature of this building. Sixteen major columns are located 20 feet from their centers to the exterior wall, allowing maximum flexibility in floor planning. Cantilevered off these concrete and steel columns are the perimeter offices and curtain wall, while the internal core is hung from a moment-resisting steel frame attached to the exterior columns. These steel frames act as Vierendeel trusses connecting the columns. Their unique 42-inch-deep size, at the time of construction not available in the United States, were made in Luxembourg. The core itself is cruciform in plan, allowing unobstructed access on each floor. The exterior columns support not only the gravity loads of the building, but structurally resist the bending and shearing forces created by the wind. This structural system allowed the building to be the slenderest tall building in the world at the time of construction, with a height-to-floor area ratio of 7:1.

The building remains the tallest in Dallas, and is the third-tallest in Texas.

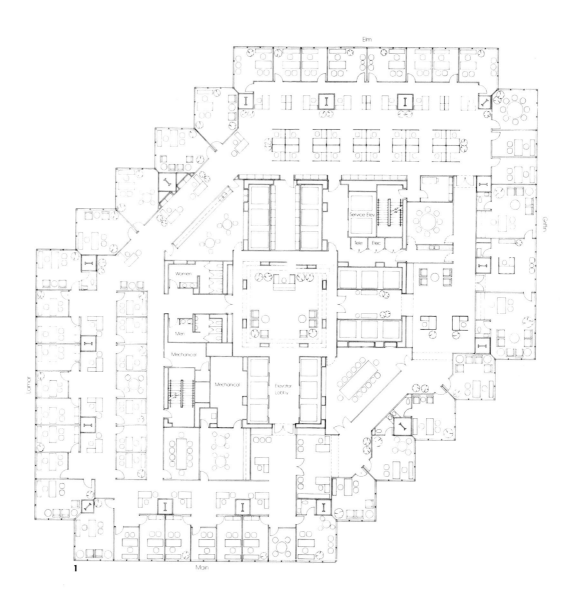

3

4

2

1	Typical floor plan
2	General view
3&4	At night, more than 2 miles of green argon tubing illuminate the building

Photography: Coll. G Binder/Buildings & Data SA

Location Dallas, Texas, USA

Completion date 1985

Architect Jarvis Putty Jarvis (JPJ Architects)

Developer Bramalea Texas, in association with Prudential Reality Group

Structural engineer LeMessurier Associates in association with Brockette

Mechanical engineer Purdy McGuire, Inc.

Contractor Austin Commercial

Height 921 ft/281 m

Above-ground stories 72

Use Office

Area of above-ground building 1,916,550 sq ft/178,047 sq m (rentable area)

Area of typical floor plate 14,746–28,502 sq ft/1370–2648 sq m (rentable area)

Basic planning module 5 ft/1.5 m

Principal structural materials Mixed

Other materials Glass and aluminum curtainwall

OUB Centre

This skyscraper in Raffles Place, Singapore, was designed as the home of the Overseas Union Bank (UOB), and as a prestigious center for commercial, rental office, and car parking spaces.

OUB Centre stands as one of the three tallest skyscrapers in Singapore. The tower is conceived as two distinct, but structurally integral, triangular volumes. The slight space between the forms creates a sense of a shift in a once-whole form.

The triangular towers face each other on the hypotenuse. The taller tower is supported by a service core and a triangular column in one corner. Imposed on the towers are square and circular designs that animate the exterior of the building. The façade is etched with a grid overlaid with larger rectangles, composed of smaller window units. These elements produce a successful rhythmic effect.

The structure rises to 919 feet and contains 1.1 million square feet of office space. The steel frame allows for column-free floor space. The floor system consists of reinforced concrete slab composite with a ribbed steel deck. A major portion of the space below grade is a reinforced concrete parking garage that connects to a subway station, and a shopping center. The exterior features a curtain wall of chemically treated alloy that changes color according to the light that it reflects.

The building's dramatic entrance is tucked into a 120-foot-high cutaway base. Skylights and other lighting are used to create an airy feel to the public areas.

The OUB Centre was the tallest building in Asia until the Bank of China Tower was completed in Hong Kong in 1989.

1   Skylights at the dramatic building entrance
2   View from below
3   OUB Centre, general view
4   Section and floor plans
Photography: Osamu Murai courtesy Kenzo Tange Associates

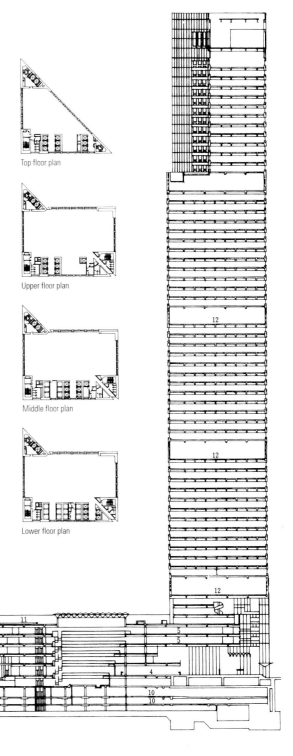

Top floor plan

Upper floor plan

Middle floor plan

Lower floor plan

3 **4**

Location Singapore
Completion date 1986
Architect Kenzo Tange Associates
Associate architect SAA Partnership
Client OUB Centre Limited
Structural engineer Bylander Meinhardt Partnership
Mechanical engineer Bylander Meinhardt Partnership
General contractors Kajima Corporation; Hazama-gumi Ltd;
Japan Development Construction Co. Ltd.

Project manager Overseas Union Project Management
Height 919 ft/280 m
Above-ground stories 66
Basements 4
Use Office, retail
Site area 81,023 sq ft/7530 sq m
Area of above-ground building 1,100,000 sq ft/102,190 sq m
Principal structural materials Steel
Other materials Aluminum

UOB Plaza

UOB Plaza is located in the business center of Singapore, adjacent to the Overseas Union Bank (OUB) Centre that was also built by the same architect. The UOB Plaza consists of two office towers: the 66-story, 919-foot UOB Tower, and a smaller, 38-story high-rise. UOB Plaza is one of Singapore's three 919-foot-tall buildings, the maximum height permitted by the Civil Aviation Authority of Singapore.

The OUB Tower tapers at its summit and is formed by square blocks, nested at 45-degree angles and sitting on an octagonal base. The articulation of the tower creates an outline that richly expresses motion, through the play of light and shadow. Each office within the multi-faceted tower has a panoramic view. A double-story sky lobby, located on the 37th and 38th floors, also provides panoramic views of the city for visitors.

The podium spans 148 feet and is supported by four large columns. It is the location for the banking hall and serves as the literal connection between the two towers. The podium is decorated with a 40-foot-high stainless steel tensile truss curtain wall, located on the first floor of the banking hall. Visitors can walk directly through the banking hall from Raffles Place to the Singapore River. This space is an active and pleasant pedestrian area; below it, an outdoor walkway provides access to the base of the towers.

In 1995, renovations to the 38-story building, originally built in 1974, were completed. The steel structural elements were untouched, but the interior, façades, and equipment were renewed. The new façade and upper levels were redesigned by Kenzo Tange Associates to match those of the main tower.

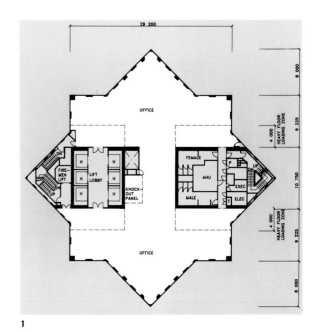

1

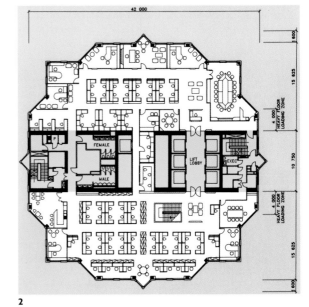

2

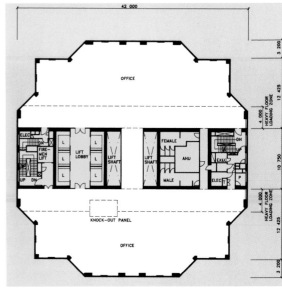

3

1   Typical floor plan, levels 52–56
2   Typical floor plan, levels 31–36
3   Typical floor plan, levels 8–18
4   UOB Plaza, with OUB Center seen between the 38- and 66-level towers

Photography: Osamu Murai courtesy Kenzo Tange Associates

Plans reproduced from the original UOB Plaza leasing brochure,
Coll. G Binder/Buildings & Data SA

4

Location Singapore, Republic of Singapore

Completion date 1992

Architect Kenzo Tange Associates

Project architect Architects 61 Pte Ltd

Client United Overseas Bank Ltd

Structural engineer Ove Arup & Partners

Mechanical engineer J Roger Preston & Partners

Vertical transportation consultant Lerch, Bates & Associates Inc.

Landscape architect Belt Collins Associates

Contractor Nishimatsu Lum Chang JV (Construction & Civil Engineering) Pte Ltd

Project manager UOB Property Management Pte Ltd

Height 919 ft/280 m

Above-ground stories 66

Basements 3

Above-ground useable levels 58

Mechanical levels 21–22, 39–40, 63–66

Use Office

Site area 1,419,104 sq ft/131,887 sq m

Area of above-ground building 1,000,000 sq ft/92,900 sq m

Nett area of typical floor plates 12,388 sq ft/1151 sq m (levels 8–18); 11,113 sq ft/1032 sq m (levels 41–51); 8413 sq ft/ 782 sq m (levels 52–56)

Basic planning module 10.5 ft/3.2 m

Number of parking spaces 421

Principal structural materials Reinforced concrete and steel composite

Other materials Metal frame granite curtain wall

Republic Plaza

This 66-story high-rise building is built adjacent to Raffles Place in the central business district of Singapore. It comprises office space in the tower and car parking in the podium. The entrance hall to the multi-story section is a four-story open atrium, in appropriate scale to the Raffles Place Park and the urban scale of the surrounding streets. The basement floor, accommodating a variety of shops and restaurants, is accessible by escalator from the covered walkway on the street level, and is linked to the subway station.

The building comprises octagonal sections created by cutting off corners from squares of the high-rise tower, producing an auspicious shape, according to Chinese Feng Shui. On the lower portions of the tower, the long sides of the octagon are aligned with the streets, whereas in the upper portions, the sides are rotated through 45 degrees to improve the view of the harbor and the sea for the tenants.

The 918-foot-high tower is made up of three portions, each narrower than the one below. The tapered shape creates a perspective that emphasizes the height of the building. The curtain wall surrounding the four sides is gradually inclined to smoothly shift from the octagonal configuration of the typical floor to the square top. The exterior walls are a combination of polished granite, blue tinted reflective glass, and black colored mullions. The top of the building is a ziggurat-styled penthouse of blue tinted glass which, when illuminated from inside at night, is a prominent feature of the Singapore skyline.

Republic Plaza was designed as an 'intelligent' building. A Building Automation System (BAS) uses Direct Digital Control, interfaced with the air-conditioning and electrical equipment, fire-fighting and detection equipment, and elevators to monitor and maintain optimum environmental control, building safety, and security.

The building is equipped to resist strong winds and even earthquakes by a combination of a core wall system and a moment-resisting frame on the exterior, including outrigger braces.

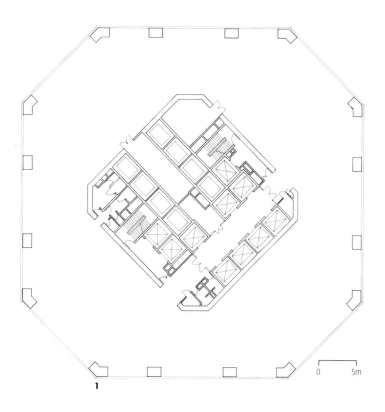

1

2

Location Singapore, Republic of Singapore
Completion date 1996
Design architect Kisho Kurokawa architect & associates
Architect RSP Architects Planners & Engineers (Pte) Ltd
Client CDL Properties Pte.Ltd.
Structural engineer RSP Architects Planners & Engineers (Pte) Ltd
Mechanical engineer Squire Mech Pte Ltd
Landscape architect Cicada Pte Ltd

Contractor Shimizu Corporation
Project manager City Project Management Pte Ltd
Height 919 ft/280 m
Above-ground stories 66
Basements 1
Above-ground useable levels 62
Use Office
Mechanical levels and level numbers 4: floors 28, 47, 65, 66
Site area 72,791 sq ft/6765 sq m

Area of above-ground building 1,068,619 sq ft/99,275 sq m
Area of typical floor plate 21,993 sq ft/2044 sq m (low rise); 14,031 sq ft/1304 sq m (mid rise); 11,857 sq ft/1102 s qm (high rise)
Basic planning module 7.87 ft/2.4 m
Number of parking spaces 504
Principal structural materials Structural steel frame, reinforced concrete
Other materials Glass curtainwall, granite
Cost ¥22,240 M/SGD$251 M

1   Typical lower floor plan, levels 19–20
2   Building's form shifts from octagonal to square
3   Contextual view
4   Lobby
5   Entry

Photography: © Albert Lim KS (2); Shinkenchiku-sha Co., Ltd. (3–5)

3

4

5

Cheung Kong Center

The design of the Cheung Kong Center was developed in response to two major project requirements: first, the local planning authority parameters for the height and massing of the proposed building in relation to its two prominent neighbors, the Hong Kong and Shanghai Banking Corporation to the west and the Bank of China to the east; and second, the study of Feng Shui principles to determine the building orientation, square plan configuration, and use of highly reflective cladding materials.

Designed within these parameters, the building takes the form of a tall, elegant, and well-proportioned square prism. The Hong Kong and Shanghai Bank and the Bank of China are both highly sculptured idiosyncratic forms, giving character to the skyline of Hong Kong. The form of the Cheung Kong Center does not attempt to compete with its neighbors; rather, it establishes its presence through its simplicity and elegance.

The reflective glass wall is modulated by a wrapping grid of stainless steel lines. The corners of the buildings are slightly chamfered to accentuate the tautness of the building envelope and the surface continuity of the stainless steel grid. At night, a dense pattern of light fixtures on the exterior of the building will make the tracery of the stainless steel grid glow softly in the night, defining the prismatic quality of the building form. A secondary, denser pattern of fiber optic lighting will allow the illumination to change color and design during times of festivities. A bright edge of light crowning the top of the building further accentuates its form against the night sky.

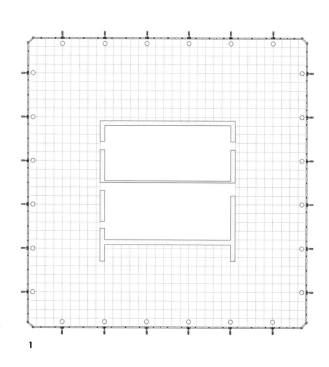

1

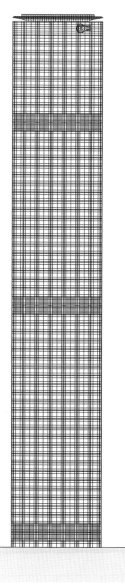

2

1   Typical floor plan
2   Typical elevation
3   Night view of west elevation

Photography: Virgile Simon Bertrand

Location Hong Kong, China

Completion date 1999

Architect Cesar Pelli & Associates (now Pelli Clarke Pelli Architects); Hsin Yieh Architects & Associates Ltd; Leo A Daly

Client Cheung Kong (Holdings) Ltd.; Hutchison Whampoa Property

Structural engineer Ove Arup & Partners Hong Kong Limited

Mechanical engineer Flack + Kurtz Consulting Engineers; Parsons Brinckerhoff

Vertical transportation consultant John Van Deusen & Associates

Landscape architect Belt Collins Hong Kong Ltd

Contractor Paul Y – Downer joint venture

Height 919 ft/280 m

Above-ground stories 62

Basements 6

Mechanical levels 6

Refuge levels 2

Use Office

Area of above-ground building 1,300,000 sq ft/120,770 sq m

Area of typical floor plate 20,157–22,454 sq ft/1873–2086 sq m

Number of parking spaces 911

Principal structural materials Concrete and steel core with unitized stainless steel and glass curtain wall

Citigroup Center

From the outset, Citigroup Center (originally Citicorp Center) was an engineering challenge. The block chosen for the site was fully purchased except for the one corner where St Peter's Lutheran Church was located. The church agreed to sell Citicorp its air rights, on the provision that a new church be designed and constructed on that corner, with no connection to Citicorp and no columns passing through the church.

The resulting design was a masterpiece. In order to provide light at street level, the columns that support the office tower were shifted to the centers of the façades. The four columns and a central core support the tower, which is cantilevered 72 feet off each side of the four columns. These columns rise to 114 feet, where the first floor of the tower begins. Located partially under the tower is a seven-story low-rise portion, which steps back as it rises.

The 59-story tower is a square-shaped sheath covered in alternating bands of aluminum spandrels and silver-tinted reflective glass. The aluminum-clad crown faces south and is sloped at a 45-degree angle.

The church forms a rock-like sculpture, and is covered in red-brown granite. This 'lantern' has a sloped roof that is bisected diagonally by a clear strip of glass skylight that continues down the sides to the base.

The tower's steel frame has diagonal wind bracing on the perimeter, which is repeated in eight-story modules. On the floor below, where the diagonal bracing intersects the corners, there are no vertical columns. This is to avoid accumulating gravity load in the corner columns and allows for the bonus feature of unobstructed views.

This building was one of the first in the United States to contain a tuned-mass-damper (TMD). This 400-ton, computer-controlled concrete inertia block controls wind sway movement.

As masterful in design and form as Citicorp is, its story is not complete without relating the events of summer, 1978, when the building's structural engineer, William LeMessurier discovered a previously undetected flaw in its design. It appeared that the bolted joints, weakest on the building's 30th floor, might tear apart in a severe storm—one that statistics predicted might occur once every 16 years. After three months of frenzied calculations, discussions, and overtime, steel reinforcing plates were placed over the bolted joints, permanently correcting the problem and allowing the building to preserve its place as a glittering addition to the New York skylilne.

1 Façade detail
2 The tower is supported by massive aluminum-clad columns; new church at bottom left
3 General view showing sloped aluminum-clad crown
4 Section
Photography: Courtesy The Stubbins Associates, Inc.

3

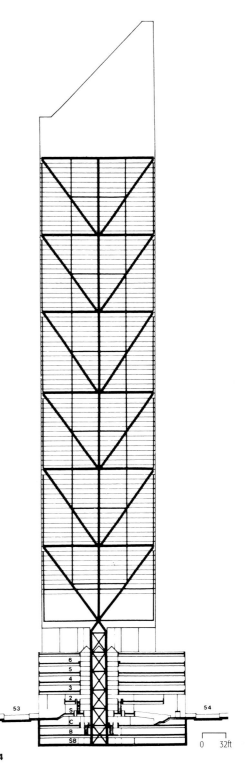

4

Location New York, New York, USA
Completion date 1977
Architect Hugh Stubbins and Associates
Associate architect Emery Roth & Sons
Client Citicorp

Structural engineer William LeMessurier and Associates; Office of James Ruderman
Services engineer Joseph R Loring & Associates
Contractor HRH Construction
Height 915 ft/279 m
Above-ground stories 59

Use Mixed
Area of above-ground building 1,569,022 sq ft/145,762 sq m
Principal structural materials Steel
Other materials Aluminum, reflective glass
Cost US$128 M

SunTrust Plaza

The striking 62-story SunTrust Plaza office tower anchors the north end of downtown Atlanta's Peachtree Center complex. The towering 1.4-million-square foot building with its bold, graphic pyramid crown has become a major icon on Atlanta's central business district skyline. A gateway to downtown Atlanta, SunTrust Plaza provides street life, park-like green space and amenities that enhance city life and anticipate future development.

The building's handsome façades are made of alternating bands of rich granite with gray glass reinforcing the tower's faceted, sculptural form. The plan is basically square with architectural interest added by stepping the building walls in and out to form five bays on each face. These dynamic projections are not merely decorative, but are also functional as they create 36 corner offices per floor and make SunTrust Plaza an ideal corporate headquarters building.

The building is designed to maximize office space. Fifty-foot-span girders supported by sloping exterior columns allow for 25,000 square feet of column-free space per typical floor. Enclosed aerial walkways link the building to retail shops, restaurants, hotels, an athletic club, and a parking structure with 2782 spaces. Express elevators to the uppermost floors are the fastest in Atlanta, rising at 1600 feet per minute.

The site's steep slope presented an opportunity to establish four major entrances into the 62-foot-high lobby, each from a different street level and each offering a distinct sense of arrival. On the upper lobby level, a balcony encircles the cylindrical elevator core and overlooks a major sculpture gallery designed for public enjoyment. Outside on the exterior plaza level, a glass and steel canopy covers the walkway encircling the tower. The spacious plazas and green space act as a public sculpture garden for the community to enjoy.

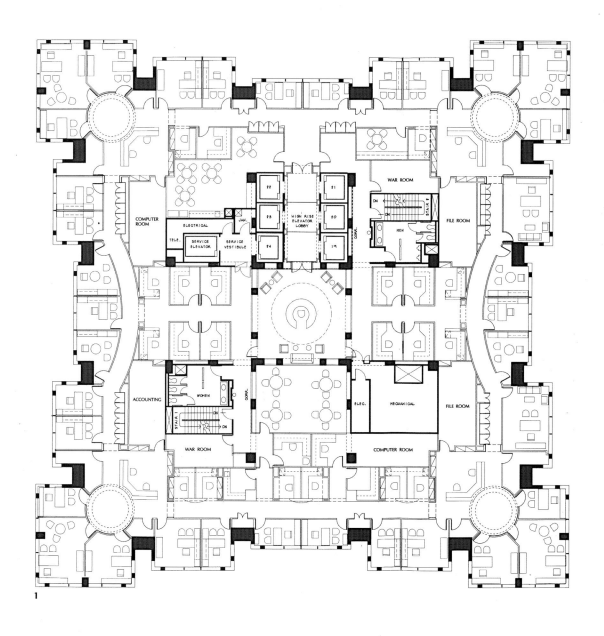

1

1 High-rise floor plan
2 Overall exterior at night
3 Bridge to SunTrust garden offices and parking garage
4 View up tower through "Ballet Olympia" sculpture by Paul Manship
5 Skyline at twilight

Photography: Michael Portman (2,3,5); Timothy Hursley (4)

3

2

4

5

Location Atlanta, Georgia, USA
Completion date 1992
Architect John Portman & Associates
Client SunTrust Plaza Associates, LLC
Developer Portman Holdings
Structural engineer John Portman & Associates
Mechanical engineer Newcomb & Boyd
Vertical transportation consultant Lerch, Bates & Associates
Landscape architect Arnold Associates

Contractor J.A. Jones Construction Company
Height 902 ft/275 m (with antenna)
Above-ground stories 62
Basements 1
Above-ground useable levels 55
Mechanical levels and level numbers 7: SL (below ground), 56–63
Use Office
Site area 2.6 acres/1.05 ha

Area of above-ground building 1,249,477 sq ft/116,076 sq m
Area of typical floor plate 25,000 sq ft/2323 sq m
Basic planning module 5 ft/1.5 m
Number of parking spaces 2782 in separate adjoining building
Principal structural materials Poured in place concrete, including post tensioning
Other materials Granite, vision glass, spandrel glass, aluminum curtainwall framing

Williams Tower

A soaring structure 901 feet high, Williams Tower (originally known as Transco Tower) rises alone from a grassy podium. Covered with mirrored and non-reflective glass, the tower looks back to a golden era of skyscrapers, recreating the Art Deco style of the 1930s. The clients wanted a landmark building and a structure that recalled the Empire State Building; the result was unique, a perfectly symmetrical tower with no front or back.

At the lower floors of the base, the architects created a huge ceremonial arched entrance, 75 feet high, covered in Spanish pink granite. The five-story base of the building provides space for a bank on the ground floor as well as extra room on the levels above. Inside, the lobby floors are lined with granite and each elevator car is lined with a different colored marble.

The shaft of the tower is arranged in a progressive series of setbacks, in the Art Deco tradition. Sheathed in two types of glass, the high-tech skin of the shaft has a stone-like appearance. The mirrored panels play the role of traditional stone; given their opaque quality, and depending on the time of day, they can appear blue, green, gray or black, or a spectacular gold at sunset.

The unusual double-pitched roof peaks 901 feet above street level to complete the tower's elegant, elongated form. Architect John Burgee described the overall effect of the building as a "steeple of a suburban village."

South of the building is a 3-acre park with a large fountain called the "Water Wall", designed by Johnson/Burgee Architects with Richard Fitzgerald and Partners. The fountain is a stunning work of hydraulic engineering and is completed by a Roman-arched pediment.

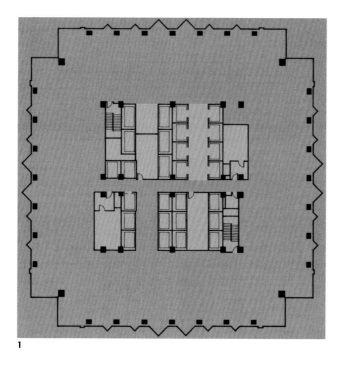

1

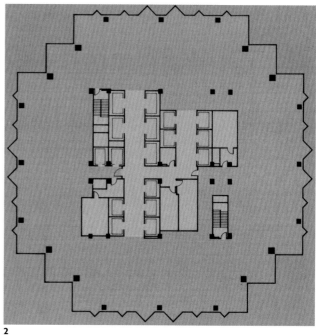

2

1   Typical floor plan, floors 10–48
2   Skylobby (51st) floor plan
3   General view

Photography: Courtesy Hines Interests Limited Partnership

Plans reproduced from original Transco Tower leasing brochure, Coll. G Binder/Buildings & Data SA

Location Houston, Texas, USA
Completion date 1983
Architect Johnson/Burgee Architects
Associate architect Morris*Aubry Architects (tower)
Associate architect Richard Fitzgerald and Partners (park and fountain)
Developer Gerald D Hines Interests
Structural engineer CBM Engineers, Inc. (tower)

Structural engineer Madeley Engineers, Inc. (park)
Mechanical engineer I.A. Naman & Associates
Landscape architect Zion & Breen Associates, Inc.
Lighting consultant Claude R Engle
Fountain consultants CMS Collaborative
Contractor JA Jones Construction Company
Height 901 ft/275 m

Above-ground stories 64
Use Office
Area of above-ground building 1,600,000 sq ft/148,640 sq m
Number of parking spaces 3200
Principal structural materials Steel
Other materials Silver gray reflective glass

Hong Kong New World Tower

Shanghai, CHINA

This mixed-use complex is located in the heart of Shanghai's Huai Hai Road, one of the most popular shopping streets in the city. The site is bounded by Huai Hai Road to the south, Ma Dang Road to the west, Huang Pi Road (N) to the east, and Jinling Road to the north.

The location and scale of the complex made it essential that it be a landmark, both in its local quarter and on the city's greater skyline. It reflects a classical elegance, and through the use of modern construction techniques and materials it celebrates the future while recognizing its history and context of the people and their culture. Along Huai Hai Road, the podium provides a definition of the street, enhancing the life and rhythm of the street as a promenade.

As the main use of this complex is an office tower, its material and aura celebrate luxury and elegance, especially along the Jinling Road entrance. Other components include 269,999 square feet of retail, and a 118,360-square-foot public parking garage. The complex's multi-story public open spaces, designed for both active and passive use, provide a place of enjoyment for the complex's users and the community.

The tower rises from a four-story podium base to 59 stories above grade, with a total height of 890 feet. The total area above grade is 1,477,735 square feet.

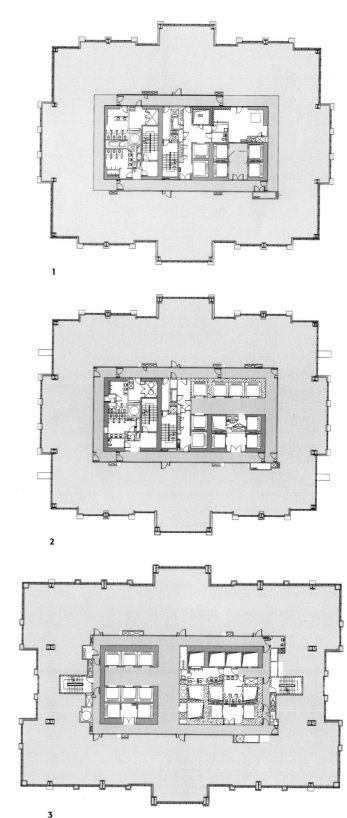

1

2

3

1 Typical floor plan high zone (levels 48–53)
2 Typical floor plan mid zone (levels 35–47)
3 Typical floor plan low zone (levels 12–33)
4 View at street level
5 Courtyard view
6 General view
7 South elevation

Photography: Kerun Ip

Plans reproduced from original Hong Kong New World Tower leasing brochure, Coll. G Binder/Buildings & Data SA

4

5

6

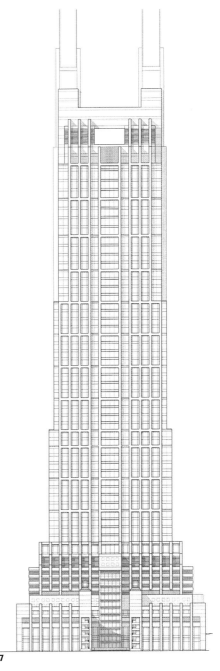

7

Location Shanghai, China

Completion date 2002

Architect Bregman + Hamann Architects

Client Shanghai New World Huai-Hai Property Development Ltd.

Structural engineer Ove Arup & Partners

Mechanical engineer J. Rogers Preston Ltd.

Landscape architect EDAW

Contractor Shanghai 7th Construction Co. Ltd.; Hip Hing Construction Co., Ltd.

Height 890 ft/271.25 m

Above-ground stories 59

Basements 3

Above-ground useable levels 54

Mechanical levels and level numbers 5: floors 10, 25, 42, 58, 59

Use Office, retail

Site area 107,094 sq ft/9953 sq m

Area of above-ground building 1,477,735 sq ft/137,336 sq m

Area of typical floor plate 17,786–21,283 sq ft/1653–1978 sq m

Basic planning module 8.5 x 12.5 ft/2.6 x 3.8 m

Number of parking spaces 256 units (25 surface; 231 in the tower)

Principal structural materials Steel, reinforced concrete, granite

Other materials Aluminum

Cost approx RMB 2.5 billion

21st Century Tower

The visually distinctive and modern 21st Century Tower was acclaimed as the tallest residential building in the world at the time of its completion in 2003. At 886 feet, it occupies a pre-eminent position on the Sheikh Zayed Road and adds a new sense of prominence with its simple clean lines and elegant form, complementing Dubai's contemporary urban landscape.

Atkins was appointed as lead consultant for architecture, interior design, structural, mechanical and electrical engineering design, construction supervision and project management.

The client's desire was for a signature tower with a modern design. The original design concept was derived from elements of the client's logo of overlapping birds in flight. A need to use durable external materials, capable of maintaining the building's appearance in the long term, was also expressed.

The concept reflects these aspects of the brief, and the front elevation features a curved silver aluminum and glass winged or 'feather' element that represents flight, grace and strength. This is complemented by the back elevation, which is a simple,

symmetrically balanced façade that does not compete with the dynamic movement of the front elevation.

The initial massing of the tower was borne out of the site constraints, in terms of maximizing both its footprint and the height restriction. The result is a ground plus 53-level residential tower and adjoining multi-story car park, with a total built up area of 925,360 square feet. The residential tower comprises 300 three-bedroom apartments and 100 two-bedroom apartments on 50 typical floors. The tower also accommodates retail space on the ground and mezzanine floors, as well as a gymnasium, swimming pool, and changing rooms on the roof, with building services taking up two floors.

The car park consists of nine floors with an overall capacity of 412 parking bays. Building services are accommodated in the car park building.

1   Typical floor plan
2&3   At 883 feet, the 21st Century Tower was the tallest residential building in the world, at the time of completion
4   Entrance reception lobby
5   Curved 'wing' element of front façade

Photography: Nick Otty (3); courtesy Atkins (2,4,5)

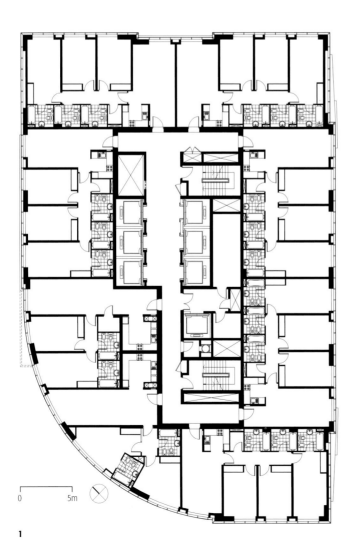

0   5m

1

2

3

4

5

Location Dubai, United Arab Emirates
Completion date 2003
Architect Atkins
Client Al Rostamani Group of Companies
Developer Al Rostamani Real Estate
Structural engineer Atkins
Mechanical engineer Atkins
Vertical transportation consultant Atkins

Contractor Arabtec & Al Rostamani Pegel (JV)
Project manager Atkins
Height 886 ft/270 m
Above-ground stories 55
Basements 1
Above-ground useable levels 54
Mechanical levels 4
Use Residential

Site area 14,200 sq ft/1319 sq m
Area of above-ground building 925,360 sq ft/86,000 sq m
Area of typical floor plate 13,773 sq ft/1280 sq m
Number of parking spaces 412
Principal structural materials Reinforced concrete
Other materials Reflective gray and blue glass and aluminum panel cladding

Al Faisaliah Complex

The Al Faisaliah Complex in Riyadh plays a key part in the city's urban development. The complex includes Saudi Arabia's first skyscraper alongside a five-star hotel, a banqueting and conference center, luxury apartments, and a three-story retail mall. The scheme carefully balances cost-effectiveness, flexibility, and architectural interest to produce buildings that are efficient in services, planning and operation, and easily maintained and responsive to the Middle Eastern climate.

The office tower is square in plan, designed around a compact central core, and tapers to a point, with four main corner columns defining its unique silhouette. Observation decks at stages up the building correspond with giant K-braces, which transfer loads to the corner columns. The building is clad in silver-anodized aluminum panels with cantilevered sunshading devices that minimize glare, allowing the use of non-reflective, energy-efficient glass. These layered façades provide maximum control over the internal environment.

Above its 30 floors of office space, the tower houses the highest restaurant in Saudi Arabia, set within a golden glass sphere 656 feet above ground level. The observation deck below the globe provides a breathtaking panorama of Riyadh and the surrounding landscape. At its pinnacle, the tower narrows to a brightly lit lantern, topped by a stainless steel finial.

The tower is set back from the King Fahd Highway to create a landscaped plaza. Beneath this is a banqueting hall, which can accommodate activities ranging from wedding ceremonies for up to 2000 people to conferences for up to 3400. A high degree of flexibility is achieved by a unique long-span arch system, which provides a column-free space with a moveable partition system that can divide the hall into a maximum of 16 separate rooms.

A five-story lobby at the tower's base forms a link between the hotel to the north and the apartments and shopping mall to the south. A spectacular colored-glass wall in the lobby by the artist Brian Clarke has a desert theme interspersed with images representing natural regional and environmental features.

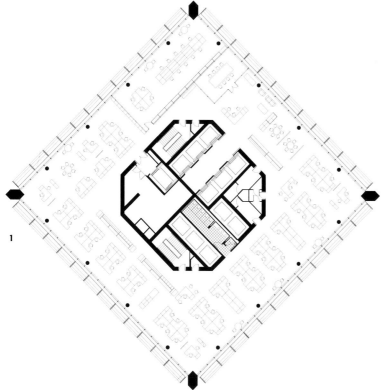

1

2

1   Floor plan
2   Interior of atrium
3   Aerial view
4   Observation deck
5   Ground floor plan

Photography: Nigel Young/Foster and Partners (2,4); Joe Poon (3)

3

4

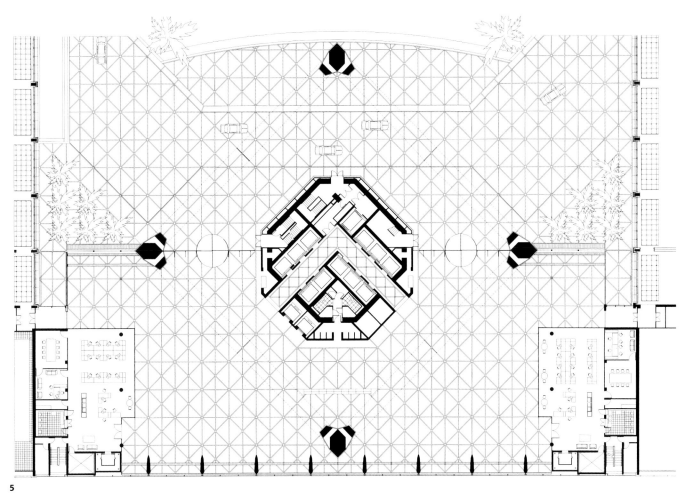

5

Location Riyadh, Saudi Arabia

Completion date 2000

Architect Foster and Partners

Client King Faisal Foundation

Structural engineer Buro Happold

Mechanical engineer Buro Happold

Vertical transportation consultant Lerch Bates & Associates Ltd

Landscape architect WET Design

Contractor Saudi Bin Ladin Group (SBG)

Height 876 ft/267 m

Above-ground stories 30 office floors plus restaurant and viewing platform

Use Office (tower); retail mall, hotel, apartments

Site area 591,800 sq ft/55,000 sq m

Area of above-ground building 582,400 sq ft/240,000 sq m (total)

Area of typical floor plate 8608–16,140 sq ft/800–1500 sq m (tower)

Number of parking spaces 1300

Principal structural materials Concrete, steel, glass

Bank of America Corporate Center

The Bank of America (formerly NationsBank) Corporate Center is in the historic, geographic and business center of Charlotte. The Center includes the 60-story corporate headquarters tower, two landscaped plazas, and Founders Hall, a large public space with retail shops lining its perimeter.

The 875-foot-tall tower is the focal point of the Charlotte skyline. Its base is clad in dark granite with marble columns at its entrances; the curved sides of the shaft have 13 setbacks. The exterior is sheathed in warm beige granite piers, progressively narrower and thinner at each setback. In contrast to the base, the upper sections become lighter and glassier. The top is composed of anodized aluminum vertical rods, which define a volume enclosed only by cage work. It is lit at night from within.

Founder's Hall, a grand civic space, is directly connected to the North Carolina Blumenthal Performing Arts Center as well as 75,000 square feet of retail, restaurant, and health club

facilities. The design allows for impromptu performances as well as programmed events; a circular monumental stair accommodates a natural stage.

Interior floors and walls of Founder's Hall are clad in marble. Structural columns and metal trusswork are painted in a gradation of golden ochers to bright yellows. The overall effect of the finishes is a warm, light-filled space throughout the year. Four large black-olive trees are grouped around a decorative granite fountain, anchoring the opposite end of the monumental stair.

Founders Hall unifies the disparate programmatic elements of the site. Acting as an entry hall for the employees of the Bank of America Tower, the space unifies the sidewalk plaza level with a skywalk level referred to as the Overstreet Mall. This large 135 x 80-foot central space is defined by four-story columns supporting a vaulted truss and skylight system. The space is fronted on two levels with retail. The second level connects to three over-street bridges, knitting the complex to the surrounding city.

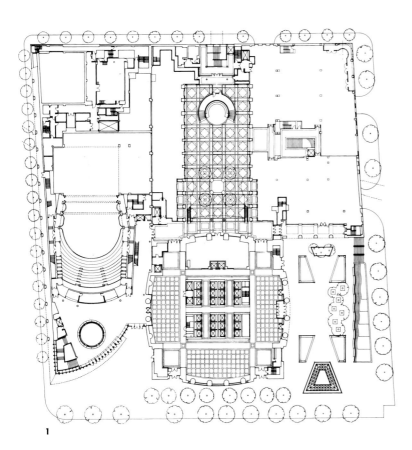

1

2

1   Site plan
2   Interior view of Founder's Hall
3   North elevation
4   Elevation

Photography: Tim Griffith (2); Tim Hursley (3)

3

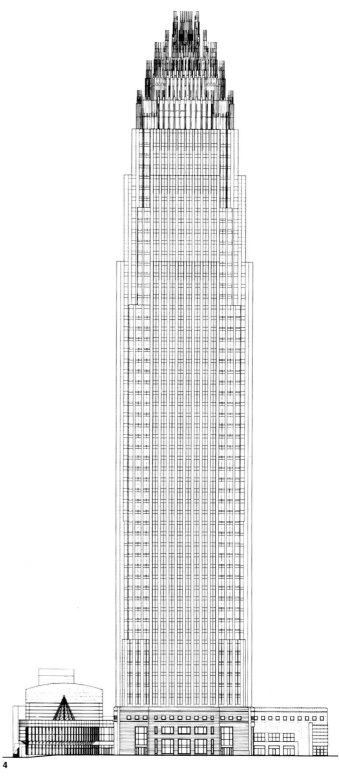

4

Location Charlotte, North Carolina, USA

Completion date 1992

Architect Cesar Pelli & Associates (now Pelli Clarke Pelli Architects)

Associate architect HKS, Inc.

Client NationsBank Corporation; Charter Properties; Lincoln Property Company

Structural engineer Walter P Moore & Associates

Mechanical engineer BL&P Engineers, Inc.

Landscape architect Balmori Associates, Inc.

Height 875 ft/266.7 m

Above-ground stories 60

Basements 100,000 sq ft/9290 sq m of below-grade service and parking

Above-ground useable levels 60

Use Mixed: office, retail, attached performing arts center and public room

Site area 150,718 sq ft/14,000 sq m

Area of above-ground building 1,400,000 sq ft/130,060 sq m

Area of typical floor plate 24,000 sq ft/2230 sq m

Principal structural materials Poured-in-place concrete core, granite, marble, reflective vision glass, anodized aluminum (top)

BOCOM Financial Towers

The building is essentially two solid, very slim columns, 755 feet and 656 feet high, connected by a huge 525-foot atrium with a podium beneath. The two columns are supported by a steel space frame structure within the atrium. The main entrance and the vertical services are oriented to the central atrium.

The dynamic, sloping, triangular shape of the top area of each tower deflects the extreme vertical proportions of the main façade. These top areas are almost free of technical uses to allow conference and leisure users to take advantage of the great panoramic view over Pudong and the Shanghai Bund. A counterpoint to the strong verticality is the horizontal structure of the façade, emphasized by metal louvers in front of the façade. The façade is clad in gray granite.

The design of the project was the result of an international competition.

1   Typical floor plan
2   Aerial view shows triangular shape of the towers
3   View to the 525-foot atrium; the two buildings can be connected by bridges through the atrium at a later date, if required
4   The lower podium of the towers, seen from the river side
5   Section b–b

Photography: PHOTO IMAGING DESIGN, Werner Kirgis

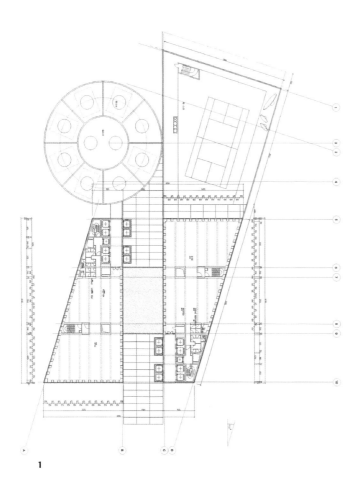

1

2

Location Shanghai, China

Completion date 2001

Architect ABB Architekten; East China Architectural Design & Research Institute Co. Ltd. (ECADI)

Client Bank of Communications

Structural engineer Obermeyer Planen & Beraten

Mechanical engineer Obermeyer Planen & Beraten

Vertical transportation consultant Obermeyer Planen & Beraten

Height 656 ft/200 m and 755 ft/230 m; 869 ft/265 m to tip of spire

Above-ground stories 42 and 50

Basements 4

Mechanical levels and level numbers 3: floors 13, 16, 39

Use Office

Area of above-ground building 1,097,520 sq ft/102,000 sq m

Area of typical floor plate 17,646 sq ft/1640 sq m

Principal structural materials Concrete

3

4

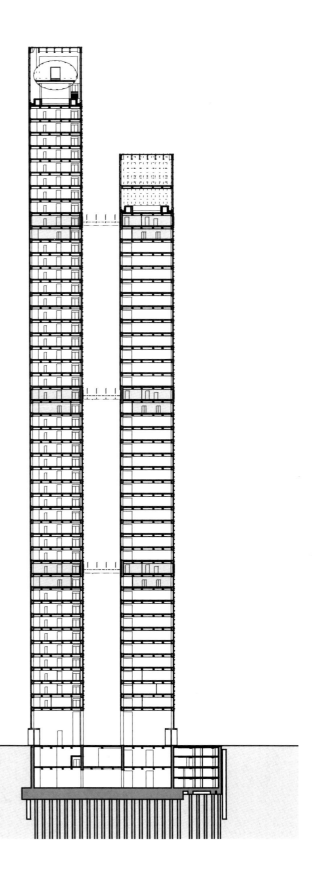

5

Triumph-Palace

At 866.5 feet (including its spire), Triumph-Palace is Europe's tallest residential building. Located in the prestigious historical borough of Sokol, Triumph-Palace commands impressive views of downtown Moscow, Leningrad Avenue, and surrounding parks and recreation zones. The design of Triumph-Palace continues the glorious tradition of the monumental architectural style of the Russian capital's seven high-rise buildings built in the late 1940s.

All nine building sections are integrated into a single composition by a five-story stylobate. The central building is the dominant element of the composition, with its proportionate vertical sections that gradually decrease as the building climbs higher. The front entrance of the central building is accessed from Chapayevski Park, though each building also has an independent entrance. The façades are paneled with light-toned natural stone and ceramic tiles of warm brown shades. The building has a Eurofox ventilated façade system. Vertical stained glass windows are a striking detail on the façades. Stained-glass corner glazing systems provide more natural light for the living quarters.

All apartments, each of which can accommodate a winter garden, include floor-to-ceiling corner glazing, bay windows, and French-style balconies protected by strong multi-layer triplex glass. Each section has two terraced apartments on the 25th level. Twelve unique penthouses, with panoramic windows and spacious terraces, crown the eight sections of the estate.

The infrastructure of the estate is oriented to an active lifestyle: the fitness center includes a 25-meter swimming pool, Finnish saunas and Turkish baths, aerobics gymnasiums and sports halls.

The construction phase was completed by a unique technical operation to install a spire on the central building. Eight structural components, each weighing 4 to 8 tons, were transported to the building and each was installed in five to ten minutes, while six days were required to assemble the spire as a whole. Using an original technique, an active lightning conductor on the spire attracts lightning and deflects it away from the building. The spire rests on an octagonal, three-story-deep foundation, and special stairs inside the foundation access maintenance areas.

1

1   Penthouse apartment with terrace, rendering
2   Façade detail
3   General view
Photography: Courtesy DON-Stroy

2

Location Moscow, Russia	**Height** 866.5 ft/264.1 m
Completion date 2005	**Above-ground stories** 57
Architect TROMOS	**Basements** 2
Client DON-Stroy	**Mechanical levels** 4
Structural engineer SMU-1	**Use** Residential, office, entertainment, retail
Mechanical engineer SMU-1	**Site area** 14.8 acres/6 ha
Contractor SMU-1	**Area of above-ground building** 2,970,115 sq ft/276,033 sq m, including 1,814,491 sq ft/168,633 sq m of residential area
Developer DON-Stroy	**Principal structural materials** Natural stone, brick, steel, iron

Tower Palace Three

Tower Palace Three promotes a new standard of high-rise living for the people of Seoul, South Korea. The tower's design and image is derived from natural forms and influences, which integrate state-of-the-art building technology to provide a landmark structure for the city. This building also owes much of its conceptual image to a 1920's scheme for a tower on the Fredrichstrasse in Berlin by Mies Van de Rohe.

The tower's tripartite arrangement provides maximum view corridors at the lower floors and evolves at the top to present a tall slender face to the city while allowing residents to have views of both the dynamic northern cityscape and the tranquil natural landscape to the south.

The structural concept includes a central core with three walls that form a tripod-like structure. Both the core and the walls were designed to take as much gravity load and lateral load as possible, reducing the need for massive columns at the exterior wall. The exterior columns were thus limited to gravity loads that are tied together at the third points of the tower by massive belt-like walls to help transfer the lateral forces to the core and corridor wall structure. The columns at the perimeter and all the floor framing within the units are constructed of steel.

The tower is clad in a light blue-green tinted high-performance glass to allow for maximum light transmission and bright views. Natural anodized panels provide a metallic quality to the solid surfaces and polished stainless steel rods that function as window-washing tiebacks add brilliance to the exterior surface. Where the tower meets the ground, the column structure is exposed to reveal the lobby and core wall. The exterior wall at this level is glass and spider bolt supported and the core is clad in a green antique marble. The exterior columns are clad in textured stainless steel. The main feature at grade level is the drop-off and its glass canopy structure that protects visitors from wind and rain. The circular drop-off provides a convenient ramp to and from the below-grade parking.

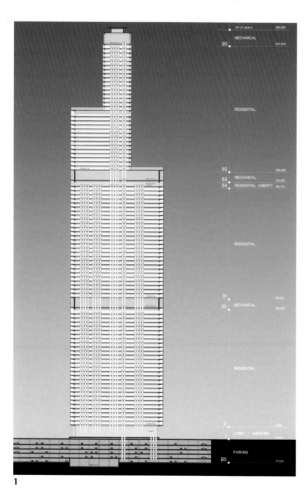

1

2

1   Elevation
2   View looking up
3   General view

Photography: HG Esch Photography, courtesy Skidmore, Owings & Merrill LLP

3

Location Seoul, South Korea

Completion date 2004

Architect Skidmore, Owings & Merrill LLP, Adrian D Smith, FAIA, Design Partner

Associate architect Samoo Architects & Engineers

Client Samsung Corporation; Samsung Construction Co. Ltd

Structural engineer Skidmore, Owings & Merrill LLP; Samoo Architects & Engineers

Mechanical engineer Skidmore, Owings & Merrill LLP; Samoo Architects & Engineers

Vertical transportation consultant Edgett/Williams Consulting Group Inc.

Landscape architect SWA Group

Contractor Samsung Construction Co. Ltd

Height 861 ft/262.425 m (exclusive of antennas)

Above-ground stories 72

Basements 6

Above-ground useable levels 67

Mechanical levels 7: levels B6, B5, B1 Mezz, 16, 55, 70, 71

Use Mixed

Site area 18 acres/7.3 ha

Project gross area 1,952,860 sq ft/181,421 sq m

Principal structural materials Steel

Other materials Glass and aluminum curtain wall

Water Tower Place

Water Tower Place bears the name of its illustrious neighbor, the historic Chicago Water Tower and Pumping Station, built in 1869 in imitation Gothic. The Water Tower Station—which Oscar Wilde called a 'castellated monstrosity'—survived the Great Fire of 1871 and remains a part of Chicago's colorful history.

Water Tower Place was the world's tallest concrete building at the time of its completion in 1976, and retained that title until 1990 when it was surpassed by the 961-foot 311 S Wacker Drive building, also in Chicago.

The Tower rises from the back of a retail shopping mall with its 74 stories wrapped around a central atrium. It houses a Ritz-Carlton hotel, condominiums, office space, parking, and entertainment facilities. The shopping mall is centered around an eight-story terraced atrium with the most famous elevators in Chicago, housed in three bundled hexagonal glass tubes. The main entrance to the mall is a two-story set of escalators, with a waterfall between them and winding staircases at the sides. In 2002 the entrance was renovated and show windows were inserted into the façade above the arcade.

Water Tower Place was the first new mixed-use development in the area, and a pioneer in the use of high-strength concrete. By using concrete instead of steel, the building could be 90 feet shorter for the same number of floors, thus saving the substantial cost associated with the enclosing of the exterior envelope in marble and glass.

1   Street level plan
2–4   General views
5   Twilight view with historic Chicago Water
     Tower and Pumping Station in foreground

Photography: Tom Cramer (2); David Clifton
(3,4,5), courtesy Loebl Schlossman & Hackl

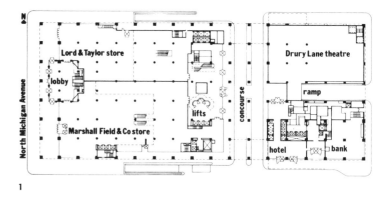

1

2

3

4

5

Location Chicago, Illinois, USA

Completion date 1976

Architect Loebl Schlossman, Bennett & Dart (now Loebl Schlossman & Hackl); C.F. Murphy Associates

Consultant architect for shopping mall Warren Platner Associates

Developer JMB/Urban Investment & Development Company

Structural engineer C.F. Murphy Associates

Services engineer C.F. Murphy Associates

Contractor Inland Robbins Construction, Inc.

Height 859 ft/262 m

Above-ground stories 74

Basements 4

Above-ground useable levels 73

Mechanical levels and level numbers 2: floors 13A, 74

Use Mixed: Office, retail, hotel, residential, entertainment

Site area 113,936 sq ft/10,585 sq m

Area of above-ground building 3,100,000 sq ft/287,990 sq m

Basic planning module 30 x 30 ft/9.1 x 9.1 m

Number of parking spaces 640

Principal structural materials Concrete, marble cladding

Grand Gateway

Grand Gateway is one of the largest, most complex projects developed in Shanghai. Twin, 52-story, 859-foot office towers rise over a 1.1-million-square-foot retail and entertainment podium. The 3.3-million-square-foot, mixed-use complex incorporates retail, residential, transit and office uses. It is one of Shanghai's largest shopping destinations, and occupies a premium site above the Xu Hui subway station, which accommodates approximately 250,000 daily commuters.

The project's components were planned and designed so that each could thrive independently, a strategy that allows each component to be implemented according to market demands. As a result, Grand Gateway was one of the few projects that remained on a steady build-out course and maintained strong occupancy over the last decade. Even the office towers reflect this flexible planning approach, designed with the ability to be built either as offices or serviced apartments above the 35th floor, according to market demand.

The project is also carefully integrated to leverage synergies among uses. To encourage high-volume patronage of Grand Gateway's shopping center, the office towers connect to the subway through the retail component. The entertainment component serves as both an anchor for the shopping center and an amenity to the nearby residential towers.

Grand Gateway is a commercially successful development thanks to painstaking integration of uses, careful phasing, keen retail thinking and a design that integrates a high degree of flexibility to hedge against a highly dynamic market environment.

1   Typical office floor plan, levels 40–46
2   Entrance, day
3   Grand Gateway, Shanghai, China
Photography: Chris Eden, Callison

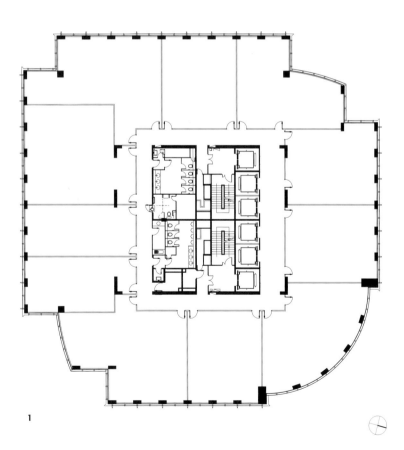

1

2

3

Location Shanghai, China

Completion date 2005

Design architect Callison

Local architect East China Architectural Design & Research Institute Company Ltd.

Client Hang Lung Development Co. Ltd.; Henderson Development; Hysan Development Co. Ltd.

Developer Hang Lung Development Co., Ltd.

Structural engineer Maunsell Structural Consultants Ltd.

Mechanical engineer Associated Consulting Engineers (ACE)

Lighting designer Horton Lees Brogden

Vertical transportation consultant Lerch Bates & Associates, Inc.

Landscape architect Stamper Whitin Works

Contractor Fujita Corporation

Height 859 ft/262 m (including lantern top)

Above-ground stories 52

Basements 3

Above-ground useable levels 46

Mechanical levels and level numbers 6: levels 7, 23, 37, 50, 51, 52

Use Office, retail, residential

Site area 408,880 sq ft/38,000 sq m

Area of above-ground building Office: 1,069,062 sq ft/99,315 sq m in two 52-story towers

Area of typical floor plate 17,517 sq ft/1628 sq m

Basic planning module 9.8 ft/3 m

Number of parking spaces 1250 cars; 7000 bicycles

Principal structural materials Reinforced concrete

Other materials Glass, granite, stainless steel

Aon Center

When the initial news release was issued in 1972, this building, then known as United California Bank (UCB) Building (and later as First Interstate Tower), was touted to be the tallest in the United States, west of Chicago. When completed, it would punctuate the downtown skyline of Los Angeles at 858 feet.

The location of the tower, in the northwest corner of Wilshire Boulevard at Hope Street, is the former site of one of Los Angeles' first commercial skyscrapers, which served as the headquarters for the Western Bancorporation

Aon Center sits on a spacious landscaped plaza paved in gray granite. It tapers inward 5.5 feet from the street level to the top. At its base, massive L-shaped, aluminum-clad, 12-foot-wide piers anchor the building at its four corners. Above it, projecting bronze aluminum mullions and bronze solar glass windows and spandrels rise the full height of the structure, dramatizing the verticality of its design. The steel frame

structure features one of the largest steel columns ever used in Los Angeles, measuring three feet at the lower level and weighing more than one ton per foot. The foundation for the tower is a structural steel frame on mat and bell cassions.

At the ground level an uninterrupted space serves as the banking floor, revealed through glass walls that accentuate the lobby's 43-foot-high ceiling. The building's 27 high-speed elevators start from the mezzanine lobby area above the banking level and are reached by high-speed escalators from the street and by shuttle elevators from the parking area. The tower elevators are grouped in four banks: low-rise, mid-low-rise, mid-high-rise and high-rise. Two private elevators connect the main banking levels to the seventh floor.

An underground pedestrian concourse and vehicular tunnel connect the three below-grade levels. Three floors of underground parking accommodate 340 cars and a 10-story structure provides an additional 760 car parking spaces, and a first-floor commercial space.

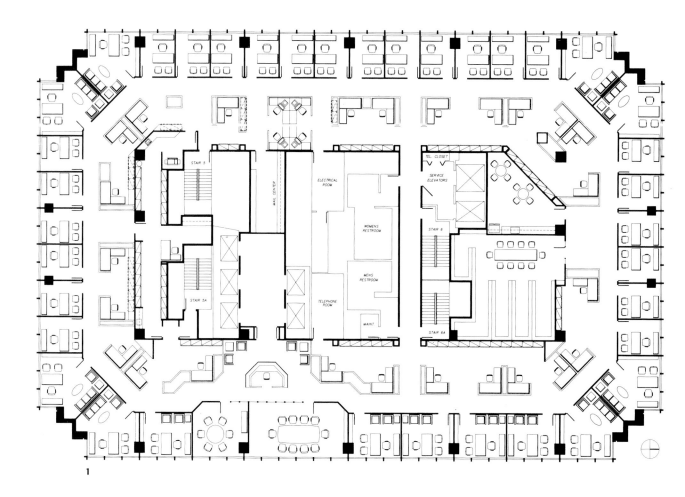

1

1   Typical floor plan
2   General view
3   Axonometric of vertical transportation system

Photography: Courtesy The Luckman Partnership

Plans reproduced from original UCB Building leasing brochure,
Coll. G Binder/Buildings & Data

2

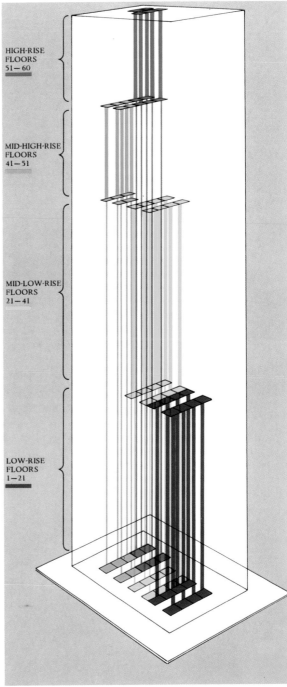

HIGH-RISE
FLOORS
51–60

MID-HIGH-RISE
FLOORS
41–51

MID-LOW-RISE
FLOORS
21–41

LOW-RISE
FLOORS
1–21

3

Location Los Angeles, California, USA

Completion date 1974

Architect The Luckman Partnership

Client United California Bank Realty Corporation and
The Equitable Life Assurance Society of the United States

Structural engineer Erkel Greenfield Associates Inc.

Mechanical engineer Levine and McCann

Electrical engineer Michael Garris & Associates

Elevator consultant Charles W Lerch & Associates

Construction consultant Carl A Morse, Inc.

Contractor CL Peck Contractor

Height 858 ft/262 m

Above-ground stories 62

Mechanical levels and level numbers 6: floors 4, 5, 22, 42,
61, 62

Use Office

Area of above-ground building 1,250,000 sq ft/116,125 sq m

Area of typical floor plate 17,500 sq ft/1626 sq m

Number of parking spaces 340 below grade; 760 in separate
building

Principal structural materials Steel

Other materials Aluminum, glass

TD Canada Trust Tower at BCE Place

The BCE Place complex consists of two office towers: the 856-foot TD Canada Trust Tower and the 679-foot Bay Wellington Tower. Several historically significant buildings on the site are linked to the towers by a glass-enclosed gallery. Below ground, the complex is connected to Union Station, the underground pedestrian walkway system, and parking garages. The 42-foot-wide, 380-foot-long Allen Lambert Galleria was designed by architect Santiago Calatrava. The galleria links the two towers, a garden court, the below-grade retail concourse, and the Hockey Hall of Fame.

Both towers are clad in flamed Rockville pink granite with polished Cambrian black granite accents and green-tinted glass. Inside, the two-story retail podium at the base of the TD Canada Trust Tower is richly adorned with marble floors and walls. Typical floors have full-height windows and 9-foot ceilings. The tower's location on the outskirts of the central business district provides panoramic views in all directions, and the overlapping squares of the floor plans allows for numerous corner offices.

2

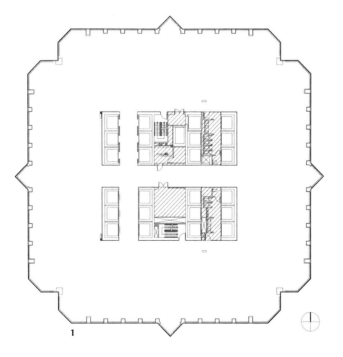

1

3

1 Floor plan example
2 Entrance to the galleria designed by Santiago Calatrava
3 TD Canada Trust Tower
4 TD Canada Trust Tower (left) and Bay Wellington Tower (right) are part of the BCE Complex
5 Elevation

Photography: Lenscape (2); Robert Burley/Design Archive (3,4)

4

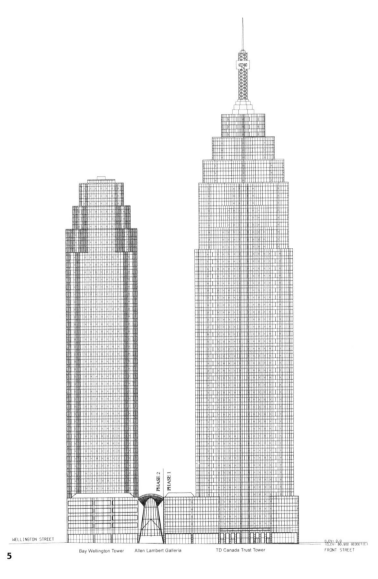

5

WELLINGTON STREET

Bay Wellington Tower   Allen Lambert Galleria   TD Canada Trust Tower   FRONT STREET

Location Toronto, Ontario, Canada

Completion date 1990

Architects Bregman + Hamann Architects and Skidmore, Owings & Merrill LLP (architects in joint venture)

Client Brookfield Development Corporation

Structural engineer M.S. Yolles & Partners

Mechanical engineer The Mitchell Partnership

Vertical transportation consultant Katz Drago & Company Inc.

Landscape architect Moorehead Fleming Corban McCarthy

Contractor PCL Constructors Eastern Inc.

Project manager Brookfield Development Corporation

Height 856 ft/261 m (to top of spire)

Above-ground stories 53

Basements 5

Above-ground useable levels 51

Mechanical levels and level numbers 2: floors 52, 53

Use Office

Site area 5.5 acres/2.2 ha (entire BCE Place complex)

Area of above-ground building 1,120,526 sq ft/104,097 sq m (rentable space)

Area of typical floor plate 22,300–23,400 sq ft/2072–2174 sq m (rentable space)

Basic planning module 5ft/1.5 m

Number of parking spaces 1465

Principal structural materials Steel, reinforced concrete

Other materials Granite, marble, glass

Cost $1.2 billion (entire BCE Place complex)

Transamerica Pyramid

Since the 530,000-square-foot, 48-story Transamerica Pyramid opened, it has become a landmark on the San Francisco skyline. Its sweeping form brought a new look to the city's financial district and fulfilled Transamerica's desire for a structure that would reflect the company's modern corporate image.

Rising from a structural steel base that forms a cloister-like arcade surrounding the building, the tower reaches a height of 853 feet from a terraced, granite-paved, public plaza. The pyramid, ideally suited to its urban environment, casts a smaller shadow than a conventional office tower, thus allowing more light and air to reach the public street level. The tapering building form also lowers the center of gravity, increasing structural resistance to seismic forces.

Having become one of San Francisco's more prestigious locations, the building compares favorably to conventional office towers in terms of the efficiency ratio of lettable space to gross floor area. Every floor in the building is different in size. The largest floor, the fifth, contains 21,025 square feet; the smallest floor, the 48th, contains only 2025 square feet.

Transamerica Corporation initially occupied roughly one third of the building's total area, the remaining space being leased to a variety of tenants ranging from law firms to financial institutions. A restaurant and lounge were located at the building's base. Parking is provided for 280 cars in a three-level underground garage.

The Transamerica Pyramid is no longer the headquarters of Transamerica Corporation, although the company retains a small presence as a tenant and still uses the building's image as its registered trademark logo. The Transamerica Pyramid is part of the Transamerica Center, home to three office buildings: the Transamerica Pyramid, Two Transamerica Center and Transamerica Redwood Park, built in 1927 and renovated in 1997. An observation area previously open to the public on the 27th level is now closed.

1

2

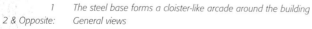

1   The steel base forms a cloister-like arcade around the building
2 & Opposite: General views

Photography: Courtesy Johnson Fain (1, opposite); Coll. G Binder/Buildings & Data SA (2)

Location San Francisco, California, USA
Completion date 1972
Architect William L Pereira Associates
Client Transamerica Corporation
Structural engineer Chin and Hensolt Inc.
Mechanical engineer Simonson & Simonson
Landscape architect Anthony M Guzzardo & Associates

Interior design Morganelli-Heumann & Associates
General contractor Dinwiddie Construction Company
Height 853 ft/260 m (including 212 ft/64.6 m spire)
Above-ground stories 48
Basements 3
Use Office
Area of above-ground building 530,000 sq ft/49,237 sq m

Area of typical floor plate 2025–21,025 sq ft/188–1953 sq m
Number of parking spaces 280
Principal structural materials Concrete encasing steel reinforcing rods
Other materials White precast quartz aggregate
Cost US$32 M

Shenzhen Special Zone Press Tower

Shenzhen Special Zone Press Tower is the headquarters building of the largest local newspaper. This 48-story tower is 853 feet to its mast. Levels 9 through 40 accomodate office space; levels 41 and 42 are assigned to conference and club facilities; and the four-level-high podium houses exhibition space and a 700-seat auditorium.

The site is strategically located to the west of the new CBD of Shenzhen and adjacent to Shennan Boulevard, one of the city's main arterial roads. In response to future developments in the new CBD, this modernistic tower's architectural expressions include a tilted line, a globe, and a ship-like veranda, in keeping with the client's wishes. The tower has a two-core typical plan, allowing space to be partitioned freely, providing a flexibility that allows the floors to accommodate large open layouts and smaller units. Every third floor there is a shared sky garden. A 39-foot-high board meeting room occupies the glass sphere. The ship-like loggia in front of the podium provides generous semi-open outdoor spaces with a sense of tropical culture.

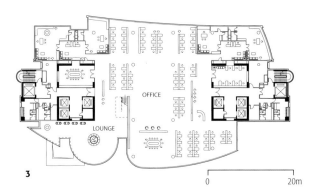

2

3

0   20m

1

4

1   View of front plaza
2   Typical office floor plan
3   Floor plan – level 38
4   Skylight at main entrance
5   Lobby interior
6   View of tower from south
7   Section

Photography: Courtesy The Institute of Architecture Design & Research, Shenzhen University (SUIADR)

5

6

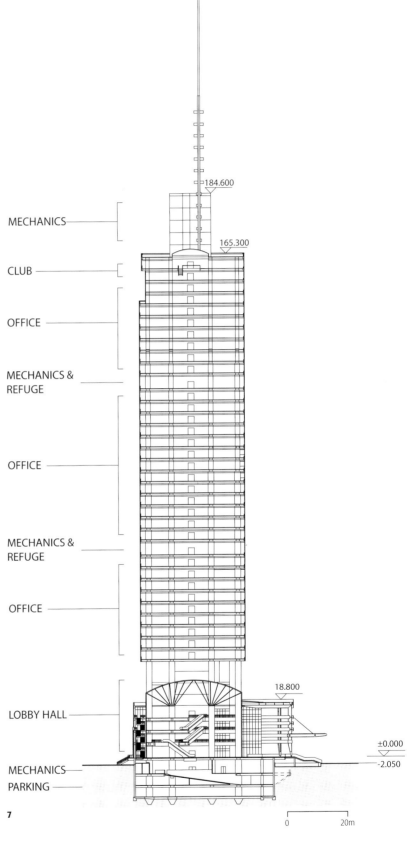

MECHANICS

CLUB

OFFICE

MECHANICS &
REFUGE

OFFICE

MECHANICS &
REFUGE

OFFICE

LOBBY HALL

MECHANICS

PARKING

260.000

184.600

165.300

18.800

±0.000
-2.050

7

0   20m

Location Shenzhen, China

Completion date 1998

Architect Gong Wei Min, Lu Yang, The Institute of Architecture Design & Research, Shenzhen University (SUIADR)

Client Shenzhen Special Zone Daily.

Structural engineer Fu Xue Yi, The Institute of Architecture Design & Research, Shenzhen University (SUIADR)

Mechanical engineer Liu Wen Bin, Meng Zu Hua, Lian Jian She, Wen Yi Bing, The Institute of Architecture Design & Research, Shenzhen University (SUIADR)

Landscape architect Gong Wei Min, Lu Yang, The Institute of Architecture Design & Research, Shenzhen University (SUIADR)

Contractor China Construction Third Engineering Bureau; Shenzhen Company

Height 853 ft/260 m (including spire)

Above-ground stories 48

Basements 3

Above-ground useable levels 44

Mechanical levels and level numbers 4: floors 18, 32, 45, basement 1

Use Office

Site area 52,724 sq ft/4900 sq m

Area of above-ground building 807,000 sq ft/75,000 sq m

Area of typical floor plate 20,444 sq ft/1900 sq m

Number of parking spaces 270

Principal structural materials Reinforced concrete (main structure), steel (veranda, sphere), curtain wall

Other materials Glazed aluminum, glass, granite

Cost RMB500 M

GE Building

The 70-story GE Building (originally known as the RCA Building) is the centerpiece of the Rockefeller Center complex, built by John D Rockefeller, Jr, founder of Standard Oil. In 1985, the New York City Landmark Preservation Committee bestowed landmark status upon the Rockefeller Center, referring to it as 'the heart of New York, a great unifying presence in the chaotic core of midtown Manhattan.'

The GE Building, with its 850-foot slender silhouette, marked the emergence of a new form of the skyscraper. This thin slab was based on the principle of 27 feet of lighting depth to give optimum working conditions around the central elevator core. Facing north and south, the building presents its huge, broad sides to the street—it was for this reason that the *New York City Guide* of 1939 nicknamed the structure 'the slab.'

The main lobby of the GE Building is decorated with an immense mural depicting, in an abstract and allegorical manner, the progress of humanity. Installed in 1941, the three large figures represent Past, Present, and Future, who are shown with their feet braced against the large marble columns of the lobby. Other murals in the lobby area include the *Spirit of Dance*, installed in 1937, and *Man's Triumph in Communication—Radio, Telephone and Telegraph*, also installed in 1937.

Rockefeller Center as a whole is one of the world's largest privately owned business and entertainment centers, part of a 22-acre complex in midtown. One of the best examples of Art Deco style, it features 30 works by great artists of the 20th century. Originally, the Center included 14 buildings and covered 12 acres of land between 48th and 51st Streets. Today, 19 buildings occupy almost twice that area.

At the time of construction, it was one of the largest projects ever undertaken by private enterprise. It required the demolition of 228 buildings and the relocation of 4000 tenants. More than 75,000 workers were employed on the building site; for each of the workers actually on site, there were two others preparing material elsewhere, equalling almost a quarter of a million people employed during the worst years of the Great Depression.

1   Main entrance to GE Building
2   Site plan, with GE Building ground floor plan in upper right
3   'Slab' view
4   Period postcard view of the GE Building
5   Night view

Photography: Ivan Zaknic (1); Douglas Mason (3);
© **The Skyscraper Museum (4); Bart Barlow (5)**

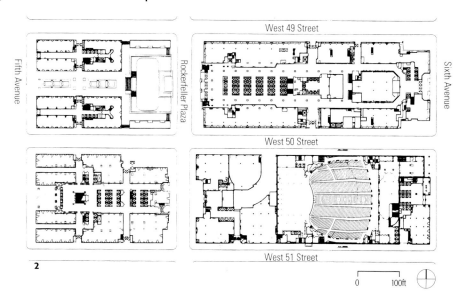

1

2

Fifth Avenue

West 49 Street

Rockefeller Plaza

Sixth Avenue

West 50 Street

West 51 Street

0   100ft

Location New York, New York, USA

Completion date 1933

Architect Associated Architects (Reinhard & Hofmeister; Corbett, Harrison & MacMurray; Raymond Hood, Godley & Foulihoux)

Developer John D Rockefeller, Jr

Builder Hegerman-Harris Company

Height 850 ft/259 m

Above-ground stories 70

Use Office

Site area 22 acres/8.9 ha (entire Rockefeller Center site)

Area of above-ground building 2,100,000 sq ft/195,090 sq m

Principal structural materials Steel

Other materials Granite, Indiana limestone façade, aluminum spandrel panels

4

3

5

Chase Tower

This 60-story building (originally One First National Plaza) was the forerunner of Chicago's downtown development boom. Born of a need for large, unobstructed banking spaces at and near street level, Chase Tower contains complete banking facilities, bank offices, and tenant spaces, as well as a cafeteria, kitchen, restaurant, and theater.

The form of the 850-foot tower sweeps up from street level in a unique tapering curve. The building sweeps from 200 feet to 95 feet at the top. The overall east–west length is 300 feet. The broad base design provides effective resistance to the horizontal forces of wind. To more effectively resist wind, loads from the floor above are transmitted to the exterior columns below on two-story trusses at the 40th floor with interior columns omitted at the 39th floor. Elevator shafts, stairs, main ducts, and pipes are housed in the utility and service cores, located at both ends of the building to allow maximum open space on the banking floors.

The nature of the building dictated the use of structural steel, which offered the most practical and the only economically feasible solution. The building used more than 40,000 tons of steel, 10,000 tons of airconditioning capacity, and some 30,000 miles of wiring.

The steel frame is sheathed in Pearl Gray granite from a quarry in south-central Texas. At the top a longitudinal row of separate penthouses enclose the cooling towers. More than 35 million pounds of stone, for 20,000 slabs, were used in the facing of the building. At the time, this was a milestone in building construction. The granite is also used on the sidewalks and plaza, and in the two-story banking room at mezzanine level.

The outdoor plaza is on two levels, covering half a city block. Fountains, landscaping, and a major artwork by Marc Chagall, *The Four Seasons*, fill the plaza. Chagall's work is a massive architectural mosaic 70 feet long, 14 feet high and 10 feet wide, covered in a bright ceramic mural, and designed as a gift to the people of Chicago.

1   Typical floor plan, floors 43–55
2   Elevations
3   General view
4   Curved form begins at street level
5   Outdoor plaza features artwork by Marc Chagall

Photography: Hedrich-Blessing, courtesy Murphy/Jahn, Inc.

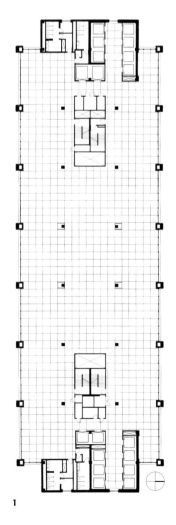

1

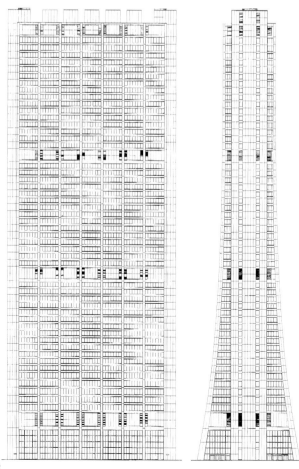

2

3

4

5

Location Chicago, Illinois, USA

Completion date 1969

Architect CF Murphy Associates (now Murphy/Jahn, Inc.); Perkins+Will Partnership (joint venture)

Client The First National Bank of Chicago

Structural engineer CF Murphy Associates; Perkins & Will Partnership

Contractor Gust K Newberg Construction Company

Height 850 ft/259 m

Above-ground stories 60

Mechanical levels and level numbers 4: 3, 23, 40, 58

Use Office

Area of above-ground building 2,191,514 sq ft/203,592 sq m

Principal structural materials Steel

Other materials Concrete, granite, glass

Cost US$117 M

Capital Tower

Capital Tower emerges as a visual signifier marking the southern extent of Singapore's CBD, and contributes toward the continuing realization of Singapore's downtown as a financial hub of international prominence.

The design integrates the programmatic functions of the tower and the urban park into one unified complex, interwoven into the city fabric. The urban park is neither an isolated retreat nor merely a theatrical forecourt for the tower; it emerges as an active component of the green belt along this busy junction.

The tower's form features a 52-story block arising from the predominantly horizontal plane of the urban plaza. The tower, strengthened by the treatment and choice of façade materials, rises as a rectilinear form up to the 35th story and gradually tapers to the top, forming a light building crown.

Functions within the tower are divided into four zones. The carparks, low-, mid-, and high-rise offices, are interspersed with recreational floors and mechanical floors, including a shuttle

lift sky lobby. An exclusive VIP drop-off is provided at the second level, next to the VIP lift lobby for private access to the premises. The ninth level provides the occupants a quick and convenient access to recreation and business facilities, which include a 230-seat auditorium, conference rooms, lecture room, gymnasium, spa, swimming pool, and clinic. Retail units, including a bank, café, florist, and wine shop are located on the first level of the building.

The penthouse at level 52 is designed as an exclusive executive lounge/dining area. The displacement of a majority of mechanical services, conventionally placed on the last floor of a building, to a floor below makes it possible to capitalize on the excellent view potential that the roof affords. Accordingly, the penthouse lounge, with its column-free structure and a 52.5-foot-tall frameless glazed façade, offers a 360-degree panoramic view of the island. The stainless steel bow trusses that support the glazed façade are located externally, allowing full utilization of the internal space, without any structural encumbrances.

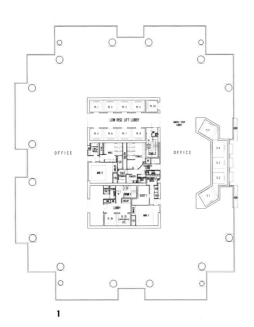

1

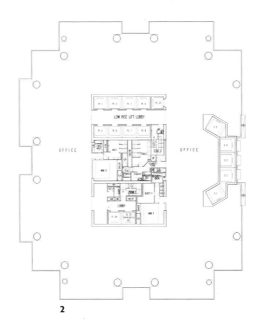

2

3

Location Singapore, Republic of Singapore

Completion date 2000

Architect RSP Architects Planners & Engineers (Pte) Ltd

Client HSBC Institutional Trust Services (Singapore) Ltd, as trustee of CapitaCommercial Trust

Structural engineer Maunsell Consultants (S) Pte Ltd

Mechanical engineer Parsons Brinckerhoff Consultants (Pte) Ltd

Landscape architect PDAA Design Pte Ltd

Contractor Ssangyong Engineering & Construction Pte Ltd

Developer Capital Tower Pte Ltd (wholly owned subsidiary of CapitaLand)

Project manager Pidemco Land Ltd (now CapitaLand Commercial Project Management Pte Ltd)

Height 846.5 ft/258 m

Above-ground stories 52

Basements 1

Above-ground useable levels 52

Mechanical levels and level numbers 4: floors 21, 36, 51 and basement

Use Office, retail

Site area 76,501 sq ft/7109.8 sq m

Area of above-ground building 997,560 sq ft/92,710 sq m

Area of typical floor plate 21,455 sq ft/1994 sq m (low rise); 19,895 sq ft/1849 sq m (mid rise); 13,547 sq ft/1259 sq m (high rise)

Number of parking spaces 415

Principal structural materials Steel, reinforced concrete, bondeck

Other materials Exterior: granite, glazed aluminium curtainwall; interior: granite, ceramic tiles, stainless steel, timber panelling

Cost SGD$317 M

Photography: © Albert Lim KS

5

6

4

Park Tower

Elegantly designed to assume a prominent place on Chicago's Magnificent Mile, the Park Tower intelligently combines a gracious hotel with high-end condominium space to serve multiple markets. All views from both the hotel and the residences are unobstructed and offer unparalleled vistas of Lake Michigan and Chicago's magnificent skyline.

The first 20 floors are occupied by the 203-room Park Hyatt Hotel, a corporate flagship for the Chicago-based chain. Located adjacent to Chicago's historic Water Tower, the Park Tower is within walking distance of world-class museums and the finest retailers and restaurants. Floors above the hotel are devoted to grand condominium residences, including eight full-floor penthouses. All hotel amenities and services are available to residents.

One of building's greatest architectural challenges was coordinating the base building design with the potential buyers' customized units. All units were sold a full year before building completion, reflecting the responsiveness of the project design to marketing studies.

The building is sheathed in buff-colored limestone and topped with a pitched copper roof. As a result of its slenderness and height, building sway posed a challenge, creatively solved with a 300-ton tuned mass damper installed under the roof. Classic design features, including setbacks and columns, soften the building's verticality and gestures to contextual elements are made at various levels.

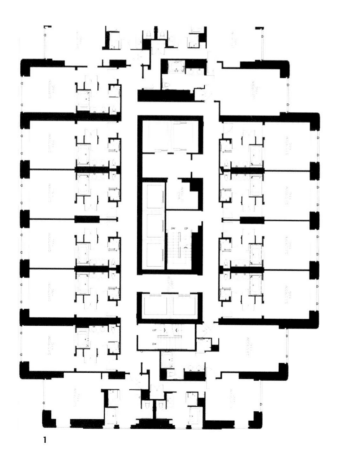

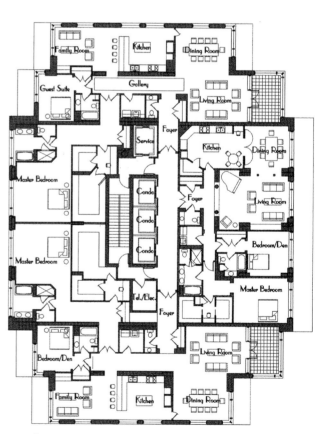

1

2

1   Typical hotel floor plan
2   Typical condominium floor plan
3   General view
4   Façade detail
5   Condominium entry at dusk

Photography: Anthony May (3,5); Barbara Karant (4)

3

4

5

Location Chicago, Illinois, USA

Completion date 2000

Architect Lucien Lagrange Architects

Production architect HKS, Inc

Client Hyatt Development Corporation; LR Development Company

Structural engineer Chris Stefanos & Associates

Mechanical engineer Environmental Systems Design, Inc.

Vertical transportation consultant Greg Davis & Associates

Landscape architect Daniel Weinbach and Partners, Ltd.

Contractor James McHugh Construction Company

Project manager John Ryden (Hyatt); Kerry Dickson (LR Development)

Height 844.3 ft/257.3 m to top of spire; 824.3 ft/251.2 m to top of roof parapet

Above-ground stories 70

Basements 1

Above-ground useable levels 68

Mechanical levels and level numbers 6: levels 8, 9, 19, 19T, (69, 70 within roof)

Use Residential, hotel, retail, restaurant, parking, spa

Site area 28,125 sq ft/2613 sq m

Area of above-ground building Residential; 475,000 sq ft/ 44,128 sq m; hotel: 193,000 sq ft/17,930 sq m; retail: 20,000 sq ft/1858 sq m; parking: 92,000 sq ft/8547 sq ft

Area of typical floor plate 9671 sq ft/898 sq m

Basic planning module 13.5 ft/4.1 m (hotel)

Number of parking spaces 200 parking spaces integrated within an adjoining building

Principal structural materials Reinforced concrete

Other materials Architectural precast concrete cladding, limestone, and granite

Cost US$94.655 M

MesseTurm

At the time of construction, the MesseTurm, at a height of 842 feet, was the tallest building in Europe. This height was the result of several factors, including the German workplace requirement that an office worker must be in the immediate vicinity of a window. This requirement reduced the size of the floor space surrounding the core of the building. The 'gate', which the tower forms at the street level, and the pyramid top, which is occupied by the cooling towers, also adds to the height.

Architecturally, the tower is derived from the great American skyscrapers of the 1920s and 1930s, rather than the modern ones of later years that compose the Frankfurt skyline today. The rigorous geometry that governs its shape begins in plan with a granite-clad, 137-foot square. This square is inscribed around a circle that is clad in glass. The circle, a cylinder in volume, is visible above the gate, at the notched corners and near the top, where the granite-clad square recedes. The glass cylinder steps back twice below the top pyramid and is articulated there by rhythmically alternating window recesses. Over the top rises a pyramid stepping three times. The corners of the pyramid are centered on the sides of the tower where triangular bay windows rise from the apex of the gate to the top.

The entrance lobby is itself a cylinder with clear glass and surrounded by powerful columns supporting the core. The entrance lobby contains six shuttle lifts in an open frame leading to the sky lobby from which twelve lifts bring the occupants to their respective floors.

The building is constructed in concrete with a façade of polished red granite columns laced with flamed stripes and profiled aluminum bands at every floor. The glass is silver reflective glass. The mullion and window frame color is metallic silver-beige baked-on paint.

1

1 Main entrance elevation
2 General view
3 Section
4 Floor plan, level 57–top office floor
5 Floor plan, levels 48–56
6 Floor plan, levels 9–28
7 Ground floor plan

Photography: Roland Halbe

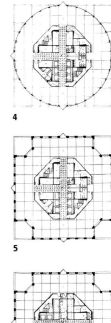

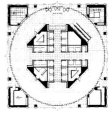

4

5

6

7

2

3

Location Frankfurt, Germany
Completion date 1990
Architect Murphy/Jahn, Inc.
Client Messe Frankfurt GmbH
Structural engineer Dr.-Ing. Fritz Noetzold
Mechanical engineer Brendel Ingenieure GmbH
Vertical transportation consultant Jappsen & Stangier GmbH
General contractor Hochtief AG
Developer Tishman Speyer Properties

Height 842 ft/256.5 m
Above-ground stories 63
Basements 2
Above-ground useable levels 60
Mechanical levels 3
Use Office
Area of above-ground building 915,000 sq ft/85,000 sq m
Structural materials Concrete
Other materials Granite, aluminum, glass

Highcliff

Highcliff is a 73-story, super high-rise residential building situated on a steeply sloping site on Hong Kong Island. The building has already been recognized with three high-rise awards: the American Council of Engineering Companies (ACEC) 2004 Engineering Excellence Award, the Silver Prize in the Emporis Skyscraper Award, and the Structural Engineers Association of Illinois 2004 Most Innovative Structure.

According to the architect, the determinant of the building's overall form is the floor layout of individual apartments. The tower's great height is thus a logical consequence, rather than primary aim, of the design process.

The design eschews superficial tokens of luxury. These are rendered particularly inappropriate and unnecessary by generous planning: apartments are large with full-width glazing. Common areas are also spacious and lofty. As a genuinely luxurious building Highcliff has no need of the 'ornamental camouflage' that characterizes much residential property in Hong Kong. While it is a striking and dramatic structure, the emphasis is upon visual simplicity, avoiding ostentation.

The plan, comprising two overlapping ellipses, offers good spatial arrangement of and natural lighting in apartments. The streamlined form, resulting from the elliptical floor layout, mitigates wind effects that are acute on the project's elevated mountainside site. Highcliff experiences lower wind-induced stresses than would be experienced by a rectangular building of similar height. Damping utilizes neither electrical nor mechanical systems. Water in interconnected rooftop tanks acts as a massive and dynamic counterweight to oscillations that occur, particularly during Hong Kong's periodic typhoons. The use of a passive damping method avoids the unnecessary complexity and high recurring maintenance costs of the alternative hydraulic systems.

The façade is clad with curtain walling. Besides weathering well, the curtain wall avoids endemic problems of cemented masonry and vitreous finishes that commonly deteriorate. The need for maintenance scaffolding, with its associated health and safety risks, is obviated by use of an automated rooftop gondola for external inspection and repairs.

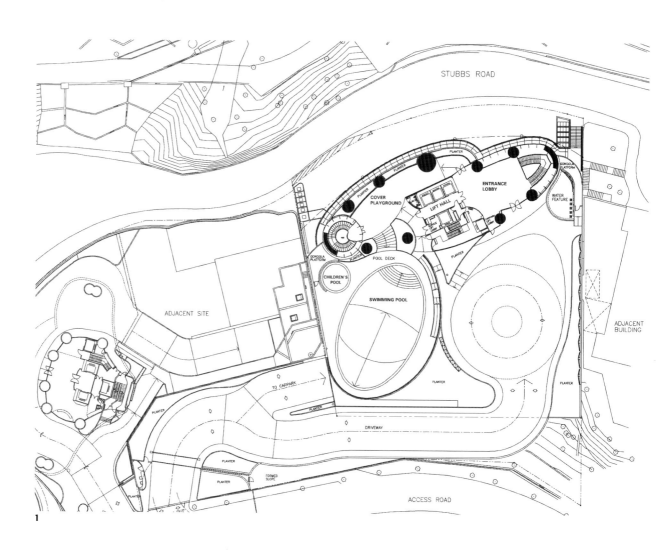

1

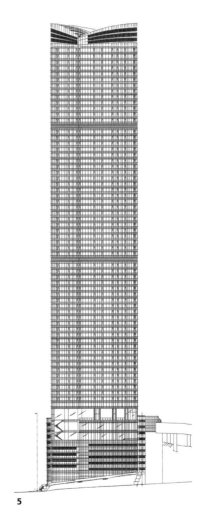

1   Site layout plan
2   Interior view of main lobby
3&4   External elevations
5   Front elevation

Photography: Frankie FY Wong

Location Hong Kong, China
Completion date 2002
Architect Dennis Lau & Ng Chun Man Architects & Engineers (H.K.) Limited
Client Highcliff Investment Ltd; Central Development Ltd
Structural engineer Canwest Consultant (Int'l) Ltd
Structural design consultant Skilling Ward Magnusson Barkshire Inc.
Services engineer Associated Consulting Engineers, Hong Kong

Curtain wall consultant CDC Limited
Landscape architect ADI Limited
Contractor Hip Hing Construction Co. Ltd
Project manager Central Development Ltd
Height 831.4 ft/253.4 m
Above-ground stories 73
Basements 0
Above-ground useable levels 71
Mechanical levels and level numbers 3: floors 71, 72, 73

Use Residential
Site area 46,978 sq ft/4366 sq m
Area of above-ground building 375,761 sq ft/34,922 sq m
Area of typical floor plate 6456 sq ft/600 sq m (approx)
Number of parking spaces 298
Principal structural materials High strength concrete
Other materials Curtain wall unitized system
Cost US$128 M

The HarbourSide

The HarbourSide is part of Union Square, a comprehensive development above Kowloon Station. It consists of three towers of 65 residential floors over a two-story clubhouse and five-story car park podium. The total area is approximately 1.4 million square feet, with 1122 residential units. Unit sizes vary from 968 square feet for two-bedroom units to more than 2582 square feet for the penthouse units.

The design conforms to the general layout of the master plan, with a curvilinear façade taking advantage of its unique location, with a south-facing panoramic harbour view toward Hong Kong Central and the Union Square Central Garden at its north. The main drop-off is at its podium roof level, which houses undulating glass lobbies. A recreation area with a

swimming pool and landscaped garden is formed on the southern part of the podium roof. A specially commissioned Italian marble sculpture acts as the focus of the entry-level garden at the north side.

The HarbourSide is one of the widest skyscrapers in the world. Four vertical openings break the scale of the façade and relieve the substantial wind stress created on such a wide structure. The openings also provide natural ventilation for the outdoor airconditioning units concealed within the two large lightwells between the building blocks.

The stainless steel features along the façade reflect the sunlight, creating an effect that resembles waves upon the sea.

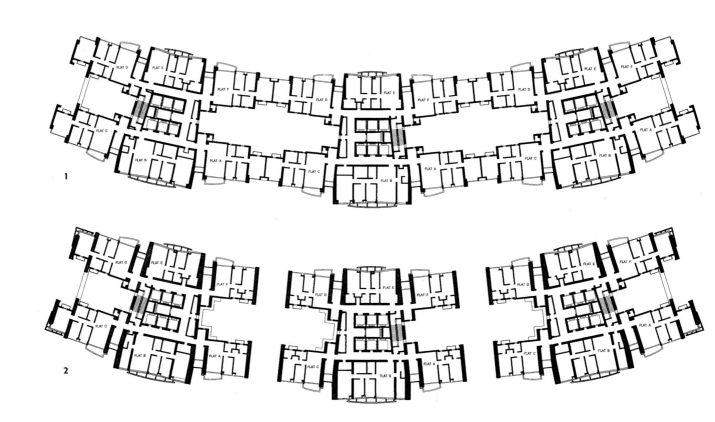

1   Typical floor plan, floors 63–71
2   Typical floor plan, floors 19–25
3–5   General and detailed views
Photography: Courtesy P&T Architects and Engineers Ltd

3

4

5

Location Hong Kong, China	Project manager Hang Lung Project Management Limited	Use Residential
Completion date 2004	Landscape architect Belt Collins International (HK) Limited	Site area 144,033 sq ft/13,386 sq m
Architect P&T Architects & Engineers Ltd	Contractor Hip Hing Construction Co Ltd	Area of above-ground building 1,386,372 sq ft/128,845 sq m
Client Hang Lung Properties Limited	Height 824 ft/251 m	Area of typical floor plate 10,068 sq ft/930 sq m (approx)
Developer Mass Transit Railway Corporation; Hang Lung Properties Limited	Above-ground stories 73	Number of parking spaces 864
	Basements 0	Principal structural materials Reinforced concrete
Structural engineer Ove Arup & Partners Hong Kong Limited	Above-ground useable levels 67	Other materials Exterior: tinted glass, metal cladding, tiles
Mechanical engineer Parsons Brinckerhoff (Asia) Limited	Mechanical levels and level numbers 2: floors 26, 53	Cost US$282 M

Condé Nast Building @ Four Times Square

New York, New York, USA

The Condé Nast Building @ Four Times Square is the centerpiece of the master plan prepared by the 42nd Street Development Corporation, a public/private consortium created to promote the redevelopment of this traditional heart of Manhattan.

Designed by Fox & Fowle Architects (now FXFOWLE ARCHITECTS), the building occupies a pivotal site at the northeast corner of Broadway and 42nd Street, straddling several great urban spaces with diverse identities. Its design embraces the essence of Times Square while meeting the needs of corporate tenants—a successful marriage of pop culture and corporate standards.

Designed with two distinct orientations, the west and north sides of the building reflect the dynamic environment of Times Square and are clad primarily in metal and glass, while along 42nd Street and the east façade, a textured and scaled masonry treatment presents a more composed personality, appropriate to the midtown corporate context and the refined style of Bryant Park. A 30 percent expansion of the original building site has enabled the architects to employ setback massing, allowing the building to evolve from a full streetwall base to a setback tower. As the main building shaft rises, the collage of volumes and surfaces evolves into a composed structure culminating in a highly energized top. The building top reflects the principal structural support system, and, with its four 70-foot square signs and a communications tower, expresses in a high-technology style the project's location at "The Crossroads of the World."

The Condé Nast Building @ Four Times Square is an environmentally responsible building. All building systems and construction technology have been evaluated for their impact on occupant health, environmental sensitivity, and energy reduction, making this the first project of its size to adopt state-of-the-art standards for energy conservation, indoor air quality, recycling systems, and sustainable manufacturing processes.

The Condé Nast Building received the American Institute of Architects New York Chapter 2000 Honor Award, the 1999 Star of Energy Efficiency Award from the Alliance to Save Energy, and the 2000 Major Achievement Award from the New York City Audubon Society. It continues to be referred to in the press as the first green tower in the United States.

1

2

1   Contextual view
2   Façade detail
3   North and west façades are clad in metal and glass
4   High-rise floor plan: 48th floor
5   Mid-rise floor plan: 11th floor
6   Masonry treatment on façade

Photography: David Sundberg/Esto (1,6); Jeff Goldberg/Esto (2,3)

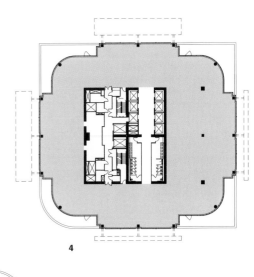

4

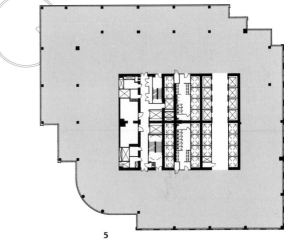

5

3

6

Location New York, New York, USA

Completion date 1999

Architect Fox & Fowle Architects, PC
(now FXFOWLE ARCHITECTS, PC)

Client The Durst Organization

Structural engineer Cantor Seinuk Group

Mechanical engineer Cosentini Associates

Vertical transportation consultant Van Deusen & Associates

Contractor Tishman Construction Corporation

Developer The Durst Organization

Height 700.75 ft/213.5 m to top of 49th floor (main) roof slab; 733.75 ft/223.6 m to top of steel cross arms & bulkhead roof; 796.75 ft/242.8 m to top of steel "cube"; 809.25 ft/246.6 m to top of steel at outside tower no. 1; 1117.75 ft/340.7 m New Broadcast Tower

Above-ground stories 48 floors plus 3-story bulkhead

Basements 2

Above-ground useable levels 47 leasable floors

Mechanical levels and level numbers 3: cellar, 4, 48

Use Office

Site area 1,600,000 sq ft/148,640 sq m

Area of typical floor plate Ranges from 24,500 sq ft/2276 sq m (high rise) to 44,300 sq ft/4115 sq m (low rise, floor 7 down)

Basic planning module 5 ft/1.5 m

Principal structural materials Steel

Other materials Curtain wall: Oconee granite; building base: Oconee and Grand Caledonia granite; lobby walls: southern pearl limestone and Grand Caledonia granite; floor: Juparana Columbo granite

Woolworth Building

Frank W Woolworth had a great dream: to build the tallest building in the world and for it to bear his name. On his many visits to London, he was impressed by the Houses of Parliament. He asked Cass Gilbert, an American architect who had studied in Europe, to design an office building in a similar Gothic style that featured spires, gargoyles, flying buttresses, stone traceries and other ornamentation. On completion, the Woolworth Building was called the 'Cathedral of Commerce' and the 'Queen of Manhattan', reflecting its ornate architecture.

An outstanding masterpiece of the American beaux-arts eclectic period, the Woolworth Building soars 792 feet above Broadway and contains 57 stories and three basement levels. The building has a U-shaped base, 29 stories high, above which the square tower rises with several setbacks. The top is a crown with pinnacles and gargoyles, one of which represents Cass Gilbert holding a model of his building.

The total cost for this Gothic Revival monument, completed in 1913, was $13.5 million. It was all paid in cash, since Mr Woolworth wished not to take a mortgage, thereby practising the same principle as his customers who paid in nickels and dimes. To this day it has been almost always fully rented and has never changed owners. Until 1930, when the Chrysler Building was completed, the Woolworth building was the tallest in the world.

The structure is covered in polychromed terra cotta blocks, at the time considered one of the most durable building materials due to its impervious vitreous glazing. The interior as well as the exterior carries the Gothic theme throughout, including polished terrazzo floors, Italian marble, wainscoting, and gilded ornamental work.

Pneumatic caissons were selected for the foundation, with an average depth of 110 feet to bedrock. The steel beams and girders were so heavy that surveyors had to test the streets to make sure that they would not collapse during deliveries to the site. The tower was also braced with portal braces for up to 200 mph wind speed.

The Woolworth Building was the first to have its own power plant, which generates enough electricity for 5000 people. The high-speed elevator system, comprising 30 cabs, was also the best in the world at the time and could rise 700 feet per minute.

In 1981 a $20 million major restoration was completed, which included the replacement of 26,000 severely deteriorated terra cotta units with architectural precast concrete, matching the originals in color and detail.

1

2

Location New York, New York, USA
Completion date 1913
Architect Cass Gilbert
Restoration architect Ehrenkrantz Group & Eckstut
Client Frank W Woolworth
Structural engineer Gunvald Aus
Restoration contractor Turner Construction Co.
Height 792 ft/241 m

Above-ground stories 57
Basements 3
Use Office
Area of above-ground building 1,300,000 sq ft/120,770 sq m
Principal structural materials Steel
Other materials Polychromed terra cotta blocks
Cost $13.5 M (1913)

1   *Façade detail*
2   *Woolworth Building, post-1981 renovation*
3   *View of Woolworth Building with Transportation Building (545 ft, 1927) at left*
4   *View from ground level*

Photography: Courtesy Ehrenkrantz Eckstut & Kuhn Architects (1,2); Reproduced from *King's Views of New York*, Manhattan Post Card Company, New York, 1926, Coll. G Binder/Buildings & Data SA (3); Courtesy Wiss, Janney, Elstner Associates, Inc (4)

3

4

Roppongi Hills Mori Tower

The 54-story mixed-use Mori Tower is the centerpiece of the 28-acre Roppongi Hills project, which is located in an important commercial and entertainment district in Tokyo. Located along the Roppongi Dori, an arterial highway, the building houses more than 3 million square feet of office space; Tokyo City View, a 360-degree public viewing area; cultural learning and meeting facilities; the Roppongi Hills private membership club; and the Mori Art Museum for contemporary art, located at the crown of the tower.

The form of the tower draws from traditions in Japanese design, where variegated natural forms are expressed in geometricized patterns. This transfer creates a faceted steel and glass curtain wall that unfolds as one moves around the project. The rooftop museum is intended to attract a high volume of visitors, at an estimated rate of 20,000 each day.

With the largest high-rise footprint in the world, approximately 60,000 square feet is reserved for office space on floors 7 through 48. The building offers cutting-edge ultra high-speed information network facilities, is built according to a comprehensive earthquake-resistant design, and provides state-of-the-art security.

The brief required the Mori Tower be multifunctional in ways far beyond the business aspect. To express the lofty cultural aims of the developer's vision, the architects took the bold step of incorporating the spectacular vistas of the city of Tokyo into an overall artistic scheme. By placing the Mori Arts Center on the top five floors, KPF was able to integrate the Mori Art Museum, an observation platform and rooftop sky deck, and an educational academy, so that visitors may experience the constant and dynamic change that is Tokyo as a virtual work of art.

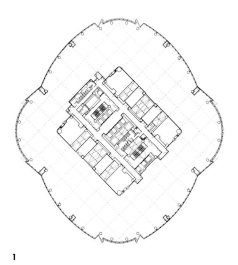

1

2

1 Typical floor plan
2 Tower detail
3 Section
4 Retail view
5 Public plaza view showing entry
6 Context view
7 View of the Mori Tower
Photography: HG Esch (2); Kohn Pedersen Fox Associates PC (4–7)

Location Tokyo, Japan
Completion date 2003
Design architect Kohn Pedersen Fox Associates PC
Associate architect Mori Biru Architects & Engineers, Tokyo
Client Mori Building Company Ltd.
Structural engineer ARUP
Mechanical engineer Mori Building Company Ltd.;
Erie Miyake Architects & Engineers
Landscape architect EDAW

Contractor Mori Building Company Ltd.
Height 781 ft/238 m
Above-ground stories 54
Basements 6
Above-ground useable levels 53
Mechanical levels and level numbers 1: floor 54
Use Office, museum, public observation deck
Site area 28.7 acres/11.6 ha (entire Roppongi Hills site)
Area of above-ground building 3,344,230 sq ft/310,679 sq m

Area of typical floor plate 60,000 sq ft/5574 sq m
Basic planning module 5.9 ft/1.8 m
Number of parking spaces 2450 (below grade)
Principal structural materials Reinforced concrete
Other materials Painted aluminum, metal and glass curtain wall, painted precast concrete panels, Jet Mist granite, metal panels, stainless steel, clear glass
Cost $2.45 billion (entire Roppongi Hills project)

6

3

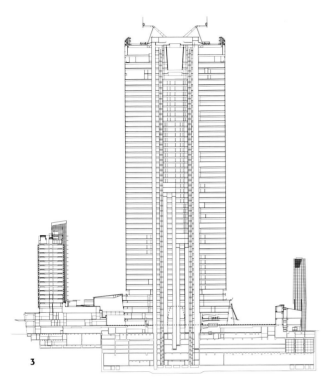

4

5

7

Buildings in Progress

Met 3

Met 3 will be Miami's tallest residential tower. Combining a modern interpretation of classic Miami architecture, its 696 distinctively designed condominiums offer unprecedented views of Biscayne Bay and the City of Miami. This 74-story building includes studios, and one-, two- and three-bedroom units in urban lofts, sky lofts, tower suites and penthouse residences, all with custom-designed floor plans. A spectacular 15th-floor sky lobby, with dramatic floor-to-ceiling windows, overlooks the lanai level and the city of Miami. A food market on the first level, and restaurants, retail venues and other amenities complete the development.

1

2

1 Northwest elevation at night
2 West elevation
3 Typical floor plan, levels 20–51
4 Podium level floor plan

Renderings: Courtesy Nichols Brosch Wurst Wolfe & Associates, Inc.

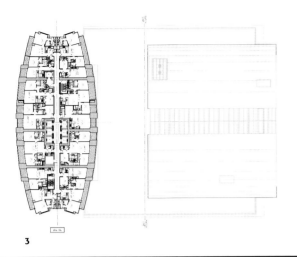

3

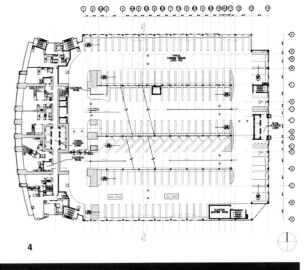

4

Location Miami, Florida, USA

Expected completion date 2008

Architect Nichols Brosch Wurst Wolfe & Associates, Inc.

Interiors RTKL

Client P & G Development, Ltd.

Structural engineer Ysrael A. Seinuk, P.C.

Mechanical engineer Hufsey Nicolaides Garcia Suarez Associates, Inc.

Vertical transportation consultant KONE, Inc.

Landscape architect Urban Resource Group (A division of Kimley-Horn & Associates, Inc.)

Height 817 ft/249 m

Above-ground stories 76

Above-ground useable levels 74

Mechanical levels and level numbers 5: levels 45, 46 (partial); 67, 75, 76

Use Residential, retail

Site area 75,776 sq ft/7040 sq m

Area of above-ground building 1,966,000 sq ft/182,641 sq m

Area of typical floor plate 65,000 sq ft/6038 sq m (parking podium, levels 1–13)18,000 sq ft/1672 sq m (residential floors 14–74)

Basic planning module 5 ft/1.5 m

Number of parking spaces 1530

Principal structural materials Steel, concrete, reinforced concrete, curtain wall

Other materials Precast concrete, aluminum, marble, granite

Torre Repsol YPF

This new headquarters building for Spanish oil and gas company Repsol continues Foster and Partners' investigations into the sustainable workplace. With this new headquarters, Repsol will be able for the first time to consolidate its 3600-strong team in one location in Madrid in a building that communicates the company's core values.

The 53-story building is located on the site of the former Real Madrid training grounds, where the city council has assigned sites for four new towers by international architects. It marks a curve in the wide boulevard of the Paseo de la Castellana—the 'backbone' of Madrid—and is carefully positioned to maximize the exceptional qualities of its site. Compositionally, the building can be thought of as a tall arch, with the services and circulation cores framing the open office floors. At ground level, a 72-foot glazed atrium provides the transition from the street, and accommodates a 'floating' glass-walled auditorium set into a mezzanine. At the top of the building, the void space beneath the uppermost section of the 'portal' frame is designed to house wind turbines capable of providing a

significant proportion of the building's power supply. This is an innovation that both signals Repsol's commitment to environmental sustainability, and indicates the company's progressive investigations into potential alternative energy sources.

Although the building is conceived as a corporate headquarters, it also has the flexibility to be partly sub-let, enabling Repsol to expand or contract its accommodation easily in the future as required. This degree of flexibility results in part from pushing the service cores to the edges of the plan to create uninterrupted 12,912-square-foot floor plates. Vertical circulation routes occupy minimal space as a result of an intelligent elevator system that requires fewer cars than conventional systems. The cores are strategically positioned so as to block west–east direct sunlight, a move that has the added benefit of framing spectacular views of the hills of Sierra de Guadarrama to the north and the center of Madrid to the south.

1

2

1   Entrance lobby
2   Visualization of elevation
3   Visualization from street level at night
Renderings: Courtesy Foster and Partners

Location Madrid, Spain

Expected completion date 2008

Architect Foster and Partners

Associate architect Reid Fenwick Asociados

Client Repsol YPF

Structural engineer SGS Tecnos SA

Mechanical engineer Aguilera Ingenieros SA

Height 820 ft/250 m

Above-ground stories 53

Basements 5

Above-ground useable levels 34 office levels

Use Office

Site area 80,700 sq ft/7500 sq m

Area of above-ground building 605,250 sq ft/56,250 sq m

Area of typical floor plate 12,912 sq ft/1200 sq m

Beijing, CHINA

Beijing Yintai Centre

With architectural details that suggest ancient Chinese architecture in a contemporary way, Beijing Yintai Centre is a comprehensive mixed-use complex located in Beijing's central business district. The three towers, square in form, are studies in simple, straightforward design. The residential tower, the focal point of the project, is flanked by twin office towers and features a five-star Park Hyatt hotel with elegant guestrooms, luxury apartments, and serviced apartments.

Topping the residential tower is a majestic cube that recalls a Chinese lantern. Express elevators sweep guests to the top of the building where the hotel registration area is located within the lantern. Other hotel public functions, such as a bar, lounge and specialty restaurant, are also located within the lantern and provide spectacular views of Beijing. The cube is a stately symbol of Chinese culture by day, and a glowing landmark at night.

On top of the podium, a landscaped roof garden ties the three towers together. Rather than attempting to copy a traditional Chinese garden, elements of historic Chinese gardens are incorporated in a symbolic way. The cool greenery and the sound of water create a welcome respite from the urban surroundings while also highlighting the forms of the architecture.

The podium base includes specialty stores and restaurants, ballrooms, a fitness center, and an enclosed pool above grade, connected with upscale retail areas below. Motor access to the site via a large monumental space under the podium gives each tower its own grand sense of entry. Supported by majestic circular columns, this covered courtyard is graced by natural light.

At Beijing Yintai Centre, timeless materials create and reinforce spaces in harmony with the urban surroundings. The symmetrical plan brings a sense of order that guides pedestrians and drivers alike, and the garden and pools bring a feeling of calmness and peace. In the capital city of a great nation with a rich architectural heritage, the elegant design and simple forms bring a sense of dignity, stateliness, and grandeur representative of the pride of Beijing's new era.

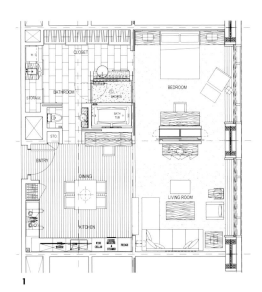

1

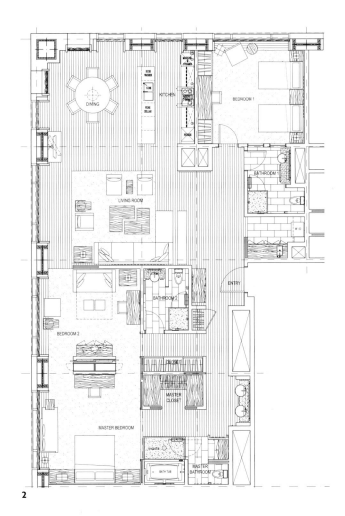

2

1 Apartment type 1 floor plan
2 Apartment type 3 floor plan
3 General view

Rendering: Courtesy John Portman & Associates
Plans: Courtesy Remedio Siembieda, Inc.

Location Beijing, China

Expected completion date 2007

Architect for initial design John Portman & Associates

Local architect China Electronics Engineering Design Institute (CEEDI)

Client Beijing Yintai Property Co., Ltd.

Structural engineer for initial design John Portman & Associates; LeMessurier Consultants

Mechanical engineer for initial design Citadel Consulting

Vertical transportation consultant for initial design Lerch Bates & Associates Inc.

Landscape design concept Arnold Associates

Final landscape design Place Media

Landscape design concept for roof garden Arnold Associates

Final landscape design for roof garden Super Potato

Interior design Remedio Siembieda, Inc. (RS)

Project manager Bovis Lend Lease

Height 820 ft/250 m

Above-ground stories 63

Basements 4

Above-ground useable levels 57

Mechanical levels and level numbers 6: levels 4, 17, 33, 34, 47, 56

Use Hotel, residential, retail, restaurants, leisure

Site area 340,328 sq ft/31,629 sq m

Area of above-ground building 1,275,264 sq ft/118,519 sq m

Area of typical floor plate 1721 sq ft/160 sq m

Basic planning module 16.4 ft/5 m

Number of parking spaces 1692 (car), 1500 (bicycle)

Principal structural materials Concrete beams, slabs, columns, and shearwalls, reinforcing steel, structural steel, steel floor deck, unitized curtainwall

Other materials Granite, glass

Dual Towers at Bahrain Financial Harbour

Bahrain Financial Harbour (BFH) is a $1.3 billion development, to be completed in several phases. It will cover more than 4 million square feet of reclaimed land on a prime, north-facing section of the Manama corniche, near the historic Bab Al-Bahrain gateway to the capital. Situated on the Kingdom's main island, BFH is located just 10 minutes away from Bahrain International Airport, and 15 minutes from the King Fahad Causeway that links the country to Saudi Arabia. The waterfront development consists of 10 projects comprising 30 individual development parcels including the Financial Centre, office towers, upmarket residences, retail and dining outlets, Bahrain Performance Centre, which will house the Bahrain Royal Opera House, seafront walkways, promenades, and marinas.

The US$270-million, phase one Financial Centre consists of three components: the Dual Towers (two 57-story buildings), the Financial Mall and the Harbour House.

At an imposing 57 stories, the uniquely designed Dual Towers will become the most visible and striking buildings on Manama's skyline. Offering beautiful panoramic views, the towers will provide office and commercial space for the financial sector. The Dual Towers will offer an expansive and efficient interior, with a balance of form, function, and flexibility adaptable to the needs of its occupiers and will provide a high-tech, sophisticated environment for regional and international financial firms offering the best IT installation opportunities and all the security and failsafe setup needed.

1,4&5   *General views of Bahrain Financial Harbour development*
2   *High-rise floor plan*
3   *Low-rise floor plan*
Renderings: Courtesy Bahrain Financial Harbour Holding Company B.S.C. (c)

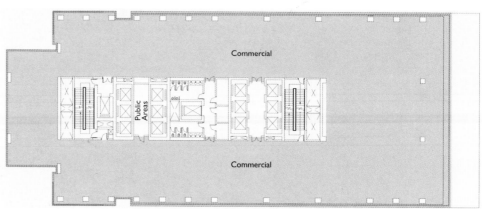

1

2

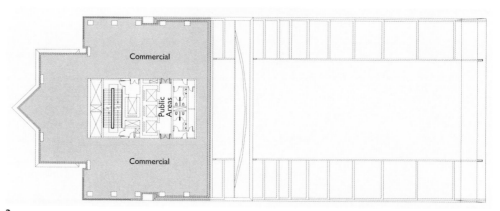

3

Location Manama, Kingdom of Bahrain

Completion date 2006 (Phase 1)

Architect Ahmed Janahi Architects S.P.C.

Client Bahrain Financial Harbour Holding Company B.S.C. (c)

Contractor (Phase 1) Al Hamad Construction and Development Company

Height 853 ft/260 m (Dual towers)

Above-ground stories 57

Basements 1

Above-ground useable levels 55

Mechanical levels 2

Use Office, retail, restaurants, entertainment

Area of above-ground building 796,240 sq ft/74,000 sq m, per tower

Area of typical floor plate 6424–18,281 sq ft/597–1699 sq m

Structural materials Reinforced concrete

Other materials Granite, aluminum panels, semi-reflective green glass

4

5

New World Building

This skyscraper, in Hanoi Road, at the heart of Tsim Sha Tsui is more than just another Hong Kong landmark. It is a high-quality urban renewal project with retail, residential and hotel functions at the heart of Kowloon's renowned commercial and residential district. The location of this prominent building, facing Victoria Harbour, demands a unique façade and excellent lighting to complement the Harbour's beauty.

The New World Building has a distinctive elevation, designed in harmony with the surrounding existing and future buildings on the Kowloon peninsula. The tower's elevation is articulated by exterior fins, creating a sleek horizontal expression, influenced by indentations and windows projected upon the façade. Lighting of the fins accentuates the horizontal expression at night.

The redevelopment consists of a 56-story tower on an eight-story podium. The podium has four basement levels with underground routes to the Mass Transit Railway's Tsim Sha Tsui Station and the KCRC East Rail – Tsim Sha Tsui Extension. A covered open space of 12,912 square feet at ground level enables pedestrians to flow easily through an organized, landscaped area. Retail areas are distributed at the basement and podium levels, providing about 100 shops and 25 restaurants with easy access to public transport and other infrastructure. On top of the podium are 15 stories of hotel guestrooms and 36 stories of serviced apartments.

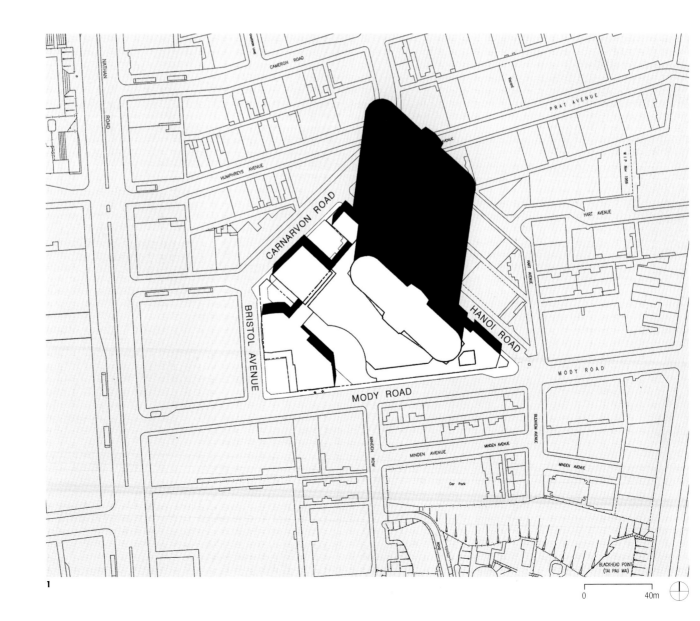

1

0   40m

ATTACHMENT D.2

SK-68 OVERALL DEVELOPMENT PERSPECTIVE FROM HANOI ROAD
PERSPECTIVE AT NIGHT TIME

2

3

4

SERVICE APARTMENT
DUPLEX

SERVICE APARTMENT
SIMPLEX

SERVICE APARTMENT

SKY GARDEN /
REFUGE FLOOR

SERVICE APARTMENT

REFUGE FLOOR
M/E FLOOR

HOTEL

SKY GARDEN
CLUB HOUSE

HOTEL

COMMERCIAL

LOADING / SERVICING
PARKING / SERVICING

256.845m

0   20m

Location Hong Kong, China

Expected completion date 2007

Principal architect Dennis Lau & Ng Chun Man Architects &
Engineers (H.K.) Ltd

Retail architect HOK International Ltd

Client New World Development Company Ltd; Urban
Renewal Authority

Structural engineer Ove Arup Partners HK Ltd

Mechanical engineer Meinhardt (HK) Ltd

Landscape architect Team 73

Contractor Main Contractor: Hip Hing Builders Co. Ltd
(main); Vibro (HK) Ltd (foundation and basement)

Height 856 ft/260.9 m

Above-ground stories Tower: 56; podium: 8

Basements 4

Use Hotel, residential, retail

Site area 89,297 sq ft/8299 sq m

Area of above-ground building 1,104,643 sq ft/102,662 sq m

Construction cost US$309 M

Capital City

Capital City is part of the Moscow International Business Center (MIBC), an investment-construction project known as Moscow-City. This multifunctional complex is one of the largest investment and construction projects in Europe, with an area of almost 27 million square feet. Its implementation is a sign that Moscow is taking its place as one of the world's leading international business centers.

The complex is located on the Krasnopresnenskaya embankment, just 2½ miles from the Kremlin. This location provides residents with panoramic city views, including the Kremlin and Moscow skyscrapers, river views, and views of the entire Moscow International Business Center development.

Capital City is composed of two residential towers, of 73 and 62 floors, named after the two capitals—Moscow and Saint Petersburg—and an adjacent office complex. The architectural approach to the complex is rooted in 20th-century Russian Constructivism, with its clear and distinct geometric forms. The square towers are twisted on axis at the technical floor levels,

adding motion to their silhouette. The unusual geometrical design of the two towers provides structural strength and allows the creation of spacious apartments with panoramic windows. Echoes of Russian Constructivism can be seen not only in the proportion of the sizes of the podiums and the towers, but also in the design of the façade. The vertical lines are highlighted by a 'mosaic' made of dark and light terra cotta tablets. The tablets also emphasize the residential part of the building, where there is again a combination of smooth and rough surfaces on the podium façade.

The building program includes 1,125,840 square feet of apartments from the 19th to 73rd floors; 907,300 square feet of offices on floors 4–17; a 238,765-square-foot shopping mall on the ground and first floors; a fitness center, swimming pool and spa on the third floor; and 1,013,110 square feet of parking on the 1st–6th floors. The apartments in Capital City are divided into six types, with floor areas ranging from 1130 square feet for the one-bedroom Deluxe apartments to 2375 square feet for the two-bedroom Royal apartments.

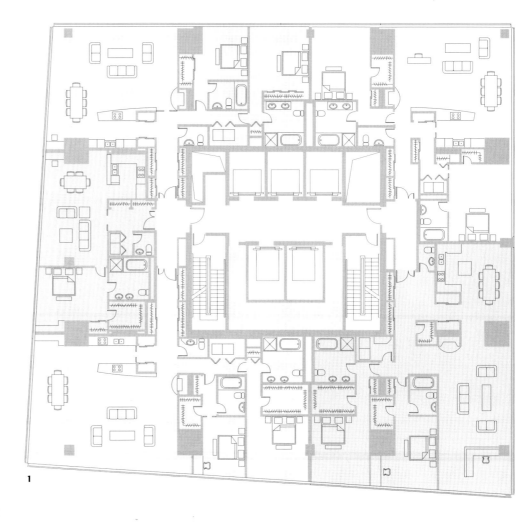

1

1 Typical residential floor plan
2 General view

Renderings: Courtesy Capital Group Holding/NBBJ

2

Location Moscow, Russia

Completion date 2008

Architect NBBJ

Client Capital Group Holding

Structural engineer Arup

Mechanical engineer Arup

Vertical transportation consultant Arup

General contractor ANT YAPI

Height 938 ft/286 m (Moscow Tower); 804 ft/245 m
(St Petersburg Tower); 233 ft/71 m (office complex)

Above-ground stories 73 (Moscow Tower); 62
(St Petersburg Tower); 18 (office complex)

Above-ground useable levels 68 (Moscow Tower); 58
(St Petersburg Tower); 17 (office complex)

Basements 6

Use Residential, offices, retail, leisure

Site area 3.14 acres/1.27 ha

Area of above-ground building 2,271,895 sq ft/211,066 sq m

Area of typical floor plate 9921 sq ft/922 sq m

Number of parking spaces 2110 underground spaces

Principal structural materials Reinforced concrete with mega
columns

Other materials Glass, terra cotta, stone, aluminum, granite

Gate to the East

This groundbreaking development will create a landmark entrance to the new central business district of Suzhou, part of the Suzhou Industrial Technology Park. Sited on the western edge of Jinji Lake, the scheme will stand some 912 feet tall and is currently hailed as the largest single building in China. It will house two world-class hotels, office accommodation, serviced apartments and 968,400 square feet of retail space.

The design and planning of the Suzhou twin towers reflects the design intent to deliver a new commercially viable public environment enriched with inviting 'places for people'. The new Suzhou CBD and Jinji Lake District will become a vibrant new urban destination in harmony with and complementing the proposed new CBD masterplan.

The Suzhou twin towers will link the external landscaped pedestrianized environment to the interior, bringing the green space up through the tower to the top presidential garden suites and creating sky gardens throughout the building. The pedestrian promenades at ground level link the new development seamlessly with the lake and its surrounds.

Responding to the unique and prominent location, and the client's ambition for the project, the Gate to the East building is formed by joining twin towers, creating a grand arch that extends the CBD axis toward the lake. Due to its streamlined geometry, the higher floors have wider frontage toward the water, thus maximizing the floor areas with lake views. Two pieces of curtain wall gently overlay the tower, reminiscent of smooth Suzhou silk.

To be coherent with Suzhou—a historical city full of traditional Chinese gardens and architecture, the colors black, white and gray were chosen for the building's main color themes. The typical Chinese garden concept is also applied to the site planning. Tight around the shell, and relaxed at the core, it makes the central pedestrian plaza more intimate and lively.

1

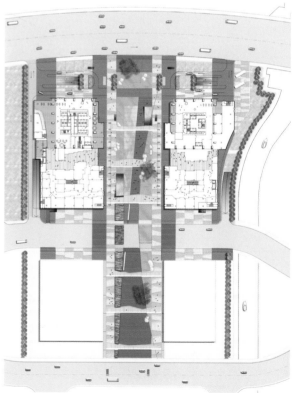

2

1   Garden perspective
2   Master plan
Opposite:
    Gate to the East aerial perspective
Renderings: Courtesy RMJM Hong Kong Limited

Location Suzhou, China
Expected completion date 2007
Design architect RMJM Hong Kong
Local architect East China Architectural Design & Research Institute (ECADI)
Client Suzhou Chinaing Real Estate Co. Ltd
Design structural, mechanical and vertical engineer Arup
Height 912 ft/278 m

Above-ground stories 68
Basements 5
Mechanical levels and level numbers LB1 to LB5
Use Office, serviced apartments, hotel, retail
Site area 258,240 sq ft/24,000 sq m
Area of above-ground building 3,643,659 sq ft/338,630 sq m
Number of parking spaces 1871

Principal structural materials Concrete, structural steel, fully toughened glass
Other materials Unitized aluminum curtain wall, clad steel mullion, aluminum cladding, insulated glazing unit, clear glass, fritted glass
Cost RMB3.5 billion

Bright Start Tower

Bright Start Tower occupies a prominent position on a plot adjacent to Dubai's main highway, the Sheikh Zayed Road. With its elegant simplicity, the tower responds to the city's demand for high-quality, stylish residential accommodation. Comprising 59 stories, the tower provides a total built-up area of 1,073,848 square feet, including a dedicated 10-story car park.

Atkins was lead consultant for architecture, interior design, structural, mechanical and electrical engineering design, construction supervision and project management.

A total of 301 three-bedroom apartments and 106 two-bedroom apartments are provided on 55 typical floors with retail space on the ground and mezzanine floors. Apartment layouts are standardized to maximize functional and cost efficiency.

The 471-bay car park building accommodates a 25-meter swimming pool, gymnasium, squash courts and changing rooms on the roof level.

The building satisfies the client's dual requirements of aesthetics and functionality. The architectural design concept is based on a symmetrically balanced assembly of two separate massed forms, displaying both minimalism and sophistication. A solid frame element anchors the building to the ground while a second, lighter, more transparent central body expresses a vertical upward movement. This is further emphasized both by the deep recess at the base, which creates a weightlessness to the main body of the tower, and the culminating fin-shaped feature and spire at the apex.

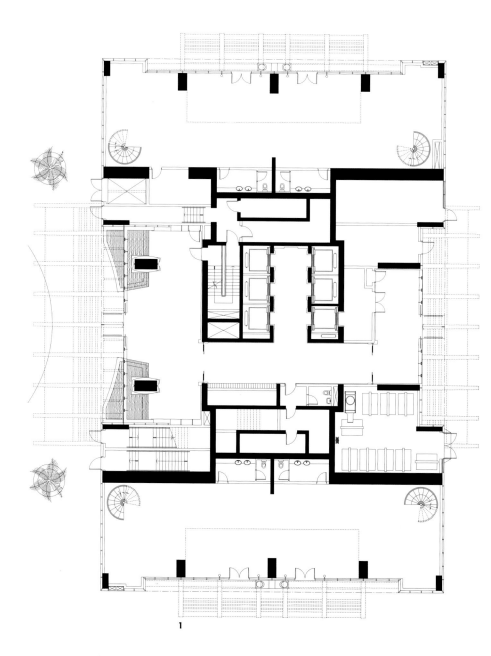

1   Ground floor plan
2   Tower view
3   Upper roof plan
4&5 Lobby views

Renderings: Courtesy Atkins

1

Location Dubai, United Arab Emirates
Completion date 2006
Architect Atkins
Developer Bright Start Holdings
Structural engineer Atkins
Mechanical engineer Atkins
Vertical transportation consultant Atkins
Landscape architect Atkins

Contractor Dubai Contracting Company
Project manager Atkins
Height 919 ft/280 m
Above-ground stories 60
Basements 1
Above-ground useable levels 57
Mechanical levels and level numbers 3: floors 10, 30, 50
Use Residential

Site area 15,000 sq ft/1394 sq m
Area of above-ground building 1,073,848 sq ft/99,800 sq m
Area of typical floor plate 14,536 sq ft/1351 sq m
Number of parking spaces Separate 10-story building with 433 parking bays
Principal structural materials Steel, reinforced concrete and aluminum curtain wall
Other materials Stone, timber, stainless steel, aluminum, exposed aggregate precast concrete

2

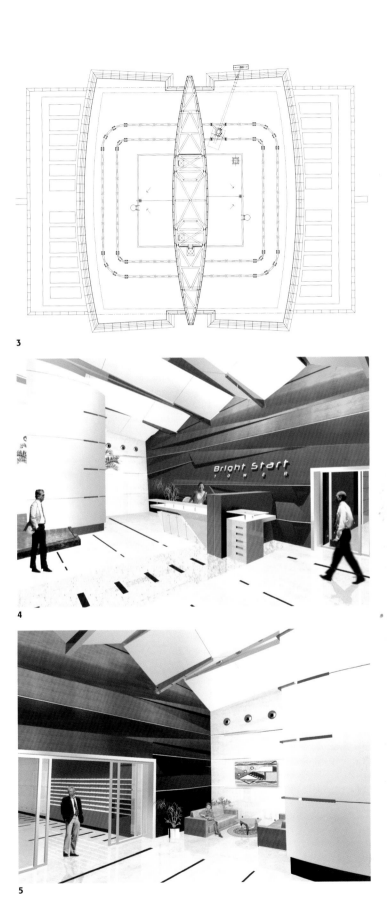

3

4

5

I & M Tower

I & M Tower is part of the City of Arabia, situated in a new suburb in the heart of Dubailand, developed by Ilyas and Mustafa Galadari Group. The project is a 40.4-million-square-foot development on a 20-million-square-foot parcel of land about 11 miles from Dubai International Airport. The main features of the City of Arabia development include the huge Mall of Arabia, the largest retail facility in the region and among the largest in the world; the Restless Planet dinosaur theme park, developed in collaboration with the Natural History Museum of London; a canal flowing between apartment buildings, and lined with shady walkways, cafés, restaurants, convenience stores and places to relax; and finally, 34 elegant towers. The aim of the project is to build a community and create a desirable new suburb of Dubai.

I & M Tower stands at the prominent frontage toward the Emirates Road and contributes to the continuous row of elite towers along this major urban spine that connects to the city center. Being one of the major symbolic icons in the City of Arabia, the tower is easily identified by the distinct geometrical form of its roof features. The quarter cutaway from the top and the sloping secondary roof become defining features of the tower. Two white triangular-shaped forms in front articulate the sky-blue colored curtain walls.

1

1   View of I & M Tower within the City of Arabia development
2   Typical floor plan (high zone)
3   Typical floor plan (low zone)
4   General view

Renderings: P&T Architects and Engineers Ltd.

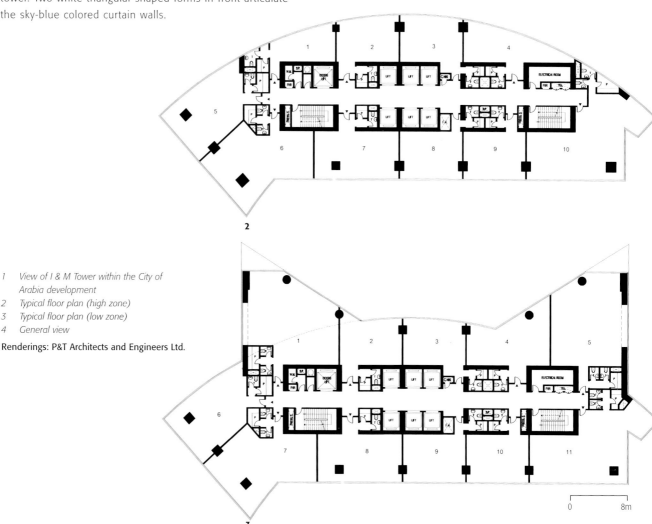

2

3

0   8m

4

Location Dubai, United Arab Emirates

Expected completion date 2008

Architect P&T Architects & Engineers Ltd; Alex Vacha Architects

Client Ilyas and Mustafa Galadari Management Investment & Development LLC

Structural engineer WSP Middle East Limited

Mechanical engineer WSP Middle East Limited

Project manager Hill International

Height 951.5 ft/290 m (approx)

Above-ground stories 54

Basements 1

Above-ground useable levels 46

Mechanical levels and level numbers 2

Use Office

Site area 68,750 sq ft/6387 sq m

Area of above-ground building 675,000 sq ft/62,708 sq m

Area of typical floor plate 15,850 sq ft/1472 sq m

Basic planning module 5 ft/1.5 m

Number of parking spaces 908

Principal structural materials Reinforced concrete

Other materials Metal cladding, reflective glass

Comcast Center

Comcast Center represents a major commitment to the future of Center City Philadelphia by the developer client, Liberty Property Trust, and by Comcast, the building's lead tenant. The site is next to Suburban Station, the principal commuter rail station serving Center City.

The design proposes two office towers framing a half-acre, south-facing landscaped plaza on John F Kennedy, Jr Boulevard. The taller building, Comcast Center, rises approximately 975 feet. It is set back from the boulevard, behind both the plaza and a 110-foot-high public winter garden, which serves both as a forecourt to the tower and as a light-flooded entrance to the Suburban Station concourse below. Set off from the street by a row of trees and a few steps up from the sidewalk, the plaza offers outdoor seating beneath shade trees and a playful water feature. It will be framed by the existing Suburban Station building to the east, by the winter garden and principal tower to the north, and to the west by a retail-lined pedestrian arcade in the phase two office building.

In the lower portion of the tower, a series of four three-story atrium spaces, one above the other, overlook the plaza and provide multifloor corporate tenants with the opportunity to create unified, identifiable homes. Throughout the tower, the floor-to-floor height is typically 15 feet, increasing to 17 feet at the top thirteen floors, allowing for generous finished ceiling heights of 11 and 13 feet respectively. Continuous 9-foot-high glazing permits unobstructed views and brings light deep into the office floors. The tower is clad in an aluminum-frame curtain wall with high performance Low-E glass. The double-skin glass curtain wall of the winter garden also features high-performance Low-E glazing along with aluminum sunscreens and louvers designed to maximize daylight and views while modulating thermal performance. Comcast Center will seek LEED™ certification.

1

Location Philadelphia, Pennsylvania, USA

Expected completion date 2007

Design architect Robert AM Stern Architects

Associate architect Kendall/Heaton Associates

Client Liberty Property Trust

Structural engineer Thornton-Tomasetti Engineers

Mechanical engineer Paul H Yeomans, Inc.

Vertical transportation engineer Persohn/Hahn Associates

Landscape architect Olin Partnership

Contractor LF Driscoll Co. (construction manager)

Developer Liberty Property Trust

Height 975 ft/297 m (to top of parapet)

Above-ground stories 58

Basements 3 (including concourse)

Above-ground useable levels 56

Mechanical levels and level numbers 2: floors 57, 58

Use Office

Site area 85,000 sq ft/7897 sq m

Area of above-ground building 1,610,000 sq ft/149,569 sq m

Area of typical floor plate Atrium floors: 27,700 sq ft/2573 sq m (varies); floor overlooking atrium: 27,640 sq ft/2568 sq m (varies); typical floor: 25,040 sq ft/2336 sq m (varies)

Basic planning module 5 ft/1.5 m

Number of parking spaces 120 cars on three levels of parking below grade

Principal structural materials Steel frame with concrete shear core; aluminum curtain wall with high-performance Low-E glass

Other materials Limestone and granite stone base; double skin glass curtain wall with high-performance Low-E glass; aluminum sun screen louvers on south, east, and west façades; granite paving at plaza; granite floor and wood veneer paneling in lobby

Cost US$492 M (estimated)

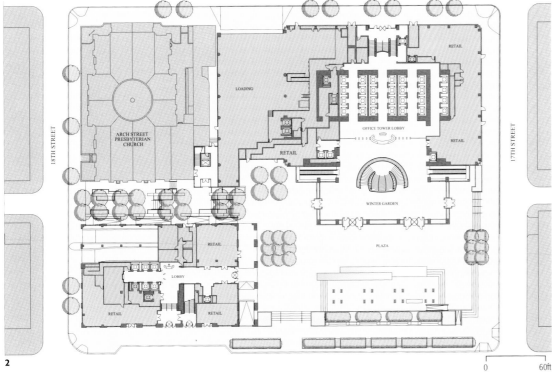

2

1 Skyline view from Schuylkill River
2 Ground floor plan on site
3 View from across 17th Street and John F Kennedy, Jr Boulevard

Renderings: Advanced Media Design

3

Moscow International Business Center

Swanke Hayden Connell Architects was commissioned by the Turkish Development Company, SUMMA, working with Russian investors, to design a 2-million-square-foot, mixed-use, 67-story tower on a 1.5-million-square-foot site. The building will have 31 floors of commercial office space based on a class 'A' US occupancy standard. Above the office space will be a sky lobby with amenities for the offices as well as the residents of 19 floors of apartments above the sky lobby. At the base of the building, four floors of retail will relate to a huge retail complex in the center of this site in central Moscow, not far from the Kremlin.

The overall mixed use development, covering 148 acres, will house 30 million square feet of retail, residential, hospitality, commercial, government offices, and a major transportation center, and is divided into 16 parcel sites that ring the retail complex. These sites are being bought and developed individually by international consortiums under the unique requirement that all the parcels must be completed by the end of 2007.

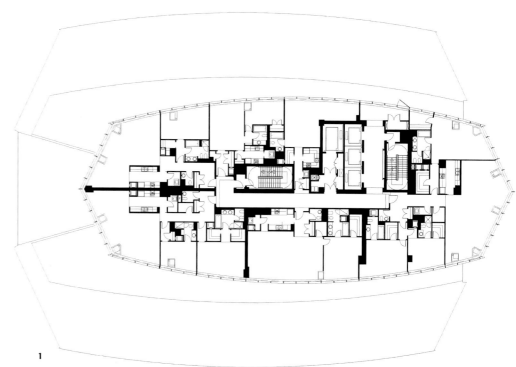

1

1   Typical residential floor plan (floors 48–66)
2   Ground floor plan
3   General view
4   Façade detail
5   Tower base

Renderings: Courtesy Swanke Hayden Connell Architects

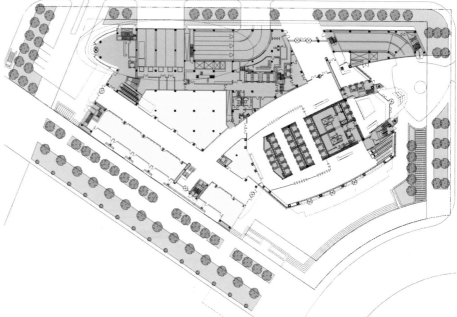

Location Moscow, Russia
Expected completion date 2007
Architect Swanke Hayden Connell Architects
Client ZAO Tekinvest
Structural engineer Thornton-Tomasetti Engineers Division
Mechanical engineer Cosentini Associates
Height 984 ft/300 m
Above-ground stories 67

Basements 5
Above-ground useable levels 64
Mechanical levels 3
Use Mixed, primarily office and residential
Site area 118,037 sq ft/10,970 sq m above ground
Area of above-ground building 1,700,080 sq ft/158,000 sq m
Area of typical floor plate 26,900 sq ft/2500 sq m (office floors); 10,760 sq ft/1000 sq m (residential floors)

Basic planning module 5 ft/1.5 m
Number of parking spaces 800
Principal structural materials Structural steel, reinforced concrete
Other materials Stainless steel, granite
Cost F 275 M

3

4

5

Northeast Asia Trade Tower

Rising more than 1000 feet above the Yellow Sea and overlooking one of the largest column-free convention centers on the Korean Peninsula, the Northeast Asia Trade Tower will be the first of many commercial buildings within New Songdo City. The new 1.5-million-square-foot tower will provide a landmark location for top tier companies as well as world-class shopping opportunities, luxury accommodation, and underground parking facilities.

The tower's retail area, contained in the basement level and the ground floor, will be home to the flagship boutiques of many famous international fashion names. Approximately 650,000 square feet of commercial office space will occupy floors 1–27. The office space will set the benchmark in northeast Asia for a prestigious, globally oriented, 24-hour business complex and will be home to many of the leading international corporations and financial institutions.

A five (or 6) star, 300-room hotel will be situated on floors 28–45. Additionally, 100 high-end serviced apartments, aimed toward the most discriminating executives, will be located on floors 46–64. This spectacular building will also feature a sky lounge on the 65th floor that will offer some of the most amazing views in Korea with sweeping vistas of the islands dotting the Yellow Sea, and nearby mountain peaks.

The tower complex will be the centerpiece for New Songdo City and will provide easy access to all associated lifestyle components including the convention center, museums, central park, Jack Nicklaus golf course, aquarium, international schools, international hospitals, canals and world-class shopping.

1   Elevations and section
2   Cut-away axonometric diagram
3   Bird's-eye view of tower in context with the convention center
Rendering: 3D-Win, Korea

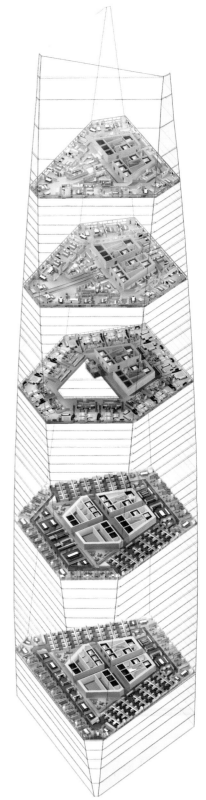

1

2

Location New Songdo City, South Korea

Expected completion date 2009

Design architect Kohn Pedersen Fox Associates PC

Associate architect Heerim Architects & Engineers

Client NSCDLLC New Songdo City Development Limited Liability Coorporation (Gale International and Posco E&C)

Structural engineer Ove Arup

Mechanical engineer Ove Arup

Vertical transportation consultant Lerch, Bates & Associates Inc.

Height 1000.7 ft/305 m

Above-ground stories 65

Basements 4

Above-ground useable levels 65

Mechanical levels 13, 33, 65

Use Mixed: office, residential, hotel, retail, and parking

Site area 50,000 sq ft/4645 sq m

Area of above-ground building 1,500,000 sq ft/139,350 sq m

Area of typical floor plate 25,000 sq ft/2322.5 sq m

Basic planning module 5.9 ft/1.8 m

Number of parking spaces 970 spaces under tower

Principal structural materials Steel structure, concrete core, aluminum and glass curtain wall

Other materials Stone, wood, glass, stainless steel

Burj Dubai Lake Hotel

The Burj Dubai Lake Hotel is a mixed-use, 63-story tower comprising a 198-key, five-star hotel and 626 serviced apartments. The imposing 1000-foot height and striking design produce a landmark project with a gross floor area of more than 1.8 million square feet that will stand at the opposite end of the lake to the anticipated world's tallest building, the Burj Dubai.

The hotel floor plate is based on an organic evolution of a series of linked arcs that present imposing interconnected double and triple volume public spaces with full views of the lake and Burj Dubai tower. This concept is also extended to the guest room levels. Rising above the hotel is a curvilinear tower topped by an aerofoil shaped roof feature that accommodates 45 levels of deluxe serviced apartments.

Extending from the promenade area, from which guests enjoy the lake panorama, is the hotel's impressive 11,836-square-foot swimming pool. Other key facilities include a specialty restaurant, ballroom and support facilities, a business center, club lounge, pool bar; health club and spa, and parking for approximately 900 vehicles.

Atkins is responsible for architectural and engineering design, in conjunction with other specialist consultants.

1   Canopy at ground level
2   Typical floor plan, floors 15–47
3   View of hotel and lake
Renderings: Courtesy Atkins

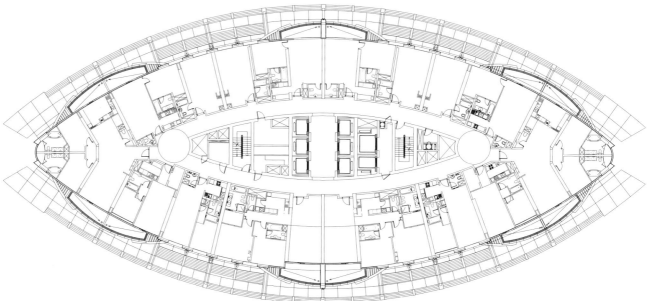

1

2

Location Dubai, United Arab Emirates

Expected completion date 2008

Architect Atkins

Client Emaar Properties PJSC

Developer, project manager and quantity surveyor Mirage Mille Leisure and Development

Mechanical engineer Atkins

Vertical transportation consultant Atkins in association with Lerch Bates

Landscape architect Shankland Cox

Contractor BESIX-Arabtec joint venture

Height 1004 ft/306 m (to top of mast); 897.31 ft/273.5 m (to top of roof feature)

Above-ground stories 61

Basements 2

Above-ground useable levels 57

Mechanical levels and level numbers 4: floors 14, 48, 61, 62

Use Hotel and residential

Site area 210,414 sq ft/19,548 sq m

Area of above-ground building 1,673,111 sq ft/155,436 sq m (total built up area from 3rd floor [ground floor] to main roof)

Area of typical floor plate 21,818 sq ft/2027 sq m (typical floors 15–47)

Basic planning module Podium: 26.2 ft x 27.8 ft/8 m x 8.5 m; Tower: radial grid system with typical angle of 4.625 degrees

Number of parking spaces 895 (podium)

Principal structural materials Reinforced concrete, structural steel for roof feature, ballroom and mast/spire

Other materials Exterior: aluminum cladding system, glazing system, stone cladding system; interior: concrete block works, drywall partitions and glass partitions

Ocean Heights

Dubai Marina will soon have a new structure added to its skyline in the form of the 1017-foot Ocean Heights tower. The project received a 2005 BENTLEY Best of Architecture International Design Award.

The 82-story tower will be easily distinguishable by its twisting form that allows each apartment unit—even those in the back—sweeping ocean views.

The building's twist starts from its base. As it rises, the tower's floor plates reduce in size, allowing the twist to become even more pronounced. At fifty stories, the building rises over its neighbors, allowing two faces unobstructed views to the ocean. The tower breaks away from the orthogonal grid and reorients the project toward one of Dubai's Palm Islands to the north.

The most challenging aspect of the design was accommodating the client's strict requirement of unit layouts within a changing envelope. The result was a rational 13-foot module, which tracks its way down through the entire building and only changes at the façade. This also considerably simplified the structural system of the project.

The main structural challenge was to minimize wind affect on the tower. The building's overall height, with its sharp edges, could have high levels of motion when subject to either low-speed, steady synoptic winds, or short duration, high-velocity thunderstorm downbursts. The wind climate in Dubai is dominated by steady afternoon sea breezes and strong smooth 'Shamal' winds, which occur in some seasons. These types of winds can cause considerable motion in tall buildings in Dubai unless appropriate measures are incorporated into the design of the project. The proposed system of continuous shear walls as 'outrigger stiffening walls' from the core, combined with mass-dampening devices significantly reduce this motion.

A central reinforced concrete core of maximum perimeter, up the full height of the building, will provide a significant contribution to the lateral and torsional stiffness of the tower. This central core will be augmented by walls, which span from the core to the perimeter for the entire height of the building. The outrigger walls will be coupled to the core with post-tensioned reinforcement. This technique allows the differential movement of the core and outrigger walls to occur during construction prior to locking them together. The floors will incorporate post-tensioned reinforcement to allow early stripping of the floor formwork and further reduce the construction time.

To ensure the stability of the tall structure on sand, the tower will be launched from a piled raft with 4-foot-diameter piles anchored into the sand and soft rock formations at approximately 50 feet below ground level.

1   Elevation
2&4   General view renderings
3   Typical low-rise (ground floor–51)
      and high-rise (52–81) floor plans

Renderings: Courtesy Aedas Limited

1

Location Dubai, United Arab Emirates
Expected completion date 2008
Architect Aedas Limited
Client DAMAC Properties Co. LLC
Structural engineer Meinhardt, Singapore
Mechanical engineer M/S Engineering Associates, Dubai
Piling contractor APCC
Developer DAMAC Properties Co. LLC

Project manager FADI GHALEB
Height 1017 ft/310 m
Above-ground storeys 82
Basements 3
Above-ground useable levels 82
Mechanical levels and level numbers 4: levels 35, 36, 65, 66
Use Residential
Site area 37,402 sq ft/3476 sq m

Area of above-ground building 858,336 sq ft/79,771 sq m
Area of typical floor plate 13,880 sq ft/1290 sq m
Basic planning module 13 ft/4 m
Number of parking spaces 685
Principal structural materials Reinforced concrete, curtain wall
Other materials Aluminum cladding, glass
Cost AED500 M

3

2

4

The New York Times Building

Renzo Piano Building Workshop and FXFOWLE ARCHITECTS have collaboratively designed a new headquarters building for The New York Times Company and Forest City Ratner, in the footprint of the southern boundary of Times Square. The building, to be located on Eighth Avenue between 40th and 41st Streets, opposite the Port Authority Bus Terminal, unites the company's employees under one roof in an exceptional signature structure.

The concept for the building, conceived during the architectural competition in which the team was chosen, incorporates a transparent glass tower that seems to float above a five-story base. The tower uses a double curtain wall technique that allows the structure to appear vibrant and transparent, while increasing energy efficiency. An exterior sunscreen of white ceramic rods and an interior system of adjustable blinds are added to the building's skin to enhance the shimmering, multi-layered effect of the façade.

At the base of the building, an atrium is surrounded on three sides to create an open urban landscape. This piazza-like space provides an arena for the Times Center, a public amenity devised by the New York Times Company. The newsroom of *The New York Times* is located above.

The New York Times Company's offices will comprise half of the building's 1.6 million square feet. One floor will be devoted to the Forest City Ratner Companies, the developer for the project, while the remainder of the building will be rented to retail and corporate tenants.

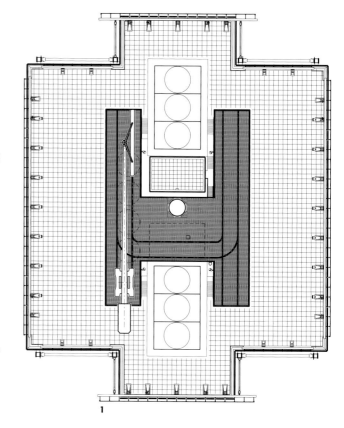

1

1 Roof plan
2 Ground floor plan
3–5 Model views

Photography: Jack Pottle/Esto

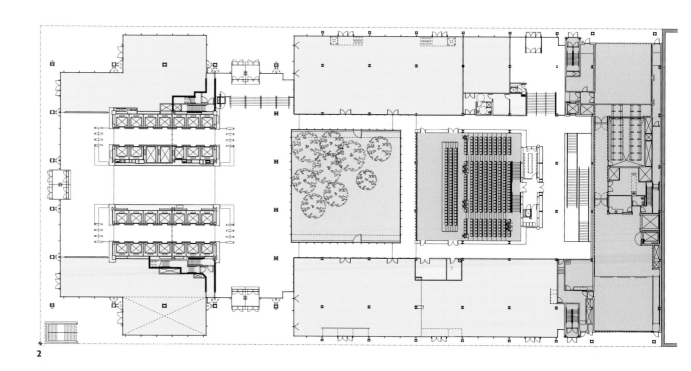

2

Location New York, New York, USA

Expected completion date 2007

Architect Renzo Piano Building Workshop, FXFOWLE ARCHITECTS, PC

Client The New York Times; Forest City Ratner Companies

Developer Forest City Ratner Companies

Structural engineer Thornton/Tomasetti Engineers

Mechanical engineer Flack + Kurtz

Vertical transportation consultant Jenkins & Huntington, Inc.

Landscape architect HM White Site Architects; Cornelia H Oberlander

Contractor AMEC

Height 1046 ft/319 m (including mast)

Above-ground stories 52

Basements 1

Above-ground useable levels 50

Mechanical levels and level numbers 2: floors 28, 52

Use Office

Site area 1,600,000 sq ft/148,640 sq m

Area of typical floor plate 32,000 sq ft/2973 sq m

Basic planning module 5 ft/1.5 m

Principal structural materials Steel

3

4

5

Waterview Tower

Waterview Tower employs a massing strategy that relates to the scale, setbacks and materials of adjacent buildings. It is composed vertically with base, middle and top, and its skin is textured to create a rich and expressive façade. On all façades the residential floors are articulated with curved bay windows that provide unparalleled multi-directional views for all units. The bays create scale and distinguish the residential component from the hotel floors. The building is topped with a band of lower and upper penthouses. These upper floors are defined by the extension of the vertical columns, creating a distinctive top and termination for the tower.

The building's shape accommodates the program as it changes from floor to floor. The base of the building is square in plan and includes lobby, restaurants, hotel, services, and parking. As the uses change higher in the building, so does the shape. The upper 60 stories, containing condominium residences, have a smaller, triangulated floor plate. This plan configuration creates the slender spire-like tower rising from a larger base, and provides south-facing units with views to the east and northeast up the Chicago River corridor to Michigan Avenue and the lake beyond.

The structural frame is constructed entirely of poured-in-place reinforced concrete. Its configuration varies as the functions vary over the height of the building. The lower part, up to the 28th floor, has a central rectangular shear core, "super-columns" (about 7 feet square) at the north edge, and conventional columns at the other three edges. The upper part, the condominium tower, which is much smaller in footprint and offset to the north from the lower part, uses conventional columns and shear walls. Gravity loads and the overturning effects of wind load from the upper part are supported primarily by the core and the super-columns below, with a 9-foot-thick concrete mat at the 28th floor helping make the transfer.

In filling the last gap in the wall of buildings along the river edge, Waterview Tower takes its place in one of the world's great architectural ensembles. The tower's articulated form and crystalline curtainwall are designed to capture magnificent views of the Chicago River, Lake Michigan and Chicago's iconic skyline.

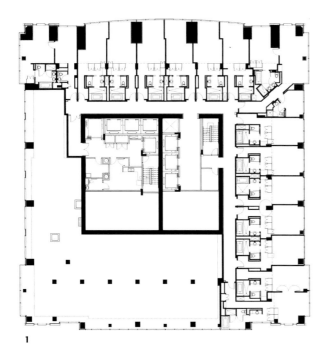

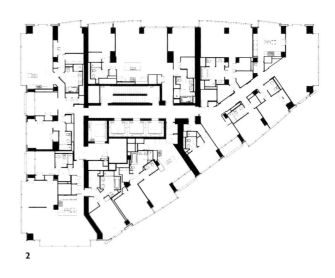

1   Typical hotel floor plan, levels 12–27
2   Typical residential floor plan
3   Looking east along Chicago River
4   Looking west along Chicago River

Photography: Courtesy Teng & Associates, Inc. (3); Russell Phillips, Russell Phillips Photography (4)

3

4

Location Chicago, Illinois, USA	Construction manager Teng Construction, LLC	Area of above-ground building 1,150,000 sq ft/106,835 sq m (approx)
Expected completion date 2009	Project manager Waterview, LLC	Area of typical floor plate 11,000 sq ft/1022 sq m
Design architect Teng & Associates, Inc., Thomas Hoepf, FAIA, Edward Wilkas, AIA	Height 1050 ft/320 m (including pinnacles)	(residential, approx); 14,000 sq ft/1301 sq m (hotel, approx); 23,000 sq ft/2137 sq m (parking, approx)
Client Waterview, LLC & Shangri-La Hotels and Resorts	Above-ground stories 90	Basic planning module 3.3 ft/1 m
Developer Waterview, LLC	Basements 4	Number of parking spaces 512
Structural engineer Teng & Associates, Inc.	Above-ground useable levels 85	Principal structural materials Poured-in-place reinforced concrete
Mechanical engineer Teng & Associates, Inc.	Mechanical levels and level numbers 5: levels M, 28, 67, 89, 90	Other materials Glass, granite, aluminum
Vertical transportation consultant Thyssen Krupp Elevator	Use Residential, hotel, parking	Cost US$400+ M
Landscape architect Teng & Associates, Inc.	Site area 24,086 sq ft/2238 sq m	

China World Trade Center Tower III

China World Trade Center Tower—embodying quiet, purposeful elegance—will mark the larger CWTC development and become the centerpiece of Beijing's Central Business District. It will also be the tallest building in the city.

The tower has a classic columnar proportion of a base, shaft/middle, and crown top integrated in the exterior surfacing and structural expression. The bold tapering profile will create a strong curved silhouette that reaches for the sky. A confident, singular soaring form will contrast with the jumble of new buildings constituting the business district's skyline.

Folded seamlessly into the urban fabric of streets and plazas, the tower's base provides both a visual strength to the lower tower levels and a welcoming transparency to the spaces within. The ground floor has clearly organized entries to the offices on the west and the hotel on the east. The tower's robust base visually and physically anchors the soaring spire.

1   View looking up
2   View from southeast corner
3   Bird's-eye view of masterplan
Renderings: Courtesy Skidmore, Owings & Merrill LLP

1

2

Location Beijing, China
Expected completion date 2007
Architect Skidmore, Owings & Merrill LLP
Client China World Trade Center Co. Ltd.
Structural engineer ARUP
Mechanical engineer PBQA
Vertical transportation consultant Edgett Williams

Landscape architect SWA Group
Height 1083 ft/330 m
Above-ground stories 85
Basements 5
Above-ground useable levels 82
Mechanical levels 8
Use Office, hotel, retail

Site area 391,890 sq ft/36,421sq m
Area of above-ground building 2,372,580 sq ft/220,500 sq m
Area of typical floor plate 32,280 sq ft/3000 sq m
Basic planning module 4.6 ft/1.4 m
Number of parking spaces 1254
Principal structural materials Glass, metal, stone

Shimao International Plaza

This 52-story, 1046-foot-high building is one of the tallest in Shanghai. It stands in the center of the city near the People's Park on Nanjing Road, which is one of China's most important shopping streets, frequented by about 1.5 million potential customers daily.

Ten stories of shopping malls with approximately 645,600 square feet of outlets, and a tower containing office levels and a 770-room five-star hotel, all focus on the central plaza, which is at the heart of the project on Nanjing Road.

Local architects took over the project after the Asian market crash and finished the building with a variation in design and construction.

1&3   General views
2   Section
Photography: PHOTO IMAGING DESIGN, Werner Kirgis (1); HG Esch (3)

1

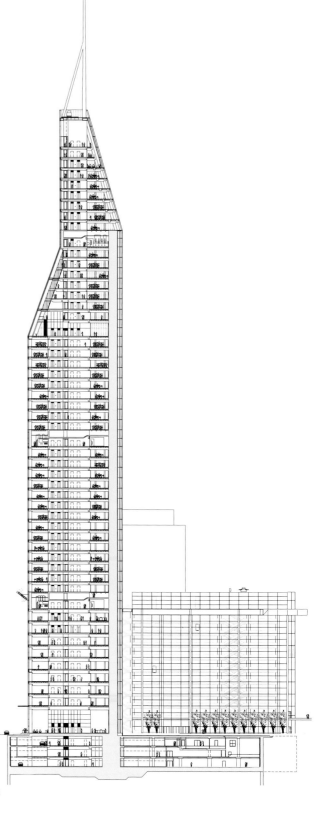

2

3

Location Shanghai, China

Completion date 2006

Design architect Ingenhoven Architects, Düsseldorf

Architect East China Architectural Design & Research Institute (ECADI)

Client Wan Xian International Plaza; Sitico

Initial concept engineer Buro Happold

Structural engineer East China Architectural Design & Research Institute (ECADI)

Mechanical engineer East China Architectural Design & Research Institute (ECADI)

Height 1093 ft/333 m

Above-ground stories 60

Basements 3

Use Retail, office, hotel

Area of above-ground building 1,038,340 sq ft/96,500 sq m

Principal structural materials Reinforced concrete, steel

Rose Rotana Suites

The project is a prestigious hospitality sector development consisting of a 1093-foot-high tower, offering 482 quality hotel-style apartments with both studio and single-bedroom configurations. The ground floor provides main reception and front office areas and the mezzanine floor accommodates administration and services sections. The restaurant and main kitchen are located on the first floor and the second and third floors are devoted to meeting rooms and conference hall. The fourth through to seventh floors comprise house keeping and staff facilities, furnished office units and studio-style residential accommodation.

A separate six-story car-park structure, health club, roof-level swimming pool and MEP systems installation are also included in the scope of the design.

1   Typical floor plan, levels 54–65
2   Typical floor plan, levels 9–28 and 31–51
3   Ground floor plan
Opposite:
    General view

Renderings: Courtesy Khatib & Alami CEC

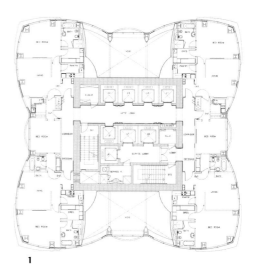

1

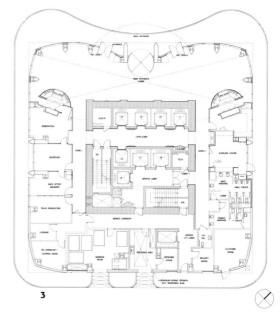

2

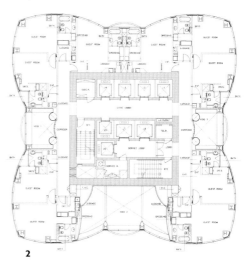

3

Location Dubai, United Arab Emirates	**Height** 1093 ft/333 m	**Area of typical floor plate** 7822.5 sq ft/727 sq m
Expected completion date 2007	**Above-ground stories** 67	**Number of parking spaces** 243
Architect Khatib & Alami CEC	**Basements** 1	**Principal structural materials** Steel
Client Sh. Maktoum Bin Khalifa Bin Saeed Al Maktoum	**Mechanical levels** 7	**Other materials** Concrete
Structural engineer Khatib & Alami CEC	**Above-ground useable levels** 60	
Mechanical engineer Khatib & Alami CEC	**Use** Hotel	
Contractor ABBCO Company	**Total built up area** 547,004 sq ft/50,817 sq m (tower); 121,749 sq ft/11,315 sq m (car park)	

Nanjing International Center

Located on one of the most prominent sites in downtown Nanjing, the 4.3-million-square-foot Nanjing International Center is designed to take advantage of its prime location and serve as a major landmark for the city. This extremely large mixed-use project's diverse program integrates retail, office, residential, hotel, and parking functions and expresses them as distinct components. This organization maximizes the project's development potential and allows for phased construction. Each project component has a strong, recognizable entry and is planned so that it is not functionally compromised by its location within the larger development.

The complex is carefully organized as a series of volumes that respond to the project's site, context and orientation toward the majestic Purple Mountain and Xuanwu Lake. Phase I features an 8-story retail podium with two 38-story symmetrical towers. The podium and towers then set the framework for the focal element of the complex, a 76-story tower, to be completed in Phase II.

The project's retail podium is set back from the street, creating a large civic plaza that activates the street edge and respects the project's urban context. The podium's curved glass façade is designed to complement this large, ceremonial plaza and establish the main entrance for the retail center. Inside, a centrally located skylight illuminates the eight-story atrium, filling the space with natural light and highlighting the retail center's organization.

Each of the two Phase I towers is composed of shifted rectilinear volumes with varying heights. The sloped rooflines of the towers help create a dynamic profile for the project along the city skyline. In order to take advantage of the views toward Purple Mountain and the lake, the towers' façades are angled to allow great exposure. Sawtoothed windows projecting from the façades not only optimize the views but also create a rich interplay of light and shadow on the building.

In Phase II, hotel, condominium, apartment, and office components are stacked in a single tower that reaches a height of 1148 feet. Topped by a sky lobby and restaurants, this signature tower will provide exceptional unobstructed views of the entire city and will define the complex on the Nanjing skyline.

1&3 Exterior rendering
2 North elevation
Renderings: Courtesy Goettsch Partners

1

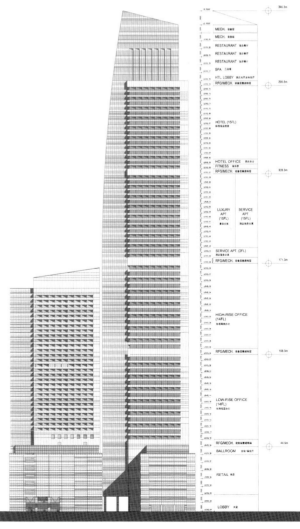

2

Location Nanjing, China

Completion date Phase I: 2006; Phase II: 2007

Architect Goettsch Partners

Client Nanjing International Group, Ltd.

Structural engineer Phase I: East China Architectural Design & Research Institute, Co., Ltd.; Phase II: Magnusson Klemencic

Mechanical engineer Phase I: East China Architectural Design & Research Institute, Co., Ltd.; Phase II: Parsons Brinckerhoff

Landscape architect Phase I: SWA Group

Contractor Phase I: Beijing Urban Construction Group, Co., Ltd.

Developer Nanjing International Group, Ltd.

Height Phase I: 551 ft/168 m; Phase II: 1148 ft/350 m

Above-ground stories Phase I: 38; Phase II: 76

Basements Phase I: 2; Phase II: 3

Above-ground useable levels Phase I: 34; Phase II: 70

Mechanical levels and level numbers Phase I: 1 (floor 24); Phase II: 5 (floors 9, 24, 39, 57, 76)

Use Hotel, office, residential, retail, parking

Site area 349,453 sq ft/32,477 sq m

Area of above-ground building Phase I: 2,438,582 sq ft/226,634 sq m; Phase II: 1,893,760 sq ft/176,000 sq m

Area of typical floor plate Phase I: 16,678 sq ft/1550 sq m; Phase II: 23,941 sq ft/2225 sq m

Basic planning module 4.92 ft/1.5 m

Number of parking spaces Phase I: 625; Phase II: 510

Principal structural materials Phase I: reinforced concrete; Phase II: steel

Other materials Exteriors: aluminum/glass curtain wall, granite

Al Mas Tower

Located 20 kilometres south of Dubai and forming the centerpiece of the Jumeirah Lakes development, the 68-story Al Mas Tower has been designed by Atkins to reflect the character and uniqueness of the Diamond Exchange facility accommodated within. The 1181-foot-tall building offers prominent views both of the Lake and the central spine of the development. The tower accommodates 63 commercial office floors above the three-story podium. Car parking for 1800 cars is provided within the five-level basement.

The design of this tower has been inspired by the requirement for an optimal environment for viewing precious stones and responds in providing two oval-shaped towers of varying height that overlap along their east–west axis. The lower, north-facing tower has a semi-transparent elevation in order to benefit from the cool, ambient north light. The taller, south facing tower is protected by a high performance treatment to its exterior.

Various aspects of the building design combine to express the tower's tendency to become lighter as it ascends. This is emphasized by the continuing height of the taller tower, the further prominence of the mast and the tapering of the narrow side elevation of both towers.

The podium design is inspired by the cut of a diamond with projecting facets. Each facet cantilevers out over the lake, making them visible from all aspects of the tower and surrounding buildings when viewed from above. The glazed elements of the retail area reflect the water surrounding the tower, creating an animated façade.

The podium accommodates a mall, conference rooms and health spa on the first floor and the Diamond Exchange Centre on the second floor. The mall extends from ground to first floor and offers magnificent views of the lake from its double-volume atrium space. The north-facing Diamond Exchange is externally treated with a high color spectrum glazing that will facilitate world-class diamond inspection and trading.

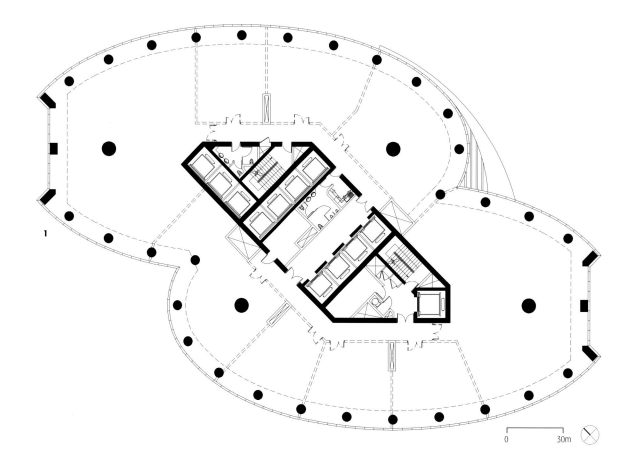

1

0   30m

1 Typical floor plan
2 Tower perspective
3 Elevation
Renderings: Courtesy Atkins

2

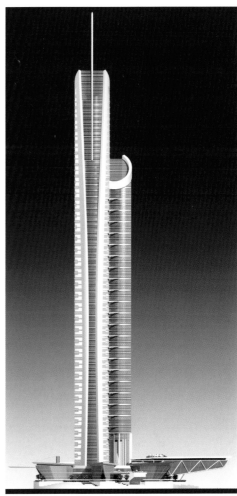

3

Location Dubai, United Arab Emirates
Expected completion date 2007
Architect Atkins
Client Nakheel
Structural engineer Atkins
Mechanical engineer Atkins
Vertical transportation consultant Atkins
Landscape architect Al Khatib Cracknell

Contractor JV Arabian Contracting Co; Taisei Corporation
Developer Dubai Metals & Commodities Centre
Project manager Faithful + Gould
Height 1181 ft/360 m
Above-ground stories 68
Basements 5
Above-ground useable levels 68
Mechanical levels 3

Use Office
Site area 165,700 sq ft/15,393 sq m
Area of above-ground building 1,973,384 sq ft/183,400 sq m
Area of typical floor plate 17,216 sq ft/1600 sq m
Number of parking spaces 1810
Principal structural materials Reinforced concrete
Other materials Reflective gray and tinted green glass
aluminum panel cladding

Bank of America Tower

Upon completion, the Bank of America Tower will be the most environmentally responsible high-rise office building in the United States, and the first to strive for the US Green Building Council's Leadership in Energy and Environmental Design (LEED) Platinum designation. The project incorporates innovative, high-performance technologies to use dramatically less energy, consume less potable water and provide a healthy and productive indoor environment.

Designed by Cook+Fox Architects of New York, the glass, steel, and aluminum skyscraper is inspired by the famed Crystal Palace—the first glass and light-frame metal building in the US, erected in Bryant Park in 1853. The tower's sculptural surfaces and crisp folds will be animated by the movement of the sun and moon, while its highly transparent glass will provide evocative views both from and through the space. The building's high-performance technologies include an on-site 5.1-megawatt cogeneration plant, and water conservation features that will save 10.3 million gallons of water annually. With floor-to-ceiling glazing, exceptionally clean air, and thermal controls at each workstation, the building will offer an office environment of unparalleled quality.

Public amenities include improvements to the surrounding pedestrian and transit circulation, and an urban garden room that will serve as an inviting extension of Bryant Park. As an integral part of the project, Cook+Fox Architects will also restore and reconstruct the historic Henry Miller's Theater, creating a state-of-the-art Broadway playhouse that captures the intimacy and proportions of the original 1918 Allen, Ingalls & Hoffman theater. The Georgian-style landmarked façade will be preserved and restored; original details will be salvaged and incorporated into the design of the new, fully modern theater.

The building will serve as the headquarters for Bank of America's operations in New York City; the bank will occupy roughly half of the 2.1-million-square-foot, 55-story tower. It is hoped that, by offering a fundamentally different vision for the urban environment, the Bank of America Tower will set the standard for a new generation of high-rise buildings.

1 View of urban garden room
2 View of tower from Bryant Park
3 Day/night time lapsed views of tower from Bryant Park
4 44th floor plan
5 34th floor plan

Renderings: ©Screampoint for Cook+Fox Architects LLP (1); © dbox for Cook+Fox Architects LLP (2,3); Cook+Fox Architects LLP (4,5)

1

2

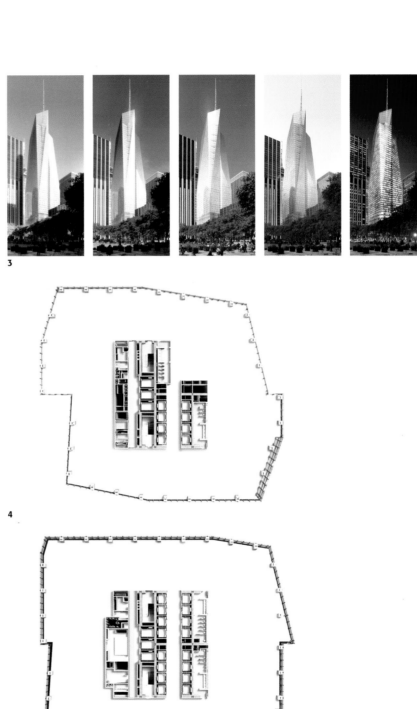

3

4

5

Location New York, New York, USA

Expected completion date 2008

Design architect Cook+Fox Architects

Executive architect Adamson Associates Architects

Client and developer Bank of America at One Bryant Park, LLC, a joint venture between The Durst Organization and Bank of America

Structural engineer Severud Associates

Mechanical engineer Jaros, Baum & Bolles

Vertical transportation consultant Van Deusen & Associates

Landscape architect Andropogon Associates Ltd.

Contractor Tishman Construction Corporation

Height approx 945 ft/288 m (to top of tower); 1200 ft /366 m (to top of spire)

Above-ground stories 55

Basements 3

Above-ground useable levels 49

Mechanical levels and level numbers 9: C3, C2, C1, 7, 7M, 52, 53, 54, 55

Use Office, theater, retail

Site area 87,864 sq ft/8163 sq m

Area of above-ground building 2,100,000 sq ft/195,090 sq m plus 50,000 sq ft/4645 sq m theater

Area of typical floor plate 36,650 sq ft/3405 sq m (tower); 71,000 sq ft/6596 sq m (podium)

Basic planning module 5 ft/1.5 m

Number of parking spaces 0

Principal structural materials Steel and concrete superstructure; glass and aluminum curtainwall

Other materials Low VOC materials, recycled and recyclable products, materials procured within 500 miles; lobby materials include bamboo, stone, leather, blackened stainless steel

23 Marina

23 Marina is an exclusive waterfront development located at the beginning of Dubai Marina, overlooking the Arabian Gulf, Sheikh Zayed Road and Dubai Media City.

It is an urbane precinct of high-rise towers overlooking the man-made waterfront and features a charming boulevard lined with exclusive retail outlets and restaurants.

Towering to 1276 feet, 23 Marina manifests itself in exposed concrete and tinted blue glass. Podiums and protruding triangular balconies that contrast with its distinct profile accentuate its powerful form. The spire at the pinnacle is embraced by triangular canopies covering the terrace, further streamlining the building's form.

The building program is a combination of luxurious two- and three-bedroom apartments, and lavish duplexes with varying vistas ranging from ocean views to views of the city, marina, and Jumeirah beach. The 90-story tower encompasses 48 exclusive duplex apartments from level 62 up to level 85. Each of these 5733-square-foot duplexes offers unique features such as private elevators, open deck plunge pools, and private Jacuzzis. All apartments feature contemporary internationally styled interiors with marble and wood finishing and a fully equipped kitchen.

The tower features an imposing six-story entrance while the residential development also boasts an elite health spa, landscaped garden and jogging track, indoor and temperature controlled pools, and a children's pool.

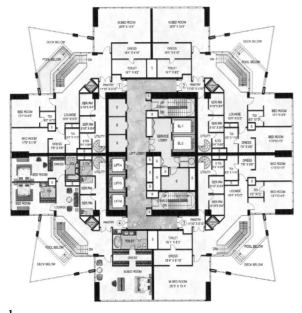

1

3

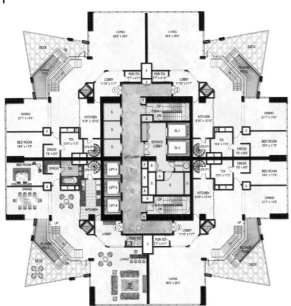

4

2

Location Dubai, United Arab Emirates
Expected completion date 2008
Concept architect Architect Hafeez Contractor
Local architect KEO International Consultants
Developer Hircon International LLC (a Hiranandani–ETA STAR joint venture)
Wind engineering consultant Rowan Williams Davies & Irwin Inc.
Project manager KEO International Consultants

Interior designer KEO International Consultants
Height 1276 ft/389 m
Above-ground stories 90
Basements 4
Use Residential
Area of above-ground building 1,489,292 sq ft/138,410 sq m

6

1   *Duplex apartment (levels 62–85), upper level floor plan*
2   *Duplex apartment, lower level floor plan*
3   *Typical floor plan, levels 35–58*
4   *Typical floor plan, levels 8–31*
5   *General view of 23 Marina tower*
6   *Lobby*

Renderings: Courtesy Architect Hafeez Contractor

Al Hamra Firdous Tower

Located in Kuwait City, Al Hamra Firdous Tower is part of a commercial complex that is comprised of offices, a health club, and a shopping mall with theaters and a food court. Reaching 1312 feet, the iconic office tower will be the tallest building in Kuwait. The total gross area of the tower with the two basement floors is more than 2 million square feet.

A quarter of each floor is removed and rotated from west to east along ascending levels. The resultant massing maximizes the sea views to the north while keeping the floor area of almost 26,000 square feet constant. This simple operation creates an illusion of a twisting building and thus achieves a complex visual perception. The apex of the building is a natural resolution of its geometry to a rising spiral.

The tower's core is covered in stone cladding, giving it a monolithic character. A glass and metal curtain wall lends transparency and light to the interior while optimizing views toward the sea.

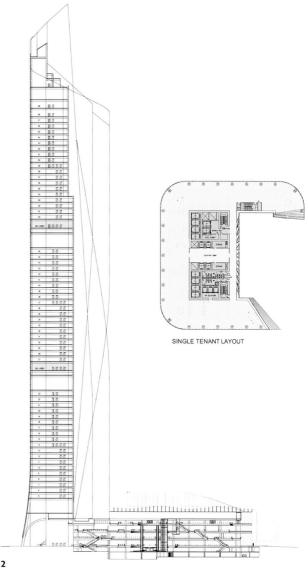

SINGLE TENANT LAYOUT

1

2

1   Skybridge
2   Section
3   Night view

Renderings: Courtesy Skidmore, Owings & Merrill LLP

Location Sharq, Kuwait
Expected completion date 2009
Architect Skidmore, Owings & Merrill LLP
Associate architect Al-Jazera Consultants
Client Al Hamra Real Estate
Structural engineer Skidmore, Owings & Merrill LLP
Mechanical engineer Skidmore, Owings & Merrill LLP
Vertical transportation consultant Van Deusen Associates

Contractor Ahmadiah Contracting & Trading Co.
Project manager Turner Construction International
Height 1312 ft/400 m
Above-ground stories 70
Basements 3
Above-ground useable levels 66
Mechanical levels 4
Use Office

Site area 118,220 sq ft/10,987 sq m
Area of above-ground building 2,098,200 sq ft/195,000 sq m
Area of typical floor plate 25,824 sq ft/2,400 sq m (gross)
Basic planning module 5 ft/1.5 m
Number of parking spaces 91 (tower) 1652 (carpark)
Principal structural materials Reinforced concrete
Other materials Glass and stone curtainwall

Trump International Hotel & Tower

The Trump International Hotel & Tower Chicago will be the tallest building project completed in the United States since the Sears Tower in 1974. The project is a unique mixture of luxury condominiums, parking for 1100 cars, 130,000 square feet of retail space, and hotel/condominiums.

The architectural design strategy is contextual: the south side of the tower parallels the bank of the Chicago River, enabling the structure to vary from Chicago's north–south grid to create a special condition. The building is shaped to reflect its functions within the tower and the need to provide as many views up and down the river as possible.

Through the contemporary synthesis of adjacent building fabrics and modulations, the tower expresses a truly modern architecture, consistent with Chicago's heritage. Setbacks in the tower's massing provide connections to the surrounding context and integrate the tower into the overall composition of its riverfront setting.

The use of clear glass and a very light palette of materials on the façade will enhance the detail and whiteness of the nearby Wrigley Building and will relate to the Mies van der Rohe-designed IBM Building to the west, with the spacing and articulation of the polished stainless steel mullion system and the tall columnar base at grade.

Materials include a light silver palette of brushed stainless steel spandrel panels and clear anodized aluminum that reflects and refracts light from the sun. At its base, the body of the building is raised 30 feet above the entrance on Wabash avenue and nearly 70 feet above the Chicago River, opening up an extensive, landscaped promenade that steps down like terraces on a hillside for three levels, until it meets the river. A suspended and cantilevered clear glass canopy at the Wabash entry will protect guests from wind and water at the automobile drop-off points. A circular ramp, clad in translucent laminated glass and back-lit during the evening, will connect the Wabash grade level to the parking levels in the tower.

1

1   Skyline view from Chicago River
2   Setbacks relate the tower to its surrounding context
3   Section

Renderings: Courtesy Skidmore, Owings & Merrill LLP

2

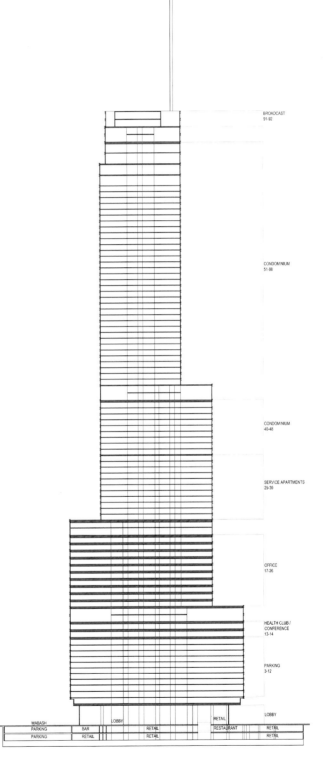

3

Location Chicago, Illinois, USA

Expected completion date 2008

Architect Skidmore Owings and Merrill LLP; Adrian D Smith, FAIA, Consulting Design Partner

Residential interior architect PMG Architects

Client Trump International Hotel & Tower

Developer Donald J Trump

Structural engineer Skidmore, Owings and Merrill LLP; William Baker, Partner in charge of Structural Engineering

Mechanical engineer WMA Consulting Engineers, Ltd

Vertical transportation consultant Lerch, Bates & Associates

Landscape architect Peter Lindsay Schaudt Landscape Architecture, Inc.

Contractor Bovis Lend Lease LMB, Inc.

Height 1361 ft/415 m (to top of spire)

Above-ground stories 92

Basements 3

Above-ground useable levels 86

Mechanical levels and level numbers 5: levels 2, 15, 28, 50, 90

Use Residential, hotel, condominium, parking, retail

Site area 102,748 sq ft/9545 sq m

Area of above-ground building 2,380,000 sq ft/221,102 sq m

Area of typical floor plate 44,410 sq ft/4126 sq m; 35,150 sq ft/3265 sq m; 24,880 sq ft/2311 sq m; 16,250 sq ft/1510 sq m

Basic planning module 5 ft/1.5 m

Number of parking spaces 847 in tower, 109 in below-grade garage

Principal structural materials Reinforced concrete

Other materials Exterior curtain wall: aluminum frame with low-e double-glazed insulated glass units with brushed stainless steel spandrel panels and polished stainless steel wing shaped vertical mullions; exposed columns are brushed stainless steel

Dubai Towers – Doha

Winner of an international design competition, the Dubai Towers is a dynamic and elegantly proportioned skyscraper, rising 1460 feet above the Arabian Gulf. The development will contain world-class retail, offices, hotel, serviced apartments, and residential units.

Structured around a robust concrete core, with perimeter columns and cross-bracing, the tall crystalline tower ascends above the podium in three inclined segments, terminating at the spire. Service floors are introduced at strategic levels to satisfy structural stability and servicing requirements. The building's geometry and internal layouts are oriented to optimize views to the sea. The angled glass façades and bold sloping roofs will glow with the reflection of the changing desert sun by day, and sparkle in quiet elegance as dusk descends.

This distinctive development is set in an urban plaza with generous landscaping and water features. A circular porte-cochere leads to the hotel and office lobbies, while the retail facilities and apartments are accessed along the pedestrian corniche.

1   Typical hotel floor plan, levels 33–40
2   Typical office floor plan, levels 5–32
3   The building's orientation and geometry offer magnificent views of the sea
4   Dubai Towers rising majestically above the Arabian Gulf
5   Northeast elevation
6   Panoramic lifts scaling the north tower façade animate the building by day and by night

Renderings: Courtesy RMJM Dubai

The granite-clad podium houses exclusive shops, restaurants, and entertainment facilities. Entrances to the various building components are highlighted by projecting glass 'crystals'. The terraced podium offers inviting pedestrian access to the shops and waterfront cafés, and provides a sculpted mass to visually anchor the slender structure.

Within the lower levels of the tower, precast concrete slabs on steel beams spanning from core to perimeter produce open and flexible office space, equipped with state-of-the-art data communication and building management systems.

Located midway up the tower, the 5-star hotel and serviced apartments enjoy exclusivity and magnificent views of the Gulf. Panoramic lifts scaling the north tower façade connect the lobby to the suites, sky atrium, and dining and spa facilities, animating the building both by day and by night.

Luxury one- to four-bedroom apartments are accommodated on the uppermost floors. The design exploits the sloping roof forms as unique opportunities to create interesting loft apartments.

On completion, the Dubai Towers will be a distinguished landmark and the tallest structure in Qatar, an iconic and symbolic reference for the Emirate of Dubai.

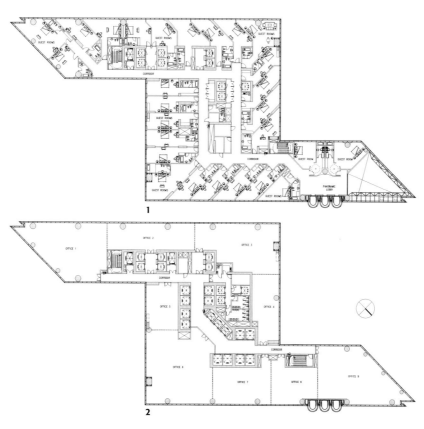

1

2

3

4

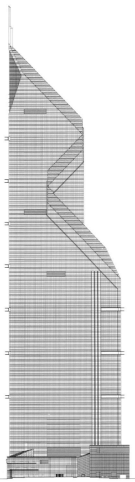

5

6

Location Doha, Qatar

Expected completion date 2008

Architect RMJM Dubai; concept design Hazel WS Wong

Client Dubai International Properties

Structural engineer RMJM Dubai

Specialist high-rise structural engineer Hyder Consulting

Mechanical engineer RMJM Dubai

Vertical transportation consultant HH Angus and Associates

Landscape architect Al Khatib Cracknell

Contractor Al Habtoor – Al Jaber Joint Venture

Project manager Hill International

Height 1460 ft/445 m (including spire)

Above-ground stories 86

Basements 4

Above-ground useable levels 80

Mechanical levels and level numbers 7: levels 4, 32 (part), 41, 57, 83, 84, 85

Use Retail (GF–2), amenities and support (3–4), office (5–32), hotel (33–40), serviced apartments (42–56), unserviced apartments (59–82)

Site area (excluding parking structure) 142,742 sq ft/ 13,266 sq m

Area of above-ground building (excluding parking structure) 2,044,400 sq ft/190,000 sq m

Area of typical floor plate 9684–27,976 sq ft/900–2600 sq m

Basic planning module 3.9 ft/1.2 m

Number of parking spaces 3500 (1000 on site; 2500 in satellite structure)

Principal structural materials Structural steel, composite steel and reinforced concrete, precast and cast in-situ

Other materials High performance low-E reflective and clear glass unitized curtain wall, stone cladding, stainless steel, aluminum panels and accents

Federation Tower

Federation Tower is part of the Moscow International Business Centre, 'Moscow-City', that includes almost 27 million square feet of office, hotel, retail and entertainment areas in several skyscrapers.

Federation Tower is a dynamic composition of two upward-reaching glass towers. The towers are formed as two spherical, equilateral triangles that narrow toward the top and grow out of a four-story stone base. The rift between the base and the towers is enhanced through a rebounding, four-story-tall lens. The central vertical axis of the complex is formed by a 'pin', comprised of glass elevators, that extends over the skyscraper and is connected to the two towers by several bridges.

Inside the base and lens is a spacious, 14-story atrium with supermarkets, conference halls, banks, shopping malls, airline offices, cafés and restaurants. The complex has many functions: it includes approximately 2.7 million square feet of office space; apartments and a hotel; retail and restaurant areas; several entertainment and wellness areas, as well as a panoramic restaurant atop the taller tower that has a spectacular view over the entire Russian capital.

1   Typical office floor plan
2   General view – night

Rendering: 'Federation Tower' Planning Association mbH

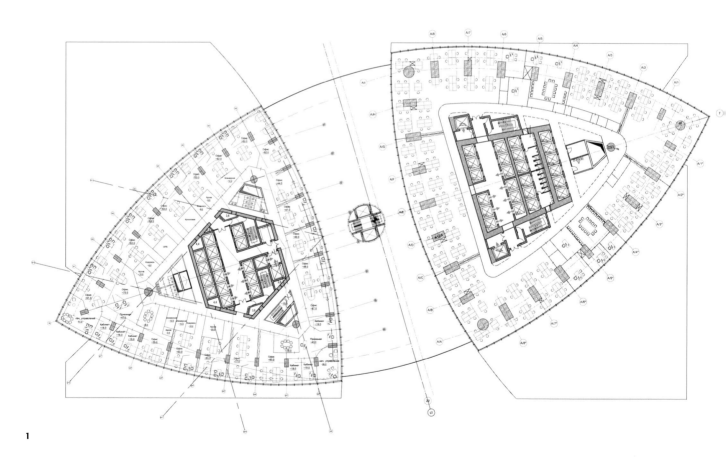

1

Location Moscow, Russia

Expected completion date 2008

Architect 'Federation Tower' Planning Association mbH: Prof. Peter Schweger, ASP Schweger Assoziierte Gesamtplanung GmbH and Sergei Tchoban, nps tchoban voss GbR Architekten BDA; AM Prasch; P Sigl; S Tchoban; E Voss

Client Mirax-City

Structural engineer Thornton Tomasetti Engineers, New York

Mechanical engineer Ebert International

Vertical transportation consultant Ebert International

Height Tower A 1162.5 ft/354.33 m; Tower B 795.3 ft/ 242.4 m (with antenna 1470.7 ft/448.25 m)

Above-ground stories Tower A 93; Tower B 62

Basements 4

Use Mixed: office, hotel, apartments, retail, entertainment

Site area 116,638 sq ft/10,840 sq m

Area of above-ground building 4,551,480 sq ft/423,000 sq m

Area of typical floor plate 26,900 sq ft/2500 sq m

Principal structural materials Reinforced concrete

Nanjing Greenland Financial Center

The Nanjing Greenland Financial Center tower form was derived from three elements of life in Nanjing: the Yangtze River; the lush green landscape environment and garden city atmosphere; and the dragon and column iconography so prevalent in Chinese culture.

The tower is shaped in a triangular form to relate to the shape and size of the building's site and to take maximum advantage of the views of the mountains, lake, and historic building features in Nanjing. The stepping of the tower relates to the functions within the tower and the desire to shape the floor plates to achieve maximum efficiency.

The curved corners of the tower present a soft, continuous surface to the exterior of the building. The tower is comprised of office, hotel, and retail above grade, with retail and parking below grade. The top of the tower houses restaurants and a public observatory.

Occupying the first seven floors of the site is a vertically organized shopping complex with a skylight atrium that runs diagonally through from street to street, allowing for interior circulation to the retail floors and pedestrian passage through the site.

The vertical and horizontal clear glass seams separating the differentially textured glass surfaces of the tower are metaphorically analogous to the clear water of the Yangtze River separating two interlocking dragon forms. The exterior treatment changes direction from one major component to the other in an effort to more clearly identify the two dragon forms interlocked around the central core of the building. The exterior wall has a distinctive directional feature. Each pane of glass is angled at seven degrees from the occupied space and the module alternates or staggers by 2.5 feet from floor to floor, giving the skin of the building a scale-like quality.

At the top of the building is a significant spire element that soars to 1503 feet, one of China's tallest structures. This feature is seen as a major identity element that will culminate the expression of the tower atrium feature and will reinforce the dominance of this tower as a landmark in the city.

1   Podium typical floor plan
2   Aerial model view
3   General view, showing scale-like appearance of building's skin
Photography: Steinkamp Ballogg Photography

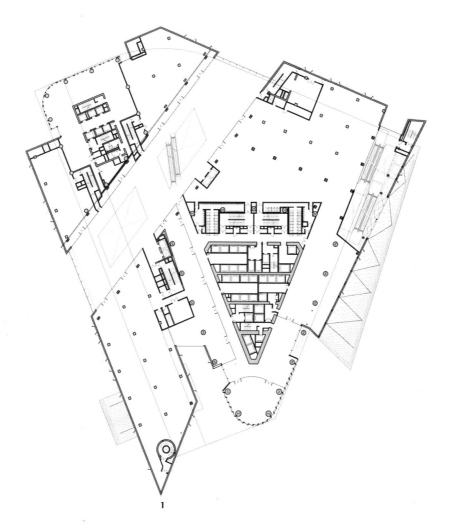

1

2

3

Location Nanjing, China

Expected completion date 2008

Architect Skidmore, Owings & Merrill LLP, Adrian D Smith, FAIA, Consulting Design Partner

Associate architect East China Architectural Design & Research Institute Co. Ltd (ECADI)

Client Nanjing State-Owned Assets & Greenland Financial Center Co. Ltd

Structural engineer Skidmore, Owings & Merrill LLP, William Baker, Partner in charge

Mechanical engineer Skidmore, Owings & Merrill LLP

Vertical transportation consultant Lerch, Bates & Associates Inc.

Landscape architect SWA Group

Project manager Robert Forest of Skidmore, Owings & Merrill LLP

Height 1085.5 ft/330.85 m to top of roof 1250 ft/380 m to top of spire roof; 1476 ft/450 m to top of spire/antenna

Above-ground stories 66

Basements 5

Above-ground useable levels 62

Mechanical levels and level numbers 4: levels 10, 35, 60, 66

Use Office, hotel, retail

Site area 201,449 sq ft/18,722 sq m

Area of above-ground building 2,118,622 sq ft/196,898 sq m

Area of typical floor plate 26,480 sq ft/2461 sq m; 19,960 sq ft/1855 sq m; 15,710 sq ft/1460 sq m

Basic planning module 5 ft/1.5 m

Number of parking spaces 989 below grade

Principal structural materials Composite reinforced concrete core and steel framing

Other materials Exterior curtain wall: aluminum frame with low-e double glazed insulated glass units with brushed stainless steel spandrel panels and polished stainless steel wing shaped vertical mullions; exposed columns are brushed stainless steel

International Commerce Center

This 118-story tower is the centerpiece of a master plan for a massive reclamation project in West Kowloon called Union Square. Facing downtown Hong Kong across Victoria Harbour, the development was conceived as a transportation hub connecting Hong Kong to Chep Lap Kok airport, and a new urban center containing residential, office, retail, hotel, and recreation facilities.

The brief for the International Commerce Center called for a 2.7-million-square-foot office provision, together with a 300-room boutique hotel, and an observation deck on the 90th floor. The office floors are generous in scale, with central cores. The hotel rooms occupy the upper levels of the tower, radiating from a cylindrical atrium topped by a restaurant. A self-contained vertical city, the tower will be one of the tallest structures in the world upon completion in 2010.

The winning entry in a design competition, the scheme succeeds in wedding the high-rise building form with a highly efficient structural and operational agenda. Square in plan, the tower's re-entrant corners taper to create a graceful profile against the sky. At its base, the tower splays out, creating an impression of a plant emerging from the ground. The walls of the tower peel away at the base, creating canopies on three sides, and a dramatic atrium on the north side. The atrium gestures toward the rest of the development and serves as a public linkage space to the retail and rail station functions.

1   Context view
2   Ground floor plan
3   Approaching the tower through the Dragon Tail
4   Bird's eye view of the Dragon Tail
5   Interior rendering of restaurant tower top
6   Hotel atrium
7   Dragon Tail

Photography: Jock Pottle (4)

Renderings: Superview (1); AMD (3,5,7); dbox (6)

1

Location Hong Kong, China
Expected completion date 2010
Design architect Kohn Pedersen Fox Associates PC
Associate architect Wong & Ouyang (HK) Ltd.
Client Harbour Vantage Management Limited
Structural engineer ARUP (HK)
Mechanical engineer JRPL
Vertical transportation consultant Lerch Bates & Associates, Inc.

Landscape architect Belt Collins & Associates
Height 1608 ft/490 m
Above-ground stories 118
Basements 4
Above-ground useable levels 100
Mechanical level numbers 6–8, 41–42, 77–78, 100–101, 117
Use Office, hotel, retail, public observation deck, Kowloon Station airport express rail link

Area of above-ground building 2,500,000 sq ft/232,250 sq m
Area of typical floor plate 27,492 sq ft/2555 sq m
Basic planning module 4.9 ft/1.5 m
Number of parking spaces 224
Principal structural materials Reinforced concrete, steel
Other materials Aluminum, glass

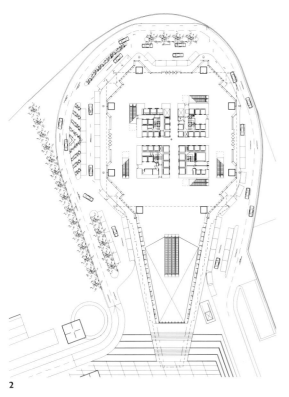

2

5

6

3

4

7

Shanghai World Financial Center

A tall building creates a link between the earth and the sky. The interaction between these two realms gives rise to the physical form and structure of the Shanghai World Financial Center tower. A square prism (used by the ancient Chinese to represent the earth) is intersected by 'cosmic arcs,' accentuating the building's vertical ascent. This geometry is further dramatized by carving a great sky portal into the upper levels of the building. Reinforcing the fundamental geometry of the building, the sky portal widens as it rises, topped by a sky bridge that joins the opposite corners of the tower into a single form.

A diverse and dynamic mixed-use development, the Shanghai World Financial Center will incorporate facilities that not only support Liujiazui's current activities as a business district, but also create a sense of vitality and activity after working hours. To this end, offices, conference facilities, and commercial establishments are coupled with a luxury hotel, high-end retail and dining facilities, and an observation deck located in the building's dramatic sky portal.

Establishing observation facilities at the very top of the building—the 101st floor at 1614 feet and the 100th floor at 1549 feet—will supersede Toronto's CN Tower, where the observatory is located at 1467 feet. In addition, the 94th floor of the Shanghai World Financial Center will host a huge observation space totaling more than 7532 square feet and will also serve as a space for entertainment events, information sessions, and other publicity-related gatherings.

The overall redesign and programmatic configuration of the Shanghai World Financial Center will support the building's role as a major Asian landmark and a symbol of redevelopment in Shanghai. The uniqueness of the Shanghai World Financial Center will establish it as a powerful new icon for the City of Shanghai.

1

Location Shanghai, China
Expected completion date 2007
Design architect Kohn Pedersen Fox Associates PC
Executive architect Irie Miyake Architects and Engineers
Project architect Mori Building Architects & Engineers
Architect of record East China Architectural & Design Research Institute Co. Ltd (ECADI)
Client Shanghai World Financial Center Corporation, a subsidiary of Mori Building Company
Structural engineer Leslie Robertson Associates RLLP
Mechanical engineer Kenchiku Setsubi Sekkei Kenkyusho

Vertical transportation consultant Otis Elevator
Landscape architect Hargreaves and Associates
Contractor China State Construction; Shanghai Construction
Developer Mori Building Company, Ltd.
Height 1614 ft/492 m
Above-ground stories 101
Basements 3
Above-ground useable levels 92
Mechanical levels and level numbers 9: floors 7, 22, 33, 44, 55, 66, 77, 89, 90

Use Mixed: office, luxury hotel, retail, gallery, and observation deck
Site area 4,059,748 sq ft/377,300 sq m
Area of above-ground building 2,394,681 sq ft/222,554 sq m
Area of typical floor plate 35,874 sq ft/3334 sq m
Basic planning module 3.9 ft/1.2 m
Number of parking spaces 1100
Principal structural materials Concrete, steel
Other materials Exterior: glass, steel, stone; interior: stone, stainless steel, glass, wood
Cost US$800 M

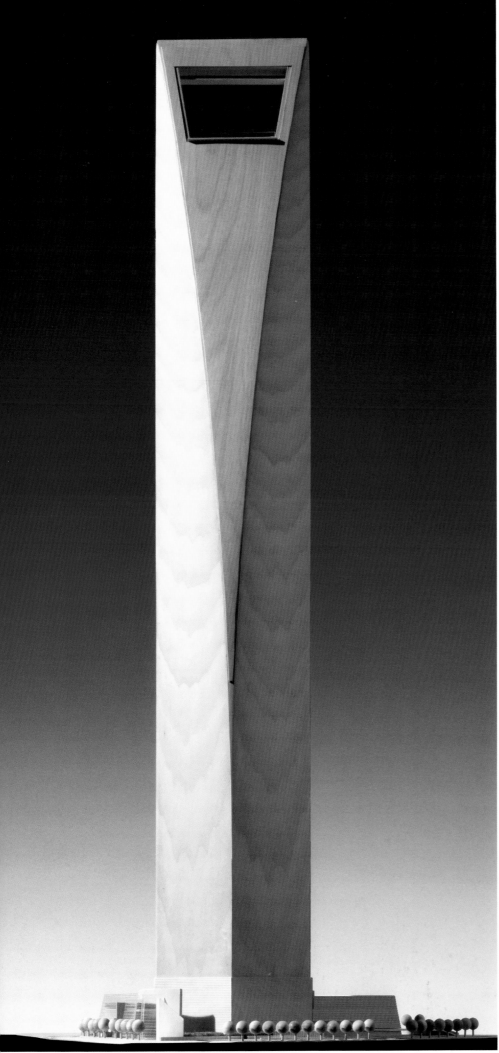

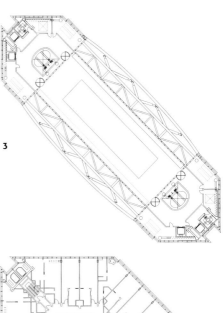

3

4

5

1   View from northwest
2   Context view
3   Upper level floor plan
4   Middle level floor plan
5   Lower level floor plan

Photography: Jock Pottle (1); Rendering: Crystal (2)

Lotte World II Tower

Lotte World II Tower is an urban entertainment center placed along Busan's harbor at a prominent site between the city of Busan and Yong Do Island. This location provides the only access to the island. This landmark facility serves as a commercial/entertainment anchor for the entire district. The combination of retail, Imax theaters, the latest in Cineplex technology, motion simulators, movie rides, nightclubs, and restaurants offers a dynamic and unique destination location.

Visibility, a critical characteristic of entertainment, was a strong stimulant for integrating the major blocks of this development. Visibility from one venue to another encourages interaction and movement while creating an energized environment. The expression of the individual retailers, venues, events and activities articulates and gives scale to an otherwise introverted facility. By purposefully exposing all of these things, Lotte World II becomes an exuberant entertainment destination.

The 107-story, 800-room five-star hotel and office component of this development will be among the tallest buildings in the world. The tower will be a landmark for the region while creating a gateway and focal point for the harbor and Busan. The site plan respects and responds to these landform issues.

The horizontal marks along the northern edge of the tower are derived from a series of references symbolic to both Busan and Korea. A spirit post or Korean totem ('ChangSung') is a figure that mediates between the earth and beyond. The spirit posts stand guard over the ancient village ensuring peace and prosperity of the inhabitants by expelling evil. The concept for the tower is to embody the nature of these primitive spirit posts within a contemporary vocabulary. Deep cuts in the wood create the mask of the totem. These cuts, with Korea's traditional color spectrum, 'Sack Dong', reinterpreted in the tower, are horizontal marks at significant programmatic points along the height of the facility. The openings at the top are observation lounges and the chairman's boardroom and office. The lower marks indicate the hotel's lobbies and lounges.

1 Typical office floor plan (levels 31–51)
2 54th floor plan
3 81st floor plan
4 82nd floor plan
5 A beacon by the sea, Lotte II will be a center of nightlife and commerce
6 Playful art provides focus to the public gathering space
7 Careful planning requires consideration of the site's relationship to the urban context

Renderings: Courtesy Parker Durrant International

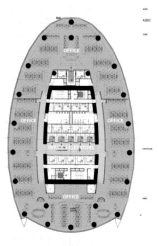
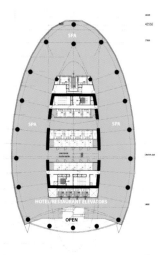

1

2

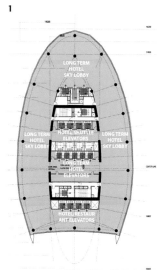
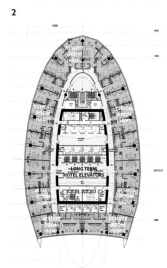

3

4

5

6

7

Location Busan, South Korea
Expected completion date 2008
Architect Parker Durrant International
Client Lotte Moolsan Co. Ltd: Lotte Shopping/Lotte Hotel
Structural engineer Magnuson Klemencic Associates
Mechanical engineer The Durrant Group, Inc.
Vertical transportation consultant Lerch Bates & Associates, Inc.
Landscape architect Parker Durrant International

Height 1673 ft/510 m
Above-ground stories 107
Basements 6
Above-ground useable levels 103
Mechanical levels and level numbers 4: floors 25,52,80,105
Use Hotel, office, retail
Site area 439,180 sq ft/40,816 sq m

Area of above-ground building Low-rise: 3,121,896 sq ft/
290,139 sq m; high-rise: 2,747,082 sq ft/255,305 sq m; total:
5,868,977 sq ft/545,444 sq m
Area of typical floor plate 25,500 sq ft/2369 sq m
Basic planning module Radial grid
Number of parking spaces 2300 below grade
Principal structural materials Steel, concrete and composite
Other materials Glass, metal panel

Burj Dubai

The Burj Dubai, planned as the world's tallest building, will be the centerpiece of a large scale, mixed-use development comprised of residential, commercial, hotel, entertainment, shopping and leisure outlets with open green spaces, water features, pedestrian boulevards, a shopping mall and a tourist-oriented old town.

The design of the tower is derived from the geometries of a regional desert flower and the patterning systems embodied in Islamic architecture. It combines historical and cultural influences with cutting-edge technology to achieve a high-performance building. Its massing is manipulated in the vertical dimension to induce maximum vortex shedding and to minimize the impact of wind on the tower's movement.

The tower is composed of three elements arranged around a central core. As the tower rises from the flat desert base, setbacks occur at each element in an upward spiraling pattern, decreasing the mass of the tower as it reaches toward the sky. At the top, the central core emerges and is sculpted to form a spire. A Y-shaped floor plan maximizes views of the Persian Gulf. Construction began in January 2004 and will be completed at the end of 2009.

1

Location Dubai, United Arab Emirates

Expected completion date 2009

Architect Skidmore, Owings & Merrill LLP, Adrian D Smith, FAIA, Consulting Design Partner

Local consultant Hyder Consulting Middle East Ltd

Client EMAAR Properties

Structural engineer Skidmore, Owings & Merrill LLP

Mechanical engineer Skidmore, Owings & Merrill LLP

Vertical transportation consultant Lerch, Bates & Associates, Inc

Contractor Samsung-BESIX-Arabtec

Construction manager Turner Construction International

Height More than 2300 ft/700 m

Above-ground stories More than 150

Use Mixed: hotel, residential, resort

Area of above-ground building 5,000,000 sq ft/464,500 sq m

Number of parking spaces 3000

Principal structural materials Reinforced concrete

Other materials Exterior: aluminum, glass; interior: granite, stainless steel, wood

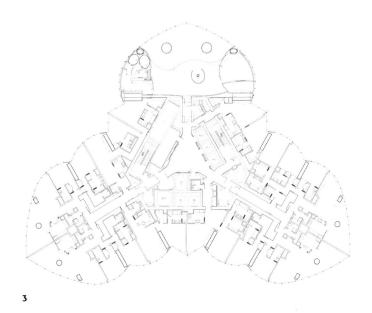

3

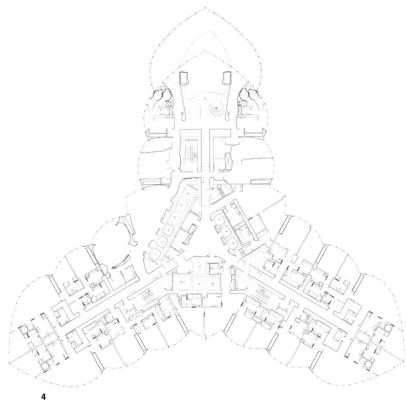

4

1   *The tower rises from a flat desert base*
2   *Model view*
3&4   *Y-shaped floor plans maximize views*

Photography: Courtesy Skidmore, Owings & Merrill LLP

2

Appendix

The World's 101 Tallest Buildings
Completed and topped-out as of April 2006

Rank	Name	City	Country	Year	Stories	Meters	Feet	Material	Use
1	TAIPEI 101	Taipei	Taiwan	2004	101	508	1667	Mixed	Office
2	Petronas Tower 1	Kuala Lumpur	Malaysia	1998	88	452	1483	Mixed	Mixed-use
3	Petronas Tower 2	Kuala Lumpur	Malaysia	1998	88	452	1483	Mixed	Mixed-use
4	Sears Tower	Chicago	USA	1974	110	442	1451	Steel	Office
5	Jin Mao Tower	Shanghai	China	1999	88	421	1380	Mixed	Mixed-use
6	Two International Finance Centre	Hong Kong	China	2003	88	415	1362	Mixed	Office
7	CITIC Plaza	Guangzhou	China	1996	80	391	1283	Concrete	Mixed-use
8	Shun Hing Square	Shenzhen	China	1996	69	384	1260	Mixed	Office
9	Empire State Building	New York	USA	1931	102	381	1250	Steel	Office
10	Central Plaza	Hong Kong	China	1992	78	374	1227	Concrete	Office
11	Bank of China Tower	Hong Kong	China	1989	70	367	1205	Mixed	Office
12	Jumeirah Emirates Towers Offices	Dubai	UAE	1999	54	355	1165	Mixed	Mixed-use
13	T&C Tower	Kaohsiung	Taiwan	1997	85	348	1140	Mixed	Mixed-use
14	Aon Center	Chicago	USA	1973	83	346	1136	Steel	Office
15	The Center	Hong Kong	China	1998	73	346	1135	Steel	Office
16	John Hancock Center	Chicago	USA	1969	100	344	1127	Steel	Mixed-use
17	Shimao International Plaza	Shanghai	China	UC06	60	333	1093	Concrete	Mixed-use
18	Minsheng Bank Building	Wuhan	China	UC06	68	331	1087	Steel	Office
19	Ryugyong Hotel	Pyongyang	North Korea	1995	105	330	1083	Concrete	Hotel
20	Q1	Gold Coast	Australia	2005	78	323	1058	Concrete	Residential
21	Burj Al Arab	Dubai	UAE	1999	60	321	1053	Mixed	Hotel
22	Nina Tower I	Hong Kong	China	UC06	80	319	1046	Concrete	Mixed-use
23	Chrysler Building	New York	USA	1930	77	319	1046	Steel	Office
24	Bank of America Plaza	Atlanta	USA	1993	55	317	1039	Mixed	Mixed-use
25	US Bank Tower	Los Angeles	USA	1990	73	310	1018	Mixed	Office
26	Menara Telekom	Kuala Lumpur	Malaysia	1999	55	310	1017	Concrete	Office
27	Jumeirah Emirates Towers Hotel	Dubai	UAE	2000	56	309	1014	Concrete	Hotel
28	AT&T Corporate Center	Chicago	USA	1989	60	307	1007	Mixed	Office
29	JPMorgan Chase Tower	Houston	USA	1982	75	305	1002	Mixed	Office
30	Baiyoke Sky Hotel	Bangkok	Thailand	1997	85	304	997	Concrete	Hotel
31	Two Prudential Plaza	Chicago	USA	1990	64	303	995	Concrete	Office
32	Wells Fargo Plaza	Houston	USA	1983	71	302	992	Steel	Office
33	Kingdom Centre	Riyadh	Saudi Arabia	2002	41	302	992	Mixed	Office
34	First Canadian Place	Toronto	Canada	1975	72	298	978	Steel	Office
35	Eureka Tower	Melbourne	Australia	UC06	91	297	975	Concrete	Residential
36	The Landmark Tower	Yokohama	Japan	1993	70	296	971	Steel	Mixed-use
37	311 South Wacker Drive	Chicago	USA	1990	65	293	961	Concrete	Office
38	SEG Plaza	Shenzhen	China	2000	71	292	957	Mixed	Mixed-use
39	American International Building	New York	USA	1932	67	290	952	Steel	Office
40	Key Tower	Cleveland	USA	1991	57	289	947	Mixed	Office
41	Plaza 66/Nanjing Xi Lu	Shanghai	China	2001	66	288	945	Concrete	Mixed-use
42	One Liberty Place	Philadelphia	USA	1987	61	288	945	Steel	Office
43	Tomorrow Square	Shanghai	China	2003	55	285	934	Concrete	Mixed-use
44	Columbia Center	Seattle	USA	1984	76	284	933	Mixed	Office
45	Cheung Kong Centre	Hong Kong	China	1999	63	283	929	Steel	Office
46	Chongqing World Trade Center	Chongqing	China	2005	60	283	929	Concrete	Office
47	The Trump Building	New York	USA	1930	71	283	927	Steel	Office
48	Bank of America Plaza	Dallas	USA	1985	72	281	921	Mixed	Office
49	UOB Plaza	Singapore	Singapore	1992	66	280	919	Steel	Office
50	Republic Plaza	Singapore	Singapore	1995	66	280	919	Mixed	Office

51	OUB Centre	Singapore	Singapore	1986	63	280	919	Steel	Office
52	Bright Start Tower	Dubai	UAE	UC07	59	280	919	Concrete	Residential
53	Citigroup Center	New York	USA	1977	59	279	915	Steel	Mixed-use
54	Hong Kong New World Tower	Shanghai	China	2002	61	278	913	Mixed	Mixed-use
55	Scotia Plaza	Toronto	Canada	1989	68	275	902	Mixed	Office
56	Williams Tower	Houston	USA	1983	64	275	901	Steel	Office
57	Wuhan World Trade Tower	Wuhan	China	1998	60	273	896	Steel	Office
58	Renaissance Tower	Dallas	USA	1975	56	270	886	Steel	Office
59	Dapeng International Plaza	Guangzhou	China	2004	56	269	883	Mixed	Office
60	21st Century Tower	Dubai	UAE	2003	55	269	883	Concrete	Residential
61	Al Faisaliah Complex	Riyadh	Saudi Arabia	2000	30	267	876	Mixed	Mixed-use
62	900 North Michigan Avenue	Chicago	USA	1989	66	265	871	Mixed	Mixed-use
63	Bank of America Corporate Center	Charlotte	USA	1992	60	265	871	Concrete	Office
64	SunTrust Plaza	Atlanta	USA	1992	60	265	871	Concrete	Office
65	BOCOM Financial Towers	Shanghai	China	1999	52	265	869	Concrete	Office
66	Triumph-Palace	Moscow	Russia	2005	61	264	866	Concrete	Residential
67	Bluescope Steel Centre	Melbourne	Australia	1991	52	264	866	Concrete	Office
68	Shenzhen Special Zone Press Tower	Shenzhen	China	1998	42	264	866	Concrete	Office
69	Tower Palace Three, Tower G	Seoul	South Korea	2004	73	264	865	Concrete	Residential
70	Trump World Tower	New York	USA	2001	72	262	861	Concrete	Residential
71	Water Tower Place	Chicago	USA	1976	74	262	859	Concrete	Mixed-use
72	Grand Gateway Plaza 1	Shanghai	China	2005	54	262	859	Concrete	Office
73	Grand Gateway Plaza 2	Shanghai	China	2005	54	262	859	Concrete	Office
74	Aon Center	Los Angeles	USA	1974	62	262	858	Steel	Office
75	TD Canada Trust Tower at BCE Place	Toronto	Canada	1990	53	261	856	Mixed	Office
76	Post & Telecommunication Hub	Guangzhou	China	2002	66	260	853	Concrete	Office
77	Dual Towers 1	Manama	Bahrain	UC06	57	260	853	Concrete	Office
78	Dual Towers 2	Manama	Bahrain	UC06	57	260	853	Concrete	Office
79	101 Collins Street	Melbourne	Australia	1991	50	260	853	Mixed	Office
80	Transamerica Pyramid	San Francisco	USA	1972	48	260	853	Mixed	Office
81	GE Building	New York	USA	1933	70	259	850	Steel	Office
82	Chase Tower	Chicago	USA	1969	60	259	850	Steel	Office
83	Commerzbank Headquarters	Frankfurt	Germany	1997	56	259	850	Mixed	Office
84	Two Liberty Place	Philadelphia	USA	1990	58	258	848	Steel	Office
85	PBCOM Tower	Makati	Philippines	2000	55	258	848	Concrete	Office
86	Park Tower	Chicago	USA	2000	67	257	844	Concrete	Mixed-use
87	MesseTurm	Frankfurt	Germany	1990	64	257	843	Concrete	Office
88	Sorrento 1	Hong Kong	China	2003	75	256	841	Concrete	Residential
89	USX Tower	Pittsburgh	USA	1970	64	256	841	Steel	Office
90	Mokdong Hyperion Tower A	Seoul	South Korea	2003	69	256	840	Concrete	Residential
91	Rinku Gate Tower	Izumisano	Japan	1996	56	256	840	Mixed	Mixed-use
92	The HarbourSide	Hong Kong	China	2003	74	255	837	Concrete	Residential
93	Langham Place Office Tower	Hong Kong	China	2004	59	255	837	Concrete	Office
94	New Century Plaza Tower 1	Nanjing	China	UC06	48	255	837	Concrete	Office
95	Capital Tower	Singapore	Singapore	2000	52	254	833	Steel	Office
96	Highcliff	Hong Kong	China	2003	73	253	831	Concrete	Residential
97	Osaka World Trade Center	Osaka	Japan	1995	55	252	827	Steel	Office
98	Bank of Shanghai Headquarters	Shanghai	China	UC06	46	252	827	Steel	Office
99	Jiali Plaza	Wuhan	China	1997	61	251	824	Steel	Office
100	Rialto Towers	Melbourne	Australia	1985	63	251	823	Concrete	Office
101	Beijing Yintai Centre	Beijing	China	UC07	63	250	820	Steel	Mixed-use

This listing is based on the Council on Tall Buildings and Urban Habitat's height criteria. Height for the above buildings is measured from the sidewalk level of the main entrance to the structural top of the building. Minor discrepancies between this and the data presented elsewhere in this book may occur when data has been provided according to other criteria.

Index of projects

Index of Architects